Sheila Paine is a world expert o~~~~ ~~~~~~~~~~~~~~~ passion for travel began when she ~~~~~~~~~~~ across the world, from Africa to ~~~~~~~~~~~~ author of several acclaimed books ~~~~~~~~~~~ *and Pakistan, Embroidered Text*~~~~~~~~~~~ *Afghan Amulet* (also Tauris Parke~~~~ ~~~~~~~~~~~~~ ~~~~~~~~~~~ writing awards from the *Independent* and *The Sunday Times*. She is currently writing a book on Afghan embroidery for the British Museum.

'*The Golden Horde* is the perfect vehicle for Paine's fresh prose.'
Independent on Sunday, Book of the Week

'This is excellent travel writing from an author who is always lively, fascinated by everything and prepared to take almost insane risks.'
Times Literary Supplement

'She is intrepid, upbeat and a keen observer of human types.'
The Scotsman

'Dalrymple and Birkett both project personal glamour. Sheila Paine couldn't be bothered with it . . . she has a lovely tenderness towards those who made or make things.'
The Guardian

'Sheila Paine is not your usual travel writer. When she comes across a piece of her precious embroidery, the prose lights up as if illuminated from within. Few travellers manage to get below the surface grottiness of Central Asia: Paine, now and again, touches something very deep indeed.'
Irish Times

'. . .an intrepid traveller and an extraordinary individual who has enriched the world of textiles through her passion, personal courage and spirit.'
Selvedge Magazine

By the same author:

The Afghan Amulet

Intrigued by an exquisite and mysterious amulet on an antique dress from Kohistan, 'land of mountains' in Pakistan, Sheila Paine began an epic quest that took her from the peaks of the Himalaya to the shores of Greece. In this, the first part of her journey, she set off alone and undaunted for the wilds of the Hindu Kush, her only possessions a tiny rucksack and a litre of vodka. Over the course of several months she followed endless clues – the patterns on a woman's dress, pendants hanging outside village houses to ward off *djinns*, scraps of embroidery in a bazaar – that took her to some of the most remote and inhospitable places in the world. She travelled to Makran, in Pakistan, an area closed completely to foreigners, and to Iran, where she was constantly watched by government minders. She was smuggled into Afghanistan by a band of mujahedin, and then forged on into Iraq and Turkish Kurdistan from Iran, before one final piece of evidence led her to the small town of Razgrad in eastern Bulgaria and news of the amulet she so tirelessly sought.

'Remarkable . . . Paine's travels have a point to them, a narrative which bespeaks a deep significance about both the history and nature of humanity. She writes beautifully . . . A spirited, perceptive exploration of some of the least-known parts of the world, conducted by a woman whose pioneering spirit and coolness under fire seem like a relic from another age.' *The Sunday Times*

'Her endurance is awesome, her courage remarkable and her prose excellent.' *The Washington Post*

'. . .armed with nothing but pluck and a good prose style, Paine traces the roots of Indo-European civilisation at the same time as writing a gripping travel book.' *The Guardian*

Tauris Parke Paperbacks is an imprint of I.B.Tauris. It is dedicated to publishing books in accessible paperback editions for the serious general reader within a wide range of categories, including biography, history, travel and the ancient world. The list includes select, critically acclaimed works of top quality writing by distinguished authors that continue to challenge, to inform and to inspire. These are books that possess those subtle but intrinsic elements that mark them out as something exceptional.

The Colophon of Tauris Parke Paperbacks is a representation of the ancient Egyptian ibis, sacred to the god Thoth, who was himself often depicted in the form of this most elegant of birds. Thoth was credited in antiquity as the scribe of the ancient Egyptian gods and as the inventor of writing and was associated with many aspects of wisdom and learning.

THE GOLDEN HORDE

From the Himalaya to the Mediterranean

SHEILA PAINE

TPP

TAURIS PARKE
PAPERBACKS

Published in 2006 by Tauris Parke Paperbacks
An imprint of I.B.Tauris and Co Ltd
6 Salem Road, London W2 4BU
175 Fifth Avenue, New York NY 10010
www.ibtauris.com

First published in 1997 By Michael Joseph
Text for this edition taken from the 1998 edition by Penguin Books Inc.

ISBN 10: 1 84511 244 X
ISBN 13: 978 1 84511 244 8

A full CIP record for this book is available from the British Library
A full CIP record is available from the Library of Congress

Library of Congress Catalog Card Number: available

Printed and bound in India by Replika Press Pvt. Ltd.

For my friends and neighbours, and the foster carers of my grandson David: all those who keep afloat while I am away the shaky barque that is my everyday domestic life.

CONTENTS

MAPS

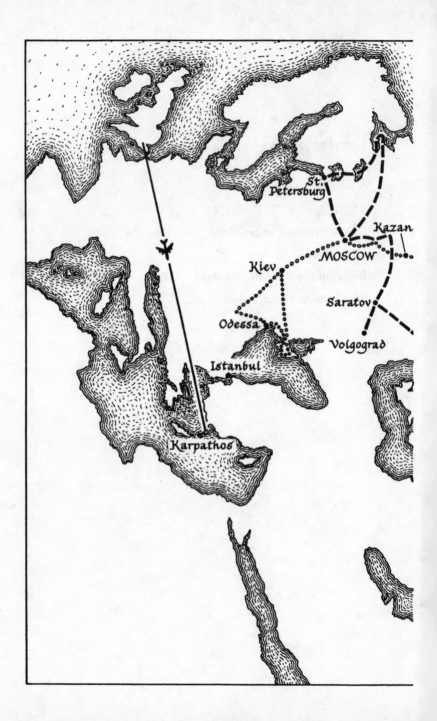

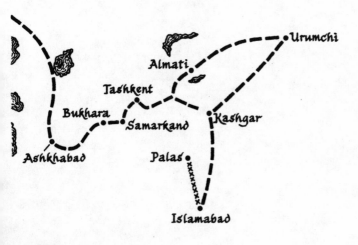

XXXXXXXX   FIRST JOURNEY

━ ━ ━ ━   SECOND JOURNEY

ooooooo   THIRD JOURNEY

Perm

Urumchi

Almati

Tashkent

Bukhara

Samarkand

Kashgar

Ashkhabad

Palas

Islamabad

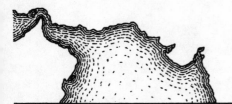

PREFACE ·

In *The Afghan Amulet* I described my journeys from the Hindu Kush to Razgrad in search of a talismanic triangle hung with tassels – three, five or seven – both when it was worn as an actual amulet or stitched as an embroidery pattern. My journeys were sadly inconclusive: I found no neat logic to explain why the amulet turned up where it did, yet was missing when I might have expected to find it; my conclusions as to its origin and meaning were, at best, woolly; I was thwarted from the very beginning by being forbidden to enter the valley of Palas, where the costume that set me on my way originated, I did not then know that the Bulgarians were related to the Chuvash people of the central Volga region, and so, worst of all, I had gone the wrong way, travelling from the mountains of northern Pakistan – the wild region of Indus Kohistan of which Palas was only one obscure valley – in a southerly swathe through Afghanistan, Baluchistan, Iran, Kurdistan and Turkey to Bulgaria, when I should have set off in a northerly direction.

So I make no apology that *The Golden Horde* is simply the tale of a dog worrying old slippers and digging up old bones. It is the tale of more journeys, still looking for the amulet, for I needed to find where people continued to believe in it and hung it round their necks or embroidered it on their clothes. But this time my journeys were to the north of Pakistan, and westward through the lands that lie north of the Caspian and Black Seas instead of south – lands that Genghis Khan had bequeathed to his grandson Batu and so once belonged to his followers, the Golden Horde.

But the first old bone to dispose of was Palas.

BEALE WILDLIFE GARDENS

✠

It had always seemed, in its tarted-up desolation, a fit setting for a Fellini film. Small columned stone bridges with classic capitals – a mish-mash of Doric, Ionic and Corinthian – spanned the artificial waterways, while peacocks strutted along the grassy banks in arcs of turquoise shimmering like a sunlit tide. This opulence of stone and feather was set in a forlorn Berkshire field between the Thames and the railway line and was visited by a few bedraggled families on wet Sundays.

But that was thirty or forty years ago and the old man, who owned the field and had invested it with bridges and peacocks with no obvious motive, had long since died. His heirs had taken over. They tidied up the place and built a shaky wooden pagoda, where tickets, teatowels printed with the college crests of Oxford and the herbs of England, stuffed toys and bags of pot-pourri were sold. They penned the peacocks and added a few rare birds, picnic tables and a model train with green livery and genuine smokestack that chuff-chuffed around the grounds. They changed its name from the Child–Beale Trust to the Beale Wildlife Gardens and moved it from the world of Fellini to the mundane one of merchandising.

Common domesticated species were brought in and labelled: donkeys, pigs, white rabbits. New attractions were added: a paddling pool of strong blue concrete and verdigris edges, a tropical house for monkeys, run up by the local carpenter. Somehow thrown into the mix were a few pheasants. But odd pheasants, odd varieties, not the 'farmyard rubbish on wings' – a phrase by which the hunting buff excuses his shot and beater – but unusual strains that, for the sake of the preservation of wildlife, should be given a home. The headquarters of the World Pheasant Association was thus settled there, as an address and a small office, a few miles from my home.

And so it was that I discovered that a rare pheasant, the western tragopan, survives only in the valley of Palas, in the last remaining forests of the Western Himalaya, high up in Indus Kohistan. And in this wild, inaccessible, forbidden valley I longed to see, that I even thought of as my own valley, the World Pheasant Association were quietly running a project to save the forests and the tragopan.

While the Pakistani police would allow no one else to cross the Indus from the Karakoram Highway to the narrow entrance of Palas, the Englishman who ran the project not only went in from time to time, but had been doing so for a few years.

I found him in Islamabad, a young man from Leatherhead, wearing a cream cabled sweater and buying croissants for his breakfast from the Afghan bakery.

HIMALAYA

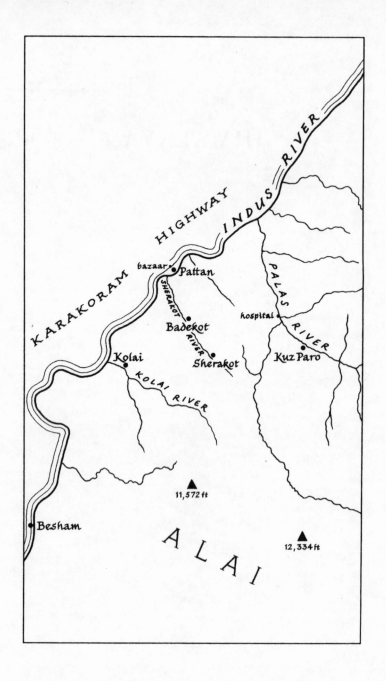

PALAS

☩

While the western tragopan, *Tragopan melanocephalus*, might be just a pheasant, a bird of the family that embraces the peacock and the barnyard rooster, it is rare. The only painting of it depicts it afluff with black feathers, dappled with white ocelli, flecked with bleached highlights and ruffed with quiffs of spiky red. It is known to inhabit the Himalayan forest, roosting high in the trees at night and pecking in the day at the shoots and acorns of the brown oak, *Quercus semicarpofolia*.

Not that anyone has actually seen it in the wild, only heard its distinctive cry, and from that alone ornithologists have pinpointed its last habitat as the valley of Palas, a valley assiduously guarded by the Pakistani police and by armed tribesmen in watchtowers. For entry to Palas is strictly forbidden. It has always been tribal territory, beyond the reach of the law, and is reputedly so dangerous that even its women are said to be armed, an image that sits uneasily with the flamboyant embroidered dresses they are also said to wear.

It was these extraordinary Kohistani dresses, their skirts flared into hundreds of godets, their bodices covered with embroidery and buttons and hung with the talismanic triangle, that I had set out to look for on my previous journeys and still had not been able to run to ground. Neither had I discovered why the women protected themselves with these triangular amulets, whether made of shells and hung on their dresses or embroidered on their marriage shawls. Nor why they stitched metal ones on the bonnets of their small boys. Such costume was reputedly from Palas, but no one I talked to had actually ever seen it being worn.

The project to save the environment of the western tragopan was an integrated ecological survival programme named The Himalayan Jungle Project. 'Jungle' seemed more tropical a

concept – creepers, lianes, tigers and so on – while this was mountain forest. But it was wild and untamed. A remote, totally isolated region that, though it was the habitat of the western tragopan, was also that of black bears, brown bears, grey langurs, red foxes, monkeys, wolves and snow leopards, of ibex, markhor and musk deer. And, on the slopes just below, of people. Of Shin tribesmen, who owned the forest but existed in primitive poverty in a regime of mono-agriculture, who still lived almost entirely off their own produce, but who needed cash for tea, sugar and cloth. And for embroidery threads and guns. And cash came from the forest, from its morel mushrooms, its medicinal plants and, most of all, from logging. To prevent the logging and the huge temptation of wealth that it brought to the valley, the Project embraced them as one: the people, the forest, the pheasants, the animals.

The women's embroidery, the young man from Leatherhead decided, could be included. A survey might establish whether it was just possible for it to be a source of cash – ('What about low-key sales to tourists on luxury trips up the Karakoram?' he suggested: 'Buy an Embroidery, Help Save a Tree.') So that if someone could look at it, assess its potential, and see whether it might, without upsetting a way of life that had existed for centuries, be used to help revert to a system of sustainable logging and keep away the outsiders careering in with their trucks ready to load up with logs. The forest as it stood, with its oak leaves for winter fodder, its morel mushrooms, its medicinal plants, could sustain the people. They just needed persuading. He would provide me with a vehicle, a porter and a guide.

Then there was Herb, who was here to build bridges and might come with me. Flash floods in 1992 had brought the villagers to the verge of starvation and destroyed the few stone bridges they had. The Project flew in supplies in helicopters borrowed from Uzbekistan, and the wondering children drew them all over the school walls, magical objects from another world, never before imagined.

For in Palas, every object of every page of every child's First Big Picture Word Book was missing: there were no helicopters and no aeroplanes, no cars and no traffic lights, no telephones and no books, no light bulbs and no taps, no bicycles and no fire engines. It was as if a cover of Mickey Mouse Elastoplast had been peeled back to leave just a dirty graze. But such a cover of colourful everyday life had never existed. The people's hold had never been more than just a dirty graze scratched on the surface of the precipitous landscape.

There was just the one school for a few small boys, with no chairs and no pencils. There were no roads, not even well-marked tracks; no shops, not even a wooden bazaar stall; no hospitals, no medicines; no electricity, no light; no windows, no glass; no

police, no doctors; no water except the snowmelt streams; and
no sound and no song. No sound of cars passing, of planes
overhead, no song of human voice, no music of any instrument,
for the local mullahs forbade them. Only the persistent, incessant
noise of the tumbling river that drowned all thought until it
faded to a rolling murmur hundreds of feet below.

Herb was a very tall thin man, his narrow face panhandled by
huge ears, his clear blue eyes pinched into each side of a beaked
nose. He wore long thin jeans, heavy suede boots on his large
slightly splayed feet, and a check lumberjack shirt, so that he
looked as if he came from the Appalachian mountains. He was
here to replace the old stone cantilevered bridges, destroyed by
the floods, with suspension bridges.

   Though grey-haired now, he had observed his fellow gradu-
ates many years ago apply for job interviews, placing themselves
right back into what he called 'the corporate society'. He had
opted out, never married, had almost lost his American accent
in an accumulation of half-learnt foreign tongues. For some
years he had busied himself building suspension bridges in a
country he called 'Neigh-pawl'. His questioning on every detail
of Palas was intense and pedantic – so we came to know all that
was missing in the valley. Was he expected to drink water from
the streams, how were the districts administered, were there any
barbers there, so where could he find one in Islamabad – in
Katmandu it had been easy – and what about a backpack mender,
for he never stepped outside without putting on a small rucksack?
Then his greatest worry of all – would his suspension bridges
have to bear the weight of seven foot of wet snow?

   It was agreed that I should go on ahead and Herb would
follow when a few technicalities, regarding concrete supplies
and barbers and backpack menders, had been sorted out.

The white jeep, like every vehicle in these parts that wasn't an
overdecorated old lorry, bore the name of an aid programme.
Usually it was UNHCR, WWFN or UNICEF that was
painted on the side, rendering suspect the scruffy driver with
woolly crocheted cap clutching the wheel. 'Birdlife International', ours said, 'Himalayan Jungle Project'. It climbed up

and up the Karakoram Highway – called by everyone the K K H – the driver's familiarity with the road evident at each sudden sharp bend, each disintegration into rutted earth, each missing edge washed away by streams in spate, each village flock headed homeward in the dusk. He was ready for them all.

We had skirted the ruins of Taxila – that splendour of decaying stupas, crumbling stones and Gandharan sculptures, abandoned in the peace of Buddha – had handed over a few dirty rupee notes for paper bags of dried apricots, figs, raisins and mulberries at the wayside stalls of Abbottabad, now hung with dim bulbs in the fading light, and had pressed on past, it was said, a refugee camp for Bosnian Muslims. 'They hate it here. Even the fighting was better.'

North and further north, small towns gave way to tiny roadside settlements straddling the highway, their rough stalls of plank and stone set out with a few piles of onions, pocked tomatoes and apples, glazed by 25-watt light. Then into Indus Kohistan, where electricity was only intermittent or had not come at all, though of course it would, they said, yes, one day, it depended on the politicians. A few villages have it, those lights high on the mountainside that look like stars, so distant are they from the unlit road, now that would be the home village of somebody or other. But here on the road, notched along the mountain flank miles below those stars and miles above the tumbling river – discernible only here and there, where it was flecked with shafts of dim light like slivers of glass – the evening grew darker and darker and the track ever stonier.

Roadbuilders' tents, shovels leant on their tied-up flies, squashed into every tiny space between the road and the fractured rockface but no one seemed to sweep the stones back and every vehicle reared and bucked aside from them closer and closer to the precipitous drop on the river side of the highway.

Then, turning a bend into a gully where a side torrent crashed down to the Indus below, the road veered through a small settlement and was suddenly crushed on both sides by a jumble of tumbled, somersaulted stone shack walls, wooden posts, iron shutters, kerosene cans, piles of mauve-tipped turnips and old men pushing carts, the scene spotlit like some clownish theatre by candles, by paraffin lamps, by torches and by the headlights of our jeep which caught, transfixed in the mayhem around, a speckled jackally dog and killed it with a yelp. The driver bent slightly forward, tightened his grip on the wheel and pressed on to Pattan, the village at the entrance to Palas.

I remembered the bazaar on the highway there, where painted trucks stood parked in droves while their drivers sat on benches around low rough wooden tables eating dinner, so many flickeringly illuminated hands and greasy bearded faces scooping spicy stews wrapped in pieces of naan into their open gossiping mouths. We zipped past, listening to Dave Brubeck on the jeep's cassette, down into Pattan itself.

From the highway, the track tipped down the hillside between crumbling stone walls past an open square facing the village police station, through the bazaar – now just a row of rusty shuttered cubicles like bathing huts closed for a cold salty winter – down almost to the Government rest house by the river. A few yards before it, the jeep stopped outside a small bungalow labelled 'Himalayan Jungle Project: Pattan Field Office' and decorated with the Project's logo of three pheasants atop each other, black, red, white.

Ghafoor had been sent along to assist me, a bureaucrat from the North-West Frontier Province Forests Division, a large young man in shalwar kameez, shawl and trainers, smouldering with resentment at having to accompany a woman looking at embroidery. Ridiculous, he thought, women's stuff. And she had managed to get access to this remote, forbidden valley just for this. It was Forests he had gone into the service for, and the status and security, of course. Not to be sent along as interpreter for some foreign woman. Not even a young and pretty one, and this one was old. He rolled out his sleeping bag on the bed opposite mine in the Pattan Field Office and glowered at me, making no attempt at conversation.

The Palas valley was not in fact one valley, but three. Not valleys that amble gently along a river's course, but three dizzying gashes cutting for miles into the western slopes of the Himalaya. It is possible to follow them along goat trails or wide paths through oak forest, or across stone footholds in icy streams, or over boulders leapt or linked by planks, or along narrow ledges cut into rock face. Where there is a river it can be crossed in one or two places, the traveller being slung above the water cradled in a wooden box pulleyed from one bank to the other or, in default of a box, sitting on a flat piece of wood like a flimsy teatray.

The northernmost valley is sliced through by the Palas river, smaller, higher side tributaries leading into it from ever more vertiginous slopes. The central valley is gentler, a vertical series of narrow terraces edged by snowmelt streams. The southernmost is a deeper cleft close to the Indus itself, a valley where the Project had not yet ventured. All are linked across the Himalaya to the east by a pattern of trails and passes that mark the rocks in summer with the delicacy of a spider's web and in winter lie buried under snow.

Ghafoor and I began with the easy central valley, led by our guide Nornaim, a quiet young man whose home was Palas. Felled logs lay everywhere, piled upon the slopes, piled along the edge of the track, piled over the track itself, a grim reminder of why we were here. One slung over the cleft of a river served as the only bridge into the rest of the valley.

The first settlement, Badekot, an hour or so's scramble upward, lay where the valley fanned out into a small platform set more or less on the level between its mountain flanks, though icy cascading streams had cut a dip through the middle of it. On each side of this dip the land had been meticulously terraced into tiny strips that had been planted with maize, now cut and drying on the rooftops. Each little parcel of terraces was centred by one small flat-topped hut, constructed of stones slatted by logs, where the family owning the terraces lived. Here and there were high towers of layered stone and wood, facing each other across the terraces. 'For the blood feuds,' said Ghafoor.

Feuds were not so often over women – girls betrothed at six years old who later decided they preferred someone else – much more often about boundaries, for the retaining stone walls and the streams delineating the maize terraces often shifted with the melting snow, enraging any man who found in the spring that he had lost an inch or two of ground. Or there were the squabbles over rights to the forest. Whatever the cause the men, all armed – usually now with Kalashnikovs – attacked one another and if

someone was injured or killed, they would repair, the men of
each family, into their own tower. 'In fort' they called it, with
some pride. They could even stay there as long as a year. They
abandoned all their agricultural tasks and took pot shots at
each other, avoiding, by tradition and civility, the women who
struggled on and ventured into the terraces to sow and reap,
though it was generally accepted that ploughing with oxen was
beyond their physical strength. So, if it was ploughing time,
crops for the year were lost.

Feuds could last a hundred years, with revenge killings still
recognized and accepted by succeeding generations. Or they
often ended with one family creeping out of the valley, over the
goat trail passes into the neighbouring valley of Alai, and never
returning. 'Form of population control,' said Ghafoor. 'Some
killed, some moved on.'

The path up the valley beyond Badekot deteriorated into
footholds on a slippery scree, or on pebbles in the beds of streams.
Up and up to the settlement of Sherakot on the fringe of the
forest. It lay on another platform of land, curled around on three
sides by the mountains and forest and edged on the other by a
precipitous drop to the rest of the valley far below. Again small
terraces of maize fields, a few cattle and goats, tumbling snowmelt
streams, thirty or so huts crudely constructed of logs and stones
and several blood-feud towers filled every inch of space. A few
women walked barefoot along the edge of the terraces in that
gentle controlled glide that a heavy metal pot of water on the
head, a narrow foothold and a lifetime of intimacy with every
step of the way impart to a woman's carriage. We stomped past
them in hiking boots and trainers into the *hujra*.

The *hujra* was a small log cabin with earth floor, like all the
other buildings in Sherakot, and was approached through a
narrow anteroom piled with firewood and guarded by a snarling
dog whose gleaming fangs and vicious eyes were all that was
visible in the dark interior. As we pushed open the heavy wooden
door a shaft of light fell on a smudge of quivering black fur
indented by a strong metal chain which tautened away from the
dog's body to the full extent of its length as he leapt towards us.

A further wooden door, hung with a padlock, led over a high
threshold into an inner windowless room. The walls were lined

with cupboards painted red, green and yellow and carved with decorative notches that were used to hang guns. Four charpoys were set close together and blankets were piled on the ground.

The *hujra* was a guest house, but free and only for men. Not that that was ever stated. It was taken for granted that any wanderer would be entitled to expect food and a bed and would only ever be a man. And, almost without exception, only a man from another village in Palas. It was a matter of honour to look after such a guest and, the same system existing in his home valley of Swat, Ghafoor stated with some pride that many a landowner there had ruined himself utterly, being driven to sell inherited land and property to feed complete strangers. So that nowadays the *hujra* did not always belong to the wealthiest man in the valley – the local khan or *malek* – as before, but was often the communal property of the village. Of course, each family was obliged to provide for its own guests, but the privilege of looking after an unknown outsider was shared, one family providing breakfast, another lunch, another dinner, unless some hapless villager found himself in the *hujra* when the wanderer arrived, in which case all the hospitality fell on him.

The *hujra* of Sherakot belonged to one man. 'It would be a slight to his honour if anything of ours was touched,' said Ghafoor, as we dumped our bags, 'so all our things are safe.'

I returned later to find him helping himself to my vodka.

'The trouble for me, it's too tasty,' he explained. Lunch was brought in for us by one of the men of the family: a bowl of honey, another of scrambled egg, another of ghee and a dish of unleavened discs of heavy bread made of maize, with one or two lighter ones of wheat that were served only to guests. We ate them off torn paper on a small table. When we had finished, the minute amounts left – Ghafoor having found everything too tasty – were placed on the floor and shared between Nornaim and three other men from the valley, a small girl bringing in more maize bread.

She had come from the women's quarters adjoining the *hujra*, where the food had been prepared, and called me back with her. The approach was through a dark outer room stacked with maize stems and then over the high earth threshold of a small doorway.

The women squatted on the dirt floor around the smouldering twig fire on which they had cooked. It was set in a shallow pit in the ground close to a wall along which ran an adobe shelf, supporting a container of straw and mud filled with the family's store of honey.

Below the shelf and close to the fire, a tiny shuttered hole in the wall gave the only light into the room, bar the bright shaft of the open door. The shutter was open, allowing some of the smoke to escape, while the rest swirled around, stinging the women's watering eyes, blackening their faces and rasping their throats. The children sitting on the earth around them were covered with sores and peered into the darkness from diseased and smarting eyes.

Hardly discernible in the thick atmosphere were the room and its meagre contents. The walls were of rough wood and logs, partly covered with dried mud, the floor of earth, the ceiling beamed. Two shelves ran the length of the back wall, lined up with blackened cooking pans and water pots. Below them stood one charpoy with a couple of sacks of flour on it. All the houses I, as a woman, was privileged to see in Palas were the same, except that if several families shared the same home, each had its own hearth.

From the dark recesses of the room the women brought a small low stool for me to sit on. They were all dressed in loose shifts and trousers, the shalwar kameez of Pakistan, enveloped in a large shawl. Mostly they wore black as it was a colour reputed to keep away the evil eye, and sometimes some worn embroidery glimmered through the dirt, but I saw no sign of any amulets on them.

They clucked and clattered, wrapped their shawls around their faces, picked up their babies for me to admire. One then balanced a stranded strip of resinous wood, thick and knotted, more a root than a branch, on top of a rusty metal canister by the fire and lit it from the embers. It spurted into life, lighting the emptiness of log walls and ceiling, earthen floor and shelves, surrounding us. It was the only light they had and, I discovered, this fibrous gnarled wood was the only source of light in all the homes of Palas. Except in the *hujra* not once did I see so much as a hurricane lamp or a torch, tokens as it were of mankind's development since the discovery of fire. Only this torchlight of wood.

The women smiled. Sons? Man? How many years? The old questions surfaced yet again. The answers were incomprehensible to them – how could I be there alone when I had a son? They fingered the cloth of my clothes and then began slowly and strongly to massage my legs. For I was a guest and to have reached there I must have walked many miles.

They themselves never left their homes or the small terraces around that belonged to their family – and property was always inherited by the men alone, contrary to Islamic law – except to go into the forest close by or to take the cattle to the high pastures in summer. On one such occasion, a young girl had glanced at a young man from another family, and on the next annual migration they had talked together for a few minutes. For this her brother had shot her dead. Of course he had to, otherwise his family's honour would be lost. It wasn't the only time such a thing had happened.

Outside the *hujra* huge stacks of maize stems leant upright in battalions waiting to be forked and pitched and stored for the winter. The agricultural cycle of Palas was immutable. It began at the end of winter, say late April, early May, when the women and children went into the forest to gather mushrooms, while the men shifted the cattle dung to the tiny terraced fields and renovated the irrigation channels. These were simply the snowmelt rivers diverted by gravity to water the maize.

At the beginning of June, unless the men were 'in fort' shooting each other, they ploughed the terraces with oxen and wooden ploughs and sowed the maize by hand. Because of their isolation, they had cultivated maize from the same seed year in, year out, so that the cobs were now tiny and of very poor quality.

By mid-June the maize had germinated and the men moved with their families and cattle to the high pastures, leaving one or two people behind to weed and irrigate the crop. At the end of September they began to move down the valley again, leaving the cattle with the women at a midway point so that they would not damage the crop. Watching over the last ripening, the men would spend their spare moments gathering grass from the forest and drying it for winter food – it tasted like radish, Ghafoor said, very tasty – and then in mid-October they harvested the maize.

This was, by now, the stage they had reached. The cobs had been separated, dried in the sun and beaten, while the stalks and husks lay piled outside the houses or on their flat earth roofs. They would be left there until men returning from the bazaar would tell the villagers it was the twentieth of November, when the next stage of the cycle would have to begin.

Meanwhile, the women trudged up and down to the two watermills at the bottom of the valley, taking the grain to be ground into flour for the heavy bread that was their staple diet. Twenty-five kilos on their head on each trip, and it was hardly a simple, level walk. There were sheer rocks to clamber up and down, but they were used to it, like goats, and only one or two fell in the river and drowned, 'dashed against the boulders of the river bed,' said Ghafoor.

From the twentieth of November, when they brought the dried maize stalks indoors, until the fifth of December they collected wood from the forest and stored it for the winter. Then snow would descend on the valley, deep deep snow, and the people would be imprisoned in their smoky, windowless homes, venturing out only to collect oak leaves from the forest for their cattle. Just some of the younger men left for the towns of the south to look for paid work, for they could not quite survive without any cash at all. Though their maize, cattle and chickens provided them with bread, milk and eggs, which together with wild honey, walnuts and small plums, and the dried beans, gourds and grasses they grew, comprised almost their entire diet, they still needed to buy tea and sugar, rice, spices and salt from the bazaar in Pattan, anything from one to three days' trek away.

Then there were boots and socks for the men, and mustard oil for their hair, cloth to make clothes, biscuits and even kerosene for special guests in the *hujra*.

'The trouble for me is it's too hard to know,' said Ghafoor, 'where they get the money for the guns and bullets they buy in Darra.'

The women's embroidery threads, now that was a different

matter, he knew about those, and they cost very little. The young men would buy the silks when they went down into Swat to find work. But now there was less work they didn't go so often and the bazaar in Pattan stocked acrylics. Nice and bright. Cheap and didn't fade. Ghafoor looked satisfied.

'A chicken, that would be good for you. Tasty,' said Ghafoor. 'You are too thin.'

He ordered one for supper – at the expense of our host, who turned out to be one of Nornaim's family – and devoured most of it with relish, leaving a few token scraps for me and the other men of the *hujra*, before we turned in for the night.

It was really quite extraordinary, it crossed my mind, for a woman to be sleeping in a room with a group of strange men, in a Muslim country. Extraordinary beyond belief. Clearly it had been more important to tackle the situation from the point of view of hospitality rather than sex. It was of prime importance to care for a guest and a guest was, it went without saying, a man. Had they regarded me as a woman they could not have looked after me correctly. In the women's quarters there would be neither bed nor food for me. I would have had to take my place on the earth floor and eat leftover scraps of maize bread. The men pointed this out to me by way of showing how honoured I was to be with them.

And so it was that my nights in Palas were spent sleeping with men in closed locked rooms with no water, no loo, no light, and any escape to the outdoors guarded by a rabidly snarling dog. There was no choice but to ask Ghafoor.

'The trouble for you is, once light, the village will watch. You go outside before sun. The dog will not break his chain.'

Days were spent trudging from one home to the next. Men and women sat outside together, sorting through stacks of maize husks. Filthy small boys ran around in jackets embroidered with bizarre plant patterns and hung with amulets, small coughing babies wore bonnets that wrapped around their shoulders like a shawl and tinkled with talismen. Men carried Kalashnikovs lovingly protected by embroidered covers. Inside the homes old women pulled back their shawls to reveal tiny embroidered skull caps with a flap that trailed down their back like a plait. I dutifully recorded everything that might serve the Project, but of the flouncy black Kohistani dress that had addressed my personal attention for the last few years, there was no sign.

Nornaim, belonging to Palas, could come into the outer room of the huts with me, though not into the women's inner sanctum, while Ghafoor ('the trouble for me is I am official of the North-West Frontier Province, Forests Division, and from Swat') had to remain outside. He stood picking his nose and spitting from boredom.

The path down again to Badekot seemed quicker and easier, but stonier, than the way up. It passed a small cemetery of wooden boxes carved with rosettes, like the ones in the pagan Kalash valleys to the west, and of holes in the ground ill-covered by wooden planks. Then it descended by clear splashing streams to the flat rooftops of Badekot. On these the maize was spread out to dry; women were bent winnowing, boys played with hoops, toddlers staggered around. ('Yes, they do sometimes fall off the edge. We lose them like that.') There was another cemetery with a small wooden mosque by the side of it where boys were taught the Koran, they said, but it seemed to be empty and was littered with stones.

By three in the afternoon the sun had vanished from the deep valley and a feeble muezzin sounded from the mosque. Along the tiny stone paths of the settlement, following the contours of the maize terraces and the streams, women led the cows home and carried the evening's water in pots on their head, men dragged along stems of maize, children threw stones. The valley hung in the swirl and smell of evening smoke and the unceasing rustle of cascading water. Then, as the light faded, the flat roofs of the houses, merged in daylight into the dusty terraces of maize around them, in the evening reflected the last glow as so many patches, squares of stuck-on fabric, like an African shaman's robe: gold where they turned to the last of the sun, mustard to the lee and bright as lemonade where they were spread with maize.

Inside the Badekot *hujra*, the floor was covered with dry grass. Hurricane lamp and wood stove were lit as we entered for the night. On one charpoy lay a paraplegic, Mohammed Suhab, injured on the Karakoram Highway some ten years previously. The fragile nature of that road and the paucity of traffic using it led one naturally to suppose that he had crashed into some stones or been hurled out of his vehicle at a particularly savage pothole, but no, his Suzuki had collided head-on with a lorry.

He leaned on one elbow on the charpoy, spitting into a metal bowl on the floor. He was well-spoken and seemed an educated man. 'You believe Jesus Christ is in the sky and will come back to earth?' he enquired.

The other men – a sharp-nosed Afghan in woolly black Chitrali cap, Nornaim, whose white teeth and white nylon kameez glimmered in the flickering light, and a fat fellow who seemed to be a professional 'guest' – paid uncomprehending attention.

'Which guns do you people prefer? Hong Kong ones?' Suhab continued. 'You make electricity out of atom bombs?'

Badekot boasted a small school but, for want of teachers and books, it was boarded up. The same with the small medical centre. There were no medicines and it would be impossible to get a doctor to live there. It was the same for Sherakot. If men or boys of the valleys were ill, they walked to Pattan on the Karakoram Highway, or carried those unable to walk, anything from one to three days' hard trekking away. There was a German doctor who called in Pattan once a month and treated all who came, for a derisory sum. The women and girls were left with no care.

'Many die, of course. What else would they do?' said Suhab.

They were not healthy, anyway. It was usual for them to have many children, ten or twelve at least, but then they never knew how many of the family would die or be killed in blood feuds.

From his charpoy, Suhab organized my enquiries around the village. He summoned people here, badgered people there, until he had unearthed the truth, convincing evidence about the Kohistani dress. It did indeed come from Palas – it was called the *jumlo*. It was first worn for marriage, then for ceremonies – circumcisions and the Eid festivity that ended Ramadan – then for every day. But, about twenty years ago when the construction of the Karakoram Highway had given the people a glimpse of the outside world, they had abandoned this cumbersome dress

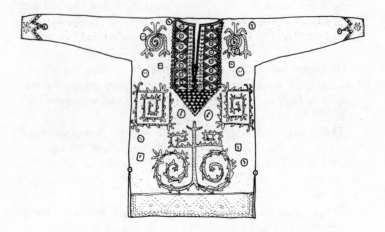

and embroidered instead the straight shifts they now wore for special occasions. During those twenty years, regularly once a year or once every two years, a couple of Afghan dealers from Peshawar had come into the valley and bought any dresses they could.

'They sold them to other dealers from London and Germany,' said Suhab. 'That's how you found yours.'

But there were no more left in the valley. Not one. And still no one from outside had seen a woman wearing one, or even seen a photograph of a woman wearing one. 'No photograph of any woman allowed anyway.' Not even of any dress on its own, in case a bride might later wear it.

Back at the Field Office, Ghafoor prepared to leave. His assignment was over. He was not to accompany me into the higher valleys of Palas, but was returning home on leave to Swat. He was on high form. He washed and oiled his black hair so that it curled even more and scrubbed his face so that it shone like a burnished apple. His shalwar kameez was clean and freshly ironed. He put on a huge pair of white trainers, inset here and there with bits of decorative blue, and proceeded to jump up and down on the bed. 'City man,' he said, with evident satisfaction.

For the really rough travelling, Nornaim and I were to be joined by the porter Azwal. Herb was still in Islamabad, busying himself with problems of concrete.

HIGH PALAS

✠

We began in the valley of the Palas river itself. The trail followed the course of the river, sometimes miles above it, sometimes descending by a tumble of insecure stones to the sandy shore where scattered boulders ensured a passageway to the next sheer escarpment. There was almost nothing visible to show the way, but Nornaim and Azwal knew every inch by heart. And all the way there was the noise of the river, always the noise of the river, never pausing, never ceasing, rolling into the emptiness.

I scrambled in total terror along an eight-inch-wide trail precariously incised into the rockface above a sheer half-mile drop to the river below, not glancing for a second to either side but concentrating only on the foothold itself. Where Nornaim trod patiently and carefully, turning with proffered hand when the going got tough, Azwal positively ran, rushing ahead as if he had no burden on his back, leaping like a gazelle from one loose stone to the next, and then waiting triumphantly on the first large boulder for us to catch up, eating dried figs and looking superior. He was a Palas man, had grown up scampering up and down these scarps and along the toe-holds scratched into this vertical landscape. He was footsure.

Where the view opened up and we could see thousands of feet above us, tiny terraces of maize clung to the precipices, and on them, here and there, unbelievably, the odd cow. If cows got up there, I had to accept, this could hardly be called real mountaineering.

I was unsuitably dressed for whatever degree of climbing it was. As I was always going into women's homes, I had to be modestly wrapped in shalwar kameez and shawl, but the rigours of November in the Himalaya had called for more protective clothing: totally rainproof, totally windproof, fleecy under-pinnings, fleecy gloves, fleecy cap, Alpine socks.

I had explained the problem to one of the staff of the Kensington specialist shop – they were all very tall, earnest young men whose names, Peter, Simon, James, appeared in computer type on the final bill. Peter frowned politely. The only suitable clothing the shop sold, he pointed out, the only thing that would give complete protection from the elements was based on a system of layering and something called 'wicking', thermal this and that and then trousers, jackets, anoraks. There was nothing for it. It would have to be such layers with the shalwar over or under the trousers, the kameez dangling around the knees below the anorak, the shawl draped across the fleecy hat. 'You'll look ridiculous, madam,' he said.

Not only did I look ridiculous but the shawl trailed dangerously at tripping level. I jettisoned it and Azwal crammed it into his huge rucksack. We soldiered on. We passed only one small hut, where the women brought out their embroideries, made us tea and massaged my legs. Then no one except a goatherd, whose savage dog hurled itself straight at me in a frenzy of snarling. I froze rigidly still, the goatherd shouted, Nornaim and Azwal attacked it with sticks. Perhaps it had been provoked by the unfamiliar outfit.

We set off again, sometimes still scrambling but sometimes strolling in a leisurely fashion along paths through verdant oak groves, until, shimmying across a wobbly plank, we entered the grounds of the hospital.

'Well, no *hujra* in the Palas valley,' the young man from Leatherhead had said. 'You'll sleep in the hospital, use it as a base.'

The wooden plank had led over a deep cleft in the rock to a small area of turfy grass and boulders surrounded by wire fencing. Nearby was a concrete platform built at the edge of the river and on it the hospital building. It consisted of several small wooden rooms around two open courtyards. The plank doors to each room were padlocked. None had a roof but were open to the sky. The place was entirely empty bar one or two piles of rubbish lying on the ground and a twig fire in the corner of one of the courtyards. Two armed men and an old *chowkidar* sat on rusty chairs warming their hands around it.

They undid the padlock on one of the doors and showed us

into the room where we were to sleep. The floors were of planking, the walls were of planking. There was one charpoy, with a filthy mattress that would clearly benefit from my flea powder, and a pile of old boots, plastic bags, bits of wood and indiscernible rubbish, swept into the corner. It seemed timely to enquire why the building was described as a hospital. It was built as such, it seemed, by a politician aiming for votes, but of course no doctor would ever come and live in such a place and there was no money for medicines, so it had never been roofed or equipped or used, or spoken of again outside the valley.

We locked our stuff inside the room and carried on along the river towards the village of Kuz Paro, to meet the women before nightfall. The valley was now darkened by the shadow of late afternoon but Kuz Paro, lying ahead slightly above the floor of the valley, caught the last rays of the sun and lay in a golden glow like an El Dorado ahead of us. The trail was worse than ever so that I almost staggered into the first house – a dark hut daubed with white painted patterns – led by a local man in a heavy woollen embroidered coat. The woman sitting at the hearth clutched her small son, wearing a fancy jacket, close to her and said she had nothing to show me. Another young girl with four small children and a husband old enough to be her grandfather pressed on me a baby's bonnet heavy with triangular metal amulets and dangling tin hearts. I gave her money for winter supplies.

It was almost dark before we got back to the hospital. Nornaim fetched me the *chowkidar*'s chair and placed it on the concrete platform where I could watch the light fade completely over Kuz Paro and gild the distant Himalayan peak of Naydikan, while he cooked our supper. He filled our metal pot with water from the river, threw in some of the rice and spices that Azwal had been carrying and heated it for hours on the twig fire. Risotto must also have come to the Italians, like pasta, from the Orient, I thought, sipping my vodka and feeling attended to like Freya Stark.

The charpoy mattress revealed itself to be already inhabited by various bugs and I spent a fitful night hurling my shoes and anything I could lay my hands on at a rat foraging in the corner rubbish pile, and dreaming of embroidered shifts being thrown over precipices and eddying down to the river miles below.

We climbed up and up, higher and higher, from one tiny settlement to the next, until we heard the golden oriole's fluty phrase, and stood facing more mountains across a cleft over a mile deep, right opposite other tiny settlements like the one we were in. Just small scratched clearings high in a wilderness of rock and forest, each a handful of stone and wood huts set in terracing, miles away from each other and seemingly impossible to reach. And still way below us the sound of the river, but now faint like those distant freight trains that rumble through the empty open spaces of the world: the Canadian prairies, the South African veld. It was easy to imagine their melancholy whistle, as melancholy and lonely as these small clusters of human life clinging to the steep escarpments.

There were no *hujra* so high up so we spent the nights with families known to Nornaim and Azwal, sitting talking by firelight, the guard dog released to prowl outside, the heavy wooden door of the house locked by a huge forked tree trunk leant against it and resting on a peg in the floor. Young women, clinking with silver anklets and bracelets, chopped wood all evening in the dark to keep the fire going. Supper was always dhal, maize bread and tea. Everyone slept on the floor after the goats and donkeys had been moved to the outer room, but if there were a charpoy it would be given to me. By dawn the women were bringing the animals back in, reviving the embers, chopping more wood, fetching water.

The women of High Palas wore nothing embroidered but were dressed only in rags, so we returned to the Pattan Field Office and then set off towards the south.

The Project had not ventured before into the southernmost valley, that lay high above the Indus on the opposite bank to the KKH. The mullahs had been more active here and the women were veiled in black. Girls spat at us and threw stones. Small boys jeered. The village of Kolai lay on the shoulder of the mountain, its terraces wrapped around it like a crinkled shawl. Gunshot reverberated across the valley. Nornaim and Azwal were uneasy. They did not belong here.

A thin, bearded man in neat grey shalwar kameez, with a pen tucked in the pocket and a black beret, appeared at the *hujra* and led me away to his family's house to sleep. It was totally different from the dark two-roomed huts I had become used to. A row of rooms flanked a verandah, each with a shuttered window and door painted in bright colours. Though the floors were still of earth and the walls of unmortared stones and adobe, there were shelves of teacups and bright metal pots. A flurry of white feathers on the verandah promised chicken for supper. An old man, his six sons and an assortment of wives and children – who opened the shuttered window to watch me undress – lived there. The men had been educated at Abbottabad and spoke English, they wore clean ironed clothes and were like messengers from the outside world.

Nornaim and Azwal fared less well and by morning Azwal refused to go any further. His pulse was racing, he said. Nornaim and I continued up over boulders, on stepping stones over cascading streams, up notched wooden planks serving as ladders, like those of the Kalash in the valleys of the Hindu Kush further west. No one asked us into their home, no one had any embroideries for me to see. The Afghan dealers had just been. We returned to Pattan.

Not once in any of the Palas valleys did I see a woman wearing the *jumlo*, nor the triangular amulet embroidered on her clothes, though they wore a beaded version on the end of their plaits. Maybe it used to mean something, they said, but not now. Horns were the same, they had lost their power. Now, to protect themselves against the evil eye, they relied on black fabric and for their homes they painted pots black and, put them on the roof. As for children, to protect them from sickness, yes, they did stitch triangular pendants of metal on their caps, but mostly they put a knife, or something of iron, in their bed.

Nor did I ever see a woman armed, though the men all carried guns. I saw pregnant twelve-year-olds, I saw a woman with leprosy, I saw many women with endemic eye diseases and many covered in sores. The Project would do its best.

As for the western tragopan, I neither saw nor heard it. It

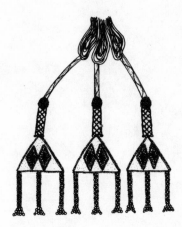

lived only in the virgin forest way, way up beyond the last shepherd's hut.

By now, winter was closing in and the Khunjerab pass to the north, that theoretically I should take into China, was blocked. I left for home just as Herb arrived in Palas to start on his first suspension bridge.

The Quest

The tasselled triangle is just one of many relics of ancient pagan superstition that link Central Asia with Eastern Europe. Horned headdresses are another. Tying rags and cloths onto trees another. Walking clockwise round fires another. The power of colour, especially red, white and black, another. Wearing trinkets of blue beads, teeth and claws, fishbones, coral, cowrie shells, garlic, bits of piercing metal, fragments of umbilical cord or scraps of prayer, another.

I now knew that in Palas, a valley as remote as any in the world, they had forgotten the meaning of the triangle and the horns they still wore. But they remembered black and piercing metal. Still, even though any kind of amulet excited me, it was the triangle that obsessed me. If the people of Palas had forgotten, the Turkmen and Uzbek settled in nearby Afghanistan had not, so what of those still in Turkmenistan and Uzbekistan? And would the Chuvash of the mid-Volga still embroider and wear amulets, though their Bulgarian kinsmen no longer did? And where, travelling north between Asia and Europe, might amulets still be found, in particular the talismanic triangle?

And then there was a subtle change in the form of the amulet itself. Through the eastern parts of my previous journeys it had been claimed to be Islamic, though its triangular shape was far more ancient than Islam, but I knew that in the West it had become more anthropomorphic and had overtones of the goddess worship of Old Europe – the neolithic culture that extended from Ukraine through the Balkans to the southern Greek islands.

Where would the amulet cease to be Islamic, where would the folded paper inside no longer be inscribed with quotes from the Koran and prayers from the mullah, but be plain or even replaced by those talismanic charms of teeth and trinkets? And where would I find it embroidered with patterns of horns or goddesses? And where in particular would the power of the

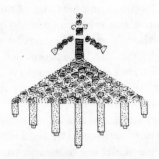

fertility goddess be dominant so that the triangle represented only her skirt? At the borders of Islam and the Orthodox Church?

How best to devise my journeys when logically my route lay northward over the Karakoram from the soaring tangle of mountains that are the nub of Central Asia, and which now lay closed until the snows melted in spring? I should go through the oasis towns of the silk route, across the sweep of the steppes, along the Volga and westward, through the lands that once belonged to the Golden Horde.

Three small events combined to settle matters for me.

The first was a crisis in the kitchen on a Monday in January when the washing machine broke down and the wine-stained, candle-grease-stiffened dinner cloths and lazily crumpled sheets of a weekend of friends swirled gently to a halt in mid-cycle.

The Hoover maintenance man frowned and then shook his head. The machine was too old, after so many years no one made the parts any more. A new one would have to be bought.

Later it became a scandal that the marketing managers of a reliable old company should ever have thought it a good idea to offer two free flights to New York or Disneyland to anyone buying even just a vacuum cleaner, let alone a washing machine. Rumbling had already been heard that they had catastrophically misjudged the promotion, but, unaccountably, they decided to extend it into January.

We arranged to meet in the Irish pub in New York, myself and the world expert in goddess figures in the embroideries of Russia and Eastern Europe. We had long corresponded on the subject of goddesses stitched in red on cloths that were then hung around graves and icons and from trees in remote birch groves. We had spoken of Berehinia, the mother goddess of Russia; of goddesses riding on horses; of goddesses horned or depicted as sirens. We had discussed the associated fertility symbols of toads and tulips and had exchanged information on trees of life, triangles, horns and maypoles, but we had never met.

The pub was packed and I looked around for my correspondent, Mary. She turned out to be a confident American lady with a shock of long wiry grey hair, wearing bright clothes over black leggings, who enthusiastically declared everything to be 'real neat'. She lectured in art and owned a sixty-acre smallholding in upstate New York, where she kept a flock of sheep whose wool she sheared, spun on her mother's old spinning wheel and wove on her mother's old loom. She had a strong aura of the back-to-earth greenness and self-sufficient feminism currently in vogue.

Tackling dishes of Gaelic chicken, we tried to converse above the racket of yelling voices, Irish songs, shouting waitresses and sloshing Guinness. Trying to further our ideas on fertility goddesses was virtually impossible, but we had made contact and resolved to meet again soon.

The second incident was receiving an invitation to present a paper on Islamic embroidery at the First International Islamic

Artisans-at-Work Festival in Islamabad in the autumn of 1994, so my next journey should end and not begin in Central Asia. I prepared material to speak for an hour or so and sent it on ahead. I could not have known then that the biggest success of the Festival was to be the dancing camels and that the speakers were to be allowed only five minutes. When I finally got there and pointed out that I had come a long way – in fact, as it turned out, from the Arctic – I was given seven minutes.

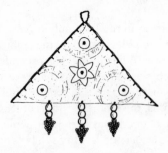

The third incident was when Mary sent a small package enclosing, wrapped in tissue paper, a triangular amulet of cheap gold brocade hung with three bunches of plastic grapes. Worn by the women of the village of Olymbos on the island of Karpathos in the Dodecanese, she said in the accompanying letter, to protect them from illness and the evil eye. This was a disturbing extension to what I had considered my territory. Should I perhaps not make one journey, beginning somewhere in the lands of the Golden Horde around the Volga, and go east and south to Islamabad, and then a second, returning to the Volga and going west as far as Karpathos?

Somewhat later, in my post after the invitation to Islamabad and the amulet from Karpathos, came a letter from Mary to say she was getting together a small group of friends to join a boat trip through the canals and rivers of Northern Russia to the White Sea, to look at the folk art of Karelia. 'There could be goddesses and triangles there. Don't you want to come along?'

'By the way', she wrote somewhat later, 'I think I've made a mistake. It seems to be some sort of a pilgrimage.'

And so these events sorted out my itinerary for me and in the summer of 1994, wearing around my neck the pagan device of a triangular amulet embroidered with horns and hung with three tassels, I set off to join a group of devout Russian Orthodox pilgrims about to set sail for the Arctic seas, when my true destination was Islamabad.

NORTHERN RUSSIA

THE PILGRIMS

✠

The welcome at Moscow airport was the same as in Communist days. My small bag, pushed off the carousel, was jammed where it was impossible to reach. The sullen, balloon-kneed woman sitting on a small kitchen chair, whose job it was to control the arrivals' baggage, looked resolutely into the middle distance and snarled '*niet*' when approached. The taxi driver, heading into town with no rear mirror or lights, opened his door in mid-traffic to see if he could change lanes. A man lay dead in the middle of the road. Nothing seemed to have changed.

But then suddenly there were hoardings advertising Rothman cigarettes and Hyundai vehicles, and a huge sign, 'Welcome to Moscow', all in English. A pristine white van overtook us, 'Jesus Loves You' painted on the side, unthinkable just a few years ago. As would have been, most of all, the presence of my companions in the taxi, a hugely obese couple with a mountain of luggage – Russians who had left in the fifties for Washington and were returning to their homeland for the first time. On a pilgrimage of the Russian Orthodox church, they confirmed.

Deciphering the Cyrillic script of the letter of invitation I had received some months before – without which it was impossible to get an individual visa for Russia – and then checking in the dictionary, it had indeed said that the visa was to be granted for a pilgrimage to the holy sites of the north. To the ancient monasteries and wooden churches where the Orthodox faith had clung to a fragile survival. The pilgrimage was to begin, it appeared, on the Saturday of the Svyatogorsk Icon of the Mother of God and end nearly three weeks later on the Wednesday of the Smolensk Icon of the Mother of God called Hodigitria.

Fellow pilgrims were also met at the airport and ferried to the hotel. Little old ladies from New Jersey who, though they had left Russia in their childhood, still spoke to each other in

Russian. They dressed in trim straight skirts, kinked slightly at the waist where they hid their moneybelts, and wore cheap white trainers or tartan slippers which they rapidly changed for high heels when each church visit began. Two of them had just been to a café, they said, and had asked for two teas. 'Only one left', they'd been told. They recounted the story rather nervously. They'd saved for several years for this trip, ever since the fall of Communism – what was it going to be like?

Last of the pilgrims to arrive was a slim, tanned man whose blond hair was now slightly tinged with grey and arranged a little more carefully than in his youth. He needed no telling that his blue jacket and bright turquoise T-shirt set off his cool looks to advantage. He attributed these, and his vigour, to a daily intake of ginseng, multivite and garlic pills. He described himself as a television producer. 'Hands-on, on the set sometimes. Name's Vladimir but call me Vlad.' Since he spoke very little Russian he was somewhat ostracized by the others, and so attached himself to the small group of Mary's friends, who had no interest in religion and had all come to see the folk art of Karelia. As I had.

Karelia had belonged to Finland and I hoped to see some of the beautiful embroidered shifts that had once been worn there. They should be like those of the Finno-Ugric peoples of the Volga – the Mordvinians, Maris and Udmurts – who were conquered by the Golden Horde along with their Turkic neighbours, the Chuvash and Tatars. Or would we see only weaving and woodcarving – distaffs and dowry chests and the like?

The daunting programme for the first day in Moscow far outstripped our interest in the Orthodox Church, covering as it did visits to the Andronikov Monastery, the Andrei Rublev Icon Museum, the Resurrection Church in Sokolniki, the Miracle-Working Iverskaya Icon of the Mother of God, the Kazansky Cathedral, the Donskoy Monastery and the Relics of St Tikhon, Patriarch of Moscow and all Rus. We set off with mixed emotions and vague thoughts of other tourists enjoying the more conventional attractions of Moscow, led by our own two priests, the one fat and portentous, the other a Jesus clone, both wearing flowing robes and heavy gold watches.

Churches that had been boarded up and used as scrap metal

dumps were being restored and rebuilt; new icons were being
painted and ancient ones cleaned by old women in white sandals,
turquoise knitted-lace socks and enveloping headscarves.
Buckets of water and scrubbing brushes were everywhere. Everyone genuflected at the passage of our priests, murmured their
names and kissed their hands.

'All wrong,' said Vlad. 'These are just priests, not gods.
That's the trouble with this place. Think how they worshipped
Lenin.'

The following day – Sunday of the Holy Fathers of the
Six Oecumenical Councils – there was no respite. The New
Jerusalem Monastery had been heavily restored on the outside,
its golden domes and silver castellated tower glinting in the
sun above the trees of its garden, where an old bag lady in a
tam-o'-shanter sat eating pickled herring out of a jar. Inside, it
was something of a shock to find no iconostasis but an immensely
lofty building of European baroque that must once have been
as ornate as Melk and Einsiedeln, but had been saved from
overblown excess by being hit by a bomb in the 1940s. Now gold
angels clung to cracked brick and fallen columns, and turquoise
tiles to flaked plaster, so that the church had a strangely haunting
beauty of life and decay, of colour and pallor, of richness and
simplicity. It was believed to be the centre of the Christian
universe, explained our interpreter, Marina, a small thin lady
in her fifties whose face lit up in conversation and in repose fell
into the weary lines etched by the tragedies of her past. Bloated
already by churches, we trooped off to dinner in a restored
monastic church, where, by some error, I was given a bottle of
Communion wine (16%, said the label) instead of Pepsi like
everyone else.

On the Monday of Finding Relics of St Seraphim, Miracle
Worker of Sarov (1903), we set sail in the motor ship *Ladoga*, a
trim white two-decker, for the waters of the far north.

The pilgrims stood quietly on the deck of the *Ladoga*, as it
crossed Lake Onega through a landscape of forest towards the
island of Kizhi. More than the monasteries and churches of
Moscow these were the holy places they had only dreamt of
and had come from Canada and the States to see.

As Kizhi came into sight the little old ladies from New Jersey stood ready in their high heels and neat skirts, dressed as though to go shopping downtown, each with her own memories of years of displaced wandering – Poland, Austria, Chile, then Manhattan, until there, too, a different kind of violence had driven them away. The men remembered the promises of jobs that then vanished, the struggles in Detroit, the sticking together in what amounted to Russian ghettos, then the calmer years of success for some and acquiescence for others.

Before them the priest loomed like a figurehead at the prow of the boat, his black robe, pinioned against his belly by a huge silver crucifix, billowing out in folds behind him. The twenty-two domes of the Church of the Transfiguration could just be discerned piercing the pale horizon of the white Arctic twilight.

The pilgrims gazed ahead and, as the strange horizontal rays pared what had seemed smooth silver domes into ashen slivers, they began to chant. They chanted the melancholy prayers of the Orthodox Church, their voices rising as the domes, illusively translucent, too translucent to be merely of wood, changed colour in the fragile light.

As the boat pulled towards the flat grassy shore of Kizhi, they fell silent and when it drew alongside only the lap of water could be heard. Across a reedy inlet lay two ethereal wooden churches, their clusters of aspen domes seeming to move in the dusk around the tented belltower that pierced the sky between them. This was the Pogost of Our Saviour, by the fifteenth century the ecclesiastical and administrative heart of a parish of hundreds of islands belonging to Novgorod and defended from the Russians by a stockade of stones and logs.

Now the whole island of Kizhi was a museum of the wooden architecture of the far north. To the churches of the Pogost had been added timber buildings brought from other islands and villages: chapels, barns, intricately carved wealthy farmers' homes, a poor peasant's house of one simple log room surrounded by a cabbage patch and a fence of slanting staves.

The pilgrims strolled around the island in the long summer night, chanting and praying at each spoor of the Holy Spirit. Beyond their path, on the further shore, lay a small fishing hamlet of log houses and picket fences skirting the shoreline, where boys played in the pale midnight sun, dogs barked and men and women raked in hay. A young man turned his back on the hamlet and walked towards a distant spinney, holding his flaxen-haired girlfriend by the hand and carrying a transistor radio blaring 'A Whiter Shade of Pale'.

The boatload of pilgrims sailed on through canals and lakes. Mary gave watercolour lessons every afternoon in the dining saloon: water, trees and churches washed and daubed from a small paintbox evocative of my schooldays with its labels 'viridian', 'cobalt', 'gamboge' and 'ochre'. She shared, too, her life experiences with those on board, giving regular little talks. These were keenly attended by her friends, as no folk art was evident anywhere.

Meanwhile, most of the pilgrims passed their time chanting and praying at each wooden church, at each good meal, at each sunrise, at each sunset and especially on Saturday night to prepare for Sunday. And nowhere did they chant and pray more poignantly than at the nineteen locks that link the Baltic with the White Sea. This Soviet 'achievement' cost one and a half million lives.

'One and a half million, you understand,' said George, a sensitive man with a forlorn bloodhound face, a bachelor in his fifties. He had had to look after his parents, he explained, since, though they had emigrated many years ago to New York, all their lives they spoke only Russian. Otherwise, he would have been an artist – he made delicate sketches of all the churches we passed and showed them to everyone – and of course it meant he had never married. But now that they had died and he was free, he had met a nice lady in Mexico, he mentioned on many occasions, only with her three daughters he feared it was too great a financial commitment for a man of his age. Though he felt he had mastered English it was only with a strong accent.

'So many they killed. A Satanic regime. All these locks, built by slave labour, by the intelligentsia of Russia, by poets and priests. Wait until you see the granite one.'

It was actually a pair of locks, hewn into solid rock. Clasping the sides of the boat were dank walls of massive boulders chipped into serried ranks, lined with a criss-crossing of logs.

'All by hand,' said George. 'Cut by writers, by artists, by teachers, by lawyers. Only with a pick and a wheelbarrow. One hundred men dead for every yard.'

The pilgrims chanted and most of them wept, as much for their lost roots as for a lost nation.

Through the Day of the Prophet Elijah, the *Ladoga* sailed silently northward, the quiet throbbing of its engine only audible when it manoeuvred into and out of locks. Occasionally the blackened chimney of an abandoned factory, the shaggy remnants of some old industrial plant, scarred the sky above the horizon, otherwise the landscape was of endless forest and water under a calm aquamarine sky.

Everywhere the priests and pilgrims chanted and intoned.

'Pseuds,' said Vlad. 'They left on a Sunday and didn't even hold a service first.'

The boat slipped through the canal past little settlements of wooden houses, the people lying sunbathing on the grass. Then out into a ruffleless lake again, past birch islands, past two men slowly paddling a small boat miles from any jetty – coming from where, going to where? They disturbed the peace with a glimpse of a life of vacant loneliness, like those passengers who get off buses in the middle of unending desert.

Further and further into the desolation of the north we sailed – trapped on a boat, with only the melancholy of the Russian soul and past, stirred by the resurgence of the Orthodox Church for company – to the tip edge of a continent where settlements had evaporated from city to town to village to hamlet to riverine shack where the sound of a radio shocked like the bite of a summer insect. The water channels became narrower, the land flatter and grassier, the trees thinner and lacier.

At night, as the sun slid towards the skyline, the water that had seemed like clear palpable, malleable glass, a simple fluidity in frigid colours as its cold slip followed the boat, now glowed in Tiffany colours. Its substance changed every second, now glaucous and opaque, now crystalline as endless light rolled into its unseen depth, now chintz-glazed on a smooth mirror of reflected sunset. The sky split into horizontal splinters, a mirage of grey-fringed trees tipped upside down above a golden mist,

then a line of dark pines and below it a sliver glowing orange
that bled slowly into the water.

'The admen call this a White Night,' said Vlad.

On the Day of the Prophet Ezekiel the *Ladoga* reached the rough
wooden jetty of Belomorsk, the village guarding the entrance
to the White Sea. A small blond ragamuffin in dirty pink sweat-
shirt ran to greet her arrival. He spent all his time there on the
jetty, the people around him said, watching for boats. His parents
were both alcoholics.

The pilgrims disembarked and took a bus into 'town'. Little
wooden houses stood in groves of birch trees, as they always
had, violated by blocks of jerrybuilt concrete flats that appeared
to have been bombarded by stones. There was once a huge
Soviet concentration camp here, so the place now had electricity.

'The plant built by slave labour again, you understand. All
those people dead,' said George.

The bus drove past the plant, past rock-strewn rivers and
acres of wild flowers, and stopped by a clearing among trees.
The open space was covered with huge flat boulders, carved
with petroglyphs from 4000 BC that told tales of hunting deer,
bear and whale and depicted figures in horned hats on skis.
Lichen and moss were now intruding and beginning to crack
the boulders.

'It's the pollution,' said Vlad.

The figures in horned hats were intriguing. Were they people
or gods? Since Neolithic times the fertility goddess had been
depicted with horns or with antlers, even giving birth to deer in
her role of mother provider to hunting communities. She could
have a triangle as a skirt and horns as a headdress, just as women
wore triangular amulets and horned caps. So were these figures
women? Like those of the Hron valley in Slovakia who bind their
hair around twigs ritually cut from the forest, fixing it into a single
horn above the forehead or into one at each side, placing over this
structure of wood and hair an embroidered bonnet. It is in this
headdress that they are buried. And like the women of Indus Kohistan who wear a peaked headdress still, and like the Bashgal Kafirs
of the Hindu Kush in Afghanistan who, until they were forced
into Islam, wore long curved horns like an antelope's.

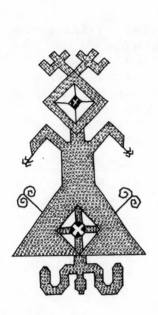

'And are any of these horned goddesses or females you're talking about ever to be seen on skis?' asked Vlad.

Perhaps then, I suggested, these figures cut into these rocks of the far north are ancestors of the Lapps and their horns are merely an earlier version of the padded caps the Lapps still wear.

'Rubbish, all that,' said Vlad.

The bus finally deposited the pilgrims at the town shop, a bleak concrete bunker with closed door, where almost the only thing to buy was alcohol: vodka and Italian amaretto at two dollars a bottle. A resounding crash of breaking glass echoed around the store as a customer fell with his purchases down the wooden entrance steps and collapsed on the ground outside. No one glanced round.

The ragamuffin was still on the jetty along with all the teenagers of town as the boat sailed on northward.

'There's nothing to do in this place,' they called from the quayside.

Belomorsk used to have a trade in evaporated salt long ago, then there were the jobs the Soviets invented.

'Now there's nothing,' they shouted. 'And nowhere to go.'

No hope for the future. Just long nights and emptiness and cheap vodka.

SOLOVKI

✠

On the Thursday of Mary Magdalene the Myrrh-Bearing Woman the *Ladoga* crossed the White Sea towards the monastery of Solovki. The water was choppier, white-crested, the sky cloudier, grey-swirled. Aspen domes again shimmered on the skyline, small grassy islands were skirted until the *Ladoga* berthed before the sinister high wall of gaunt stone, bastioned at each corner, that formed the monastic enclave along the bay. Solovki was no gentle hermitage of retreat, bequeathed by the Tsars with bells and icons. Cannons and gunpowder they had sent, to this northern defence of Russian territory. The monks might be contemplative but they were expected to fire. Attacked by an English vessel in 1855 they had none the less retaliated by bells alone. The English were impressed. 'We will pay for any cattle and the sheep we took. We do not wish to harm the monastery or any peaceful institution', wrote the vessel's captain in flowing copperplate, before he retreated.

Solovki had been too a gulag for the intellectuals exiled here, part of an entire class exterminated by forced labour. In the courtyard of the monastery, George averted his eyes from his fellow pilgrims and sketched the Preobrazhensky Cathedral. The setting of Solovki was bleak, an isolated grassy island where even the Russian birch cannot grow save so twisted by the winds that the trees are known as 'dancing birches'. The gulag prisoners used to be led from the monastery along a causeway to a small outlying island that was only a bare hillock, and there abandoned. Just as centuries before the Old Believers, who could not accept the New Believers' way of signing the cross, had been shipped off to another small outcrop and there left to die. They had merely clung to their belief that the sign should be two fingers raised, symbolizing the divine and human aspects of God, and the other three, representing the Trinity, lowered, whereas the

New Believers had elected to raise three fingers and lower two. It was an important principle, the priests pointed out.

In the forest hinterland some distance from the monastery, at the chapel on the hill of Savatjevo, political prisoners had been tortured through the twenties and thirties. They slept in the unheated chapel in layers on top of each other and, through the seasons, were made to stand outside without moving for six hours, in the summer immobile in unrelenting sun until bitten beyond the threshold of pain by mosquitoes, in the winter until frozen to death. Some were given five minutes to fetch a bucket of water from the distant sea and tortured to death if they overran their time. Others were made to sit on a thin stick without shifting and, if they failed, were thrown down a steep wooden staircase to their deaths in the forest far below. George sat on the grass above these steps, facing away from them towards the chapel, sketching meticulously, detailing each fine embrasure, each exquisite mullion built in praise of God.

Declared a UNESCO heritage site a year or two ago, the monastery itself was now abuzz. Plank walkways wobbled over precipitous holes and mounds of rubble. Volunteers – black-robed monks with high black hats, pilgrims with rucksacks and poor clothes, museum restorers, hangers-on – chopped away at stone steps, moulded and shaped them, skidded them with sand and left lazy gaps.

'Yanks,' said Vlad, 'will be falling on those and suing UNESCO for millions. Could close the whole site.'

In the Church of the Assumption workmen, surrounded by mops and buckets, scraped intrusive nineteenth-century frescoes off the walls while others scratched away in the icon repair shop. The flaked bricks of the churches and cathedrals that formed the monastery enclave were being replaced by new red ones, ferried across the courtyard in a human chain from monk to monk.

Through a dark passageway, fragrant with warm bread, was the monastery bakery. It had remained unchanged for hundreds of years, baking for the devout and the condemned. Its stone floor was scrubbed, its pine shelves sprucely set with wooden bread moulds. By two huge metal drums that were the baking ovens, one woman in white apron and mob cap stood at a deep kneading bowl, her arm muscles flexed, while another scurried to and fro with the leavened bread. Both were thin, as buxom peasant women of the fields become, confined in an intense heat and sweat that sharpens cheekbones and hollows flesh. Twice a day they turned out two hundred and seventy loaves and trundled them out of the monastery on wooden trolleys with rusty handmade wheels, to be sold in the village.

The labyrinth lay beyond the village, beyond the blue log cabins, the little wooden washhouses, the seaweed factory. The way to it led past a concrete store where a large dog sniffed us and tagged along, past the cows, the goats, the rocks, the seaweed drying on racks, past storehouses buried under grass roofs, then through woods of dancing birches, ferns and heather underfoot, and out onto a flat grassy headland. Beyond lay the sea, nothing but sea to the pack ice of the north. The only sounds were the bark of seals playing in the water and the thrash of their bodies on the white crests. Then, intermittently, a dull thud from a bomb range. The dog sat motionless on the shore, ears aprick, white tail curled around black fur, and watched the seals.

It must have been a pagan shrine, the labyrinth, this maze of crouching stones spiralling out from two low cairns, with isolated boulders placed uncasually around. The earth goddess, the fertility goddess, the goddess mother, Berehinia, was always associated with stones and cairns, with water, with trees, with dancing. It was easy to imagine the inhabitants of these remote lands, the same hunters of whale, deer and bear who had carved their trials and trophies on the boulders of the forest clearing we had seen at the southern tip of the White Sea, dancing around this 4,000-year-old labyrinth, hanging cloths on the twisted birches, plunging naked into the sea, in rituals that ensured the fertility of the land.

But what fertility was there here in this grassy waste? The people who passed through were hunters, their gods – or were they goddesses? – horned. Was the fertility they hoped for only of berries, of grasses, of mosses for the animals they hunted? And was it this shrine to the fruits of the earth and the hunt, pagan though it might be, that had led the saints Savatius and

Zosima to choose this desolate spot to found their monastery
and to designate its lake holy?

The Alsatian swam straight into it, holy or not, after the stick
his master threw him. Our dog had left us as we returned past
its home and we continued back to the monastery without him,
Mary and I. It was here that we found them – through a maze of
dank, dirty passageways – several women in dirndl skirts, and
two small girls, from St Petersburg. They were the Hand
Weaving Club of the Goddess, here to set up an exhibition of
textiles. They were camping in a small room, their sleeping bags
cheek by jowl on the floor, their saucepans, toothbrushes and
tins of meat round a small gas ring. They were weaving and
embroidering the design of the goddess on belts and cloths and
towels. The little girls pushed their needles against the wooden
floor to drive them through the thick cloth as they made dolls
wearing blouses with Berehinia worked on the sleeves, her skirt
a triangle, her headdress a triangle with horns, her hands triangles
with raised fingers.

And the triangle with pendants, was that an amulet they
believed in and used? Yes, yes, they said. It was a symbol of
fertility, the triangle with tasselly pendants, from long before
Christianity. They made it of leather and wore it hanging from
a belt to protect themselves against illness and the evil eye. Or
they wore it as jewellery. One had new earrings of wood in just
that design. They gave her a feeling of inner peace, she said.
But on their textiles they never had triangles, only the figure of
the goddess and patterns of horns.

Svetlana, founder of the club, was a curator at the Ethnography
Museum in St Petersburg. Hearing that we had seen nothing
but churches, she promised Mary and me a tour through the
museum's cupboards and drawers when the boat docked there
at the end of the pilgrimage.

Back at the *Ladoga* two smart yachts had anchored in the harbour
beside her. A yacht race round the northern seas, someone said.
A group of Italians in designer jeans and crucifixes walked past
talking about ravioli and the hour of dinner. Old women sat on
the quayside selling jars of smoked herring. The sun set that
night on a plain white sea, streaked only by the black stones of

the causeway, the sky only a shimmered creasing, the sun only a plain red disc. We sailed southward before dawn, my mind in a sleepless confusion of goddesses, triangles and horns, stone cairns and picket fences.

OF WOOD, FLAX AND GODDESSES

✙

It was, of course, the confusion of an amateur, an entanglement of iconography that threw goddesses and picket fences together when the one dated back to the Aurignacian and the other to yesterday's woodcutters. The symbolism, the women of the Hand Weaving Club of the Goddess had said, related to the peasants' view of their lives – and not just those of northern Russia – as a cultural space created out of universal chaos, an organized existence to be guarded from the wandering malevolent spirits of the natural world around them. It was the marginal areas of this existence – the fences and gates around their homes, the thresholds, the corners of the frame construction of their houses, where the overlap of the logs was sacral and often carved with mythological beings – that were the most vulnerable and needed protection from the evils beyond. Just as it was the humans in a transitional state – babies who had not yet lived the sanctified forty days, brides and fiancés, and the newly deceased – who needed to be bound with red thread and hung with triangular amulets to keep marauding witches and spirits at bay.

Trees, stones, flax even, in fact most particularly flax, the women added, belonged to the natural world until they were transformed into objects of the cultural world of humans: wood, walls, fabric. Even so, some things were never really assimilated, they remained marginal. The wooden fence was one. Whether it was of woven wattle or of staves it certainly was not there just to keep the deer away from the cabbages, it was a ritual boundary. Even the weaving of the wattle was symbolic. It was well known that tangled hair belonged to creatures of the underworld, whereas neatly plaited hair placed a woman within the context of human society. It was the same with weaving the wattle and neatly setting the staves in diagonal patterns. Such an ordered arrangement of natural materials defined the boundary of human space within chaos. That was why, when a man died, part of the fence was always removed to allow his soul to pass through to the other world. And it was not just the picket fence that defined boundaries. In these northern forests the whole cultural world of the Slavs had been created from timber. They had felled the trees and tamed them, said the women of the Goddess Weaving Club, and closed their lives around with wood.

As for stones, mysterious ancient stones litter the world – the menhir and dolmen of Western Europe, the carved heads of the Celts, the standing effigies across the steppes, the cairns that act as markers. But the labyrinth of Solovki was somewhat different. As a spiral it would have been an obvious sun symbol, but it was not a true spiral, it was a labyrinth and as such it created a small cosmos out of a greater chaos. Walking into it a human or wizard could turn to the left or the right and go in a clockwise or anti-clockwise direction. It was well known in northern Russia that wizards always go against the rotation of the sun. Moving with the sun belonged to the cultured world, withershins to the underworld, so any man wishing to approach the spirits of the underworld simply had to walk against the direction of the sun. The labyrinth offered a clear invitation to walk into it: what was its purpose? Its site on the flat grassy headland beyond the forest and at the side of the lake, in awesome isolation in a landscape that for more than half the year was frozen in ice and snow, was powerfully mysterious. It was, without any doubt, marginal.

Just as, said the weavers, a linen towel is marginal, only ever a transitional object, only part of a larger piece of linen, woven and spun from flax they had grown and, if spun by a bride, it would always be sitting at the threshold of her house or by the gate, revolving her distaff against the direction of the sun. Then, as a linen towel symbolizes life's journey, it cannot be cut from the woven piece but has to be torn away, even by beating with stones, so that the threads are sundered by natural forces. And then never is it used for so mundane a task as drying hands. It is a marker to communicate with spirits and ancestors and so is hung at crossroads and draped around trees and gravestones.

Not unique, of course. Though perhaps it was only in Russia and the Ukraine that, until the Second World War, people had chosen a birch tree standing alone in a clearing to personify the earth goddess and had girded it in women's clothing and hung a linen towel from its branches, the other ways in which towels were ritually used could still be found right into Western Europe. They are draped around doorways and windows – boundaries again between outer chaos and inner calm – around mirrors, where evil spirits hover and through which souls can escape, around washbasins, where the power of water lingers, around icons hanging in the holy corner of the room, and at the hub of the household. This was once the hearth where the goddess dwelt and then became the kitchen stove and now it is the television set over which the ritual towel is laid. And it is almost always embroidered, almost always in red and almost always with the motif of the goddess.

Her guises are many: she is mistress of the horse, queen of the animals, part-tree, part-bee, a sphinx, a siren, giving birth, blessing the crops, calming the elements. Her acolytes are birds, flowers, fire. She is stylized beyond recognition or she is realistic as a woman or a doll. And in the midst of all these goddesses on the embroidered towels of Russia, from Siberia to the Ukraine, and on textiles westward and southward to Europe and the Greek Islands, there were those that lured me to follow their trail: the ones wearing horned headdresses, the ones with club-shaped heads and raised hands, resembling the Minoan goddesses of Crete and the many, many who were nothing much more than a triangle, often with three appendages – two legs and a child being born.

In St Petersburg, the pilgrims ended their odyssey at the Chapel of St Xenia and the Alexandro-Nevsky Lavra and Necropolis, while Mary and I ferreted around the treasures of the Ethnographic Museum. The Soviet Union might have collapsed but the museum remained frozen in days of former glory. Embroideries came from every land between the Baltic States and Mongolia, between Armenia and Chukchia. They looked as if they would always be there, rather as the live crocodiles still bask in the Paris Museum of the Arts of Africa

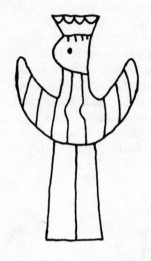

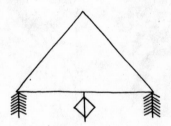

and Oceania from the days when it was the Museum of the French Colonies.

Mary had the unique ability of the fanatic to see goddesses on everything, whereas, accepting that my interest was perhaps equally limited, I observed that it was the embroidery of the Mordvinians and Chuvash in particular that was decorated with cowries, blue beads, bits of metal and coins. And that the triangle with three pendants was appliquéd in red fabric on Chuvash aprons, and that dangling from the belts of Mordvinians were triangles of beads and coins, hung with three double red tassels, a blue bead between each one.

I said goodbye to Mary, who was bent enquiringly over some rags tied to a baby's coffin, while I set off for the Hermitage. I descended into the bowels of the building below the salons of malachite and crystal, below the treasures of Western art – the familiar Madonnas of Leonardo da Vinci and the blurred snowy suburbs of pre-industrial Paris – down some badly lit steps, past a couple of massive stone carvings of goddess figures from the remote steppelands to the south, and then, opening a closed and ummarked door, entered the room containing the textiles dating from around 400 BC that had survived frozen in the tombs of Pazyryk in southern Siberia.

The great felt, so huge its purpose remains a mystery, covers, even partially rolled, one wall of the room. The goddess sits holding a sacred branch, approached by a rider on a horse, a motif repeated across the whole felt. Her face is heavy and masculine, her headgear flat and not horned. It is the skeletons of the horses that are horned. Buried in their hundreds with these nomadic European and Mongol people of the steppes, they are crowned with symbolic horns, encased in gold. The felt shabraks that lined their saddles are embroidered with the motif of an animal of the hunt attacking some pastoral beast, a design common in Scythian art and – thousands of years earlier – in paleolithic, and are edged with jazzy bits of metal foil, fringes and falderals. Even a fine piece of imported Chinese embroidery of delicate pheasants on graceful tree branches receives the same treatment, framed by the ferocity of pagan belief.

A linen shirt has also survived, edged in red, as have four flying swans made of felt, which probably hung as amulets from each corner of one of the huge wooden carts the nomads moved their women and goods in. But of the tasselled triangle there was no sign, neither embroidered on the shabraks, nor hung with the felt swans, nor sewn in red on any clothing.

I caught the night train to Moscow with Marina, the interpreter.

It was only a gentle click that woke us. The compartment door slid slowly open and revealed the silhouette of a man standing in the corridor. He shone a small shielded flashlight along the bunks with deft quick movements. Suddenly the lights of a passing station, skimming like a circling searchlight, partially illuminated his face and highlighted his glinting rapacious eyes. He started and slid the door quickly to again.

'By inserting a knife through the gap the door can be unlocked from the outside, and he acts undoubtedly with the connivance of the train guards,' said Marina, who had gleaned her English entirely from books.

'And in any case the Mafia would have the keys. The corruption here now is endemic. One of our number on the ship was not a pilgrim but a bodyguard. He conceals most efficaciously a dangerous knife inside his trouser leg. We are unable to escort foreigners without such a man. He should have accompanied us on this train.' Marina sighed. 'There is no hope for Russia.'

MOSCOW

✠

On the Friday of the Ghost of Kafka – as I felt it surely should be called – as soon as we arrived in Moscow, Marina attempted to buy my rail ticket on to Nizhni Novgorod. This took from the early morning to the late afternoon, when we set out for her flat. It was in one of a series of shabby white twelve-storey blocks set in a rough terrain of unkempt grass and disorderly trees. Built to last for twenty years the flats had survived way beyond with cardboard sheets placed over chipped defective concrete, and loose electric wires tangled around rusty piping. Dom 5, the entrance to the block was signed, flats 1–54. The doors of the paired lifts were of grey steel, as if leading to a prison, and the lifts inside were corroded and dirty, floored with three layers of worn-out lino and littered with fag-ends, though the women paid to clean the place earned more than a university professor.

'It's absurd,' said Marina, 'crazy. Those who work earn nothing, those who do nothing, prosper. And those who are cultured are ostracized.'

The door to the flat was padded in brown plastic like a cell. Inside, two small rooms – and a minute kitchen of odd wooden cupboards, piled-up pots that found no space and an empty fridge that ran noisily and ineffectually – housed three people and a curious, playful cat. The cramped confusion came not only from a desperate tucking into corners of every plastic bag of recent acquisitions, including the clothing of the new daughter-in-law who so far only visited, but also from a reluctance, born of need, to discard anything. An out-of-date advent card, an empty half-bottle of Dewar's whisky, a bent melted candle, a clay sculpture of a female torso with accidentally severed head, set in a bronze holder shaped like a long-legged wolf, stood on the piece of thin carpeting that covered a broken table.

In spite of these frivolities it was the flat of an intellectual, superimposed by the discovery of faith and the embrace of the church. Two pianos, which no one now played, were piled with bags and books. Books were everywhere, rows of them, tipsily supporting yet more, trailing snippets of paper marking favourite or scholarly references. A higgledy-piggle of bindings, spines, dust jackets, sharp clean white fore-edges and crinkly yellowed ones. The subjects they covered ranged from an explanation of Hebrew grammar in German, through Chaucer and remaindered gifts from English friends, through French histories of Ancient Christianity and French poets – Mallarmé, Baudelaire – in those soft sugar-paper volumes of the immediate post-war years, to a wealth of erudite books in Russian.

Propped up against them, against the piano, the walls, and wobbling near the torn curtains, were dozens of tawdry postcard icons. They depicted all four versions of the Mother of God – 'In Her Mercy and Tenderness' holding the Christ child to her cheek, 'Showing the Way' as she cradles Christ in the crook of her left arm, her right laid as an elongated delicate pointer across her breast, leading our eyes to Christ, who holds the scroll of the Holy Gospel in his hand.

'Read and know the gospel,' said Marina, 'and you will enter heaven.'

In others the raised and gracefully hooked fingers of Mary serenely blessed erring mankind. 'The Virgin Enthroned' appealed less to Marina and there were few that showed her in this guise. Most beautiful – though as a lurid fairground print on a card tablemat placed close to the empty whisky bottle – was Andrei Rublev's flowing Trinity, the chalice at the heart of the icon, swirled around by three angels robed in the heavenly hues of magenta, blue and ethereal transparency.

Marina was a devout follower of the Russian Orthodox Church and worshipped at the church in Moscow to which our priests and organizer, Ivan, belonged. She had leapt at the chance of accompanying our cruise without pay. In no other way could she enjoy such a feast of devotion and her old mother would look after the cat. Her husband, whose name she never mentioned, of

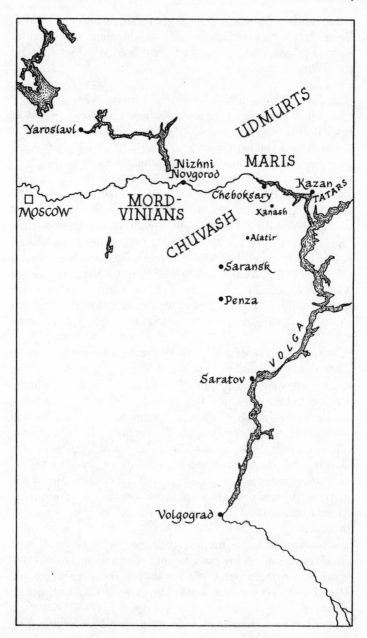

whom she could not bear to speak, and whose photo – an intense, honest face with a intelligent smile and the plumpness of youth – stood propped among the icons, had been killed long ago by the Soviet system.

The flat had been difficult to reach. A metro ride followed by two trams, changing at junctions where the tracks veered in several directions and people sat on the pavement selling cigarettes in ones and twos, then a walk through a park approached by a pair of white gates incised with hammer and sickle.

'This park was originally laid out by Peter the Great,' said Marina, 'but the authorities only placed their emblem at the entrance and then failed to look after it.'

A potholed drive led through rough grass and trees past the Lyefortova prison where Solzhenitsyn had been imprisoned before being exiled and where innumerable nameless political prisoners had preceded or followed him. I wondered whether Marina's husband had been one, but she continued talking with no suspicion of a crack in her voice. Past the park and out through a less impressive exit, another tram ride had led to the flat.

Returning to central Moscow the next day to catch the train to Nizhni Novgorod we had taken a different route and had reached the metro more quickly. Marina no longer spoke of the Church and the Soviets and we stood looking at the single huge poster in the station. It showed a sleek bronzed model in an ultra-smart swimsuit lying beside a glitzy pool, a German sun-tan oil at her side. Pushing into the train, the red digital display showing that the last one had passed only 2.14 minutes before, an eye-catching advertisement posted everywhere round the carriage promised a 1,600 per cent return on investments. Marina had insisted on accompanying me because of the risk of assault.

The approach to the mainline station was lined with countrywomen selling salami and cucumber. Drunks lay sprawled on the ground, gypsies jostled and begged, a child played a squeaky violin, kiosks displayed vodka and pirated cassettes.

'I fail to understand why your train should be leaving from

this station,' said Marina, 'and not from the one for trains to the east.'

The station was wrong, the platform was wrong, the train was wrong. Marina had been sold a ticket to Yaroslavl instead of Nizhni Novgorod.

'It's the Mafia,' she said. 'They buy all the best tickets and sell them to their friends. Other people get sent anywhere. The Mafia will kill Russia before it even begins to live. And they control the imports. Look at this' – she pointed to a kiosk – 'five thousand roubles for a bottle of vodka, but twelve thousand for a bag of children's sweets. They mostly come from the Caucasus, the Mafia, Chechens mainly, though there are some Russians,' she said. 'It's the young men of about seventeen who are the most dangerous. They have no morals and they're armed. All small businesses have to pay them protection money.'

We went from station to station, from queue to queue to try to buy the right ticket.

'But we must sell the other. Someone will need it.' Marina looked worried.

Back at the original station, we found an anxious young man in a purple T-shirt emblazoned 'Gucci' pacing up and down the platform. He had been waiting for two days with his wife – she was wearing a matching purple T-shirt, shorts and Adidas trainers and guarding two large bags and a small boy – hoping to get on the train to Yaroslavl. He would buy the ticket if he could get another.

'Look the other way,' said Marina. 'He will have to give the train guard a hefty bribe and will be reluctant to do so with a foreigner watching.'

I gazed a while into the middle distance and then turned around to see the young family gathering their baggage to get on the train. Marina and I set off to return to her flat. Perhaps the next day or the one after that or some time I would manage to get a ticket, to leave the last of my companions behind and begin my slow journey step by step, by train, by boat, by bus, east and then south through the lands of the Golden Horde into Central Asia and beyond. Just a seven-dollar ticket was all I needed.

THE LANDS OF THE
GOLDEN HORDE

NIZHNI NOVGOROD

✠

It was in 1346 that, having rampaged across the steppes and terrified Europe a century before, the Golden Horde flung its last curse at the West. Besieging the Genoese trading post of Kaffa in the Crimea – on the site of which the port of Feodosia now stands – and finding his troops decimated by some unknown pestilence, the commander of the Khan's army catapulted their corpses over the siege walls into the town, where they were left to moulder. The Genoese boats that later departed from there for Italy carried on board the Black Death that was to wipe out a third of the population of Europe.

Travelling into their lands on a slow train I noticed the old women, fattened by years of potatoes, bread and barley porridge – and the fear there may be none tomorrow – flinch at the imported curse of Tom Jones belting out 'Delilah' on someone's radio. They scowled at me, an obvious Westerner. There was also Western democracy that had brought them nothing but deeper poverty and crime – were two armed policemen not at that very moment patrolling the train? There was the humiliation of no longer being a world power, there was their unemployed, disenchanted youth. There were those who prospered under the new order and could afford to buy the Snickers bars and Sun Valley peanuts the free-enterprise kiosks sold, while their own bread and potatoes merely became scarcer and more expensive. They glowered at me as if it were indeed plunder and the Black Death I was responsible for revenging. I smiled back and wondered why they had ever been called golden, these people.

But was it they who were golden, or was it the land itself that was already rife with gold? With real gold. For the Scythians two thousand years before had mined gold in the Altai and Ural mountains and had fashioned it into plaques and ornaments that they buried with their dead in tumuli scattered across the steppes. As at Pazyryk.

Gold had poured in as tribute too when Batu was bequeathed by his grandfather Genghis Kahn in 1227 all those lands west of the Irtysh river, whether conquered or not, and then within a decade had subjugated the Bulgars of the Volga, the Coumans of present-day Ukraine and the Russians. Was it the tribute they paid that had laden this steppe khanate with golden treasure? Tribute had poured into his military camp, the Turkic word for which was *ordu*. Was it this tribute then and the wealth it brought that led the Russians to devise the name 'the Golden Horde' for the khanate founded by Batu?

And what of legend? What of Greek legend? Had the Greeks not traded with the Scythians from their outposts on the northern shore of the Black Sea, traded golden ornaments, influenced each other's style? Has Greek pottery from the sixth century BC not been found in what were Scythian settlements way up the Dnieper river, south of Kiev?

And where was the golden fleece that Jason sought? He had sailed across the Black Sea, so called because of the black mists that shroud it, to Asia. And how far did he penetrate? The Ural mountains were known to the ancient Greeks and Romans and so must their gold have been: the mountains the Romans called Rhiphaei were identified by the Russian scientist Lomonosov in 1760 as the Urals. In legend these were north of Scythia, where gorgons lived, but the name was given to any cold mountain in any northern country. Perhaps Jason's golden fleece was no fleece, let alone that of a ram supposedly the offspring of Neptune, but the solid gold of the Urals.

And did the Greeks not believe in the Arimasps, people they thought lived in the frozen north and stole the gold from the rivers of Scythia that was guarded by griffins?

Then there was simply the theory that it was called the Golden Horde because in the centre of Batu's capital at Sarai in the lower Volga stood his golden throne.

'Crap, all that,' Vlad would have said.

Of the peoples who were subject to the Golden Horde – the Coumans, the Bashkirs, the Tatars, the Mordvinians, the

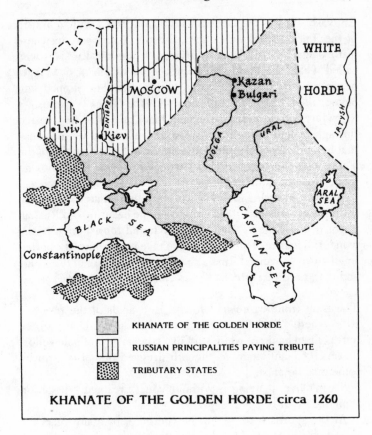

KHANATE OF THE GOLDEN HORDE

RUSSIAN PRINCIPALITIES PAYING TRIBUTE

TRIBUTARY STATES

KHANATE OF THE GOLDEN HORDE circa 1260

Chuvash – it was the Chuvash I was concerned with, a branch of the Turkic-speaking Bulgars. But the Tatars too, in whose history again Greek legend surfaced. It was the Russians who called 'Tatar' the Turkic-speaking peoples of Turkic or Mongol origin who formed the Golden Horde, but they slipped into being called Tartar, in confusion with the Greek Tartarus – a legendary hell shrouded in the same black mist Jason had crossed through to find himself in Asia, a hell inhabited by monsters, that befuddled people into equating the bellicose cruelty of the Tatar with the ogres of that particular Hades. Karpathos no longer seemed quite so far away.

As the Chuvash and Tatar were my immediate destination, my journey – instead of encompassing the beautiful old Russian towns of the Golden Ring, the new-found tourist circuits, the wonderful wastes of Siberia – was to take me through the boring small-town provincial Russia that lies in the crook of the Volga and that, until recently, had been closed to foreigners.

The train trundled on past forests, and fields of the rose-bay willow-herb I had learned to recognize on the boat journey north. Then banks of white stuff like cowparsley, of pale yellow flowers, of giant stems of rhubarb drugged out of control by some mad botanist.

'I can't live, if living is without you,' screamed Nilsson on someone's radio.

At the approach to Nizhni Novgorod – for many years the closed city of exile of Gorky, but now back with its old name and hoping for visitors – the scenery changed and the flowers wilted. We passed a tangle of power lines amid pylons and huge concrete pillars hung with electrical connectors like the flags of all nations. Everywhere were blackened factories, abandoned – or maybe not? – with broken windows and gaunt chimneys. Littered along the tracks were hundreds of railway trucks, old diesel engines, even old steam engines. It had seemed just possible in the north, because of the odd desolate, deserted coal-bunkering yard along the canal edge, that this was a country where junk was never disposed of. At Nizhni Novgorod it was obviously so.

The minute one walked through the old town, it was very clear that the idea of a closed city called Gorky to celebrate its famous son's support of the Soviet regime had been entirely shrugged off. It was as if the change of name had wiped out the exile there of so many dissidents, as if Sakharov's pleading for international understanding was now enshrined in the freedom to revive the town's historical name. The shedding of the name Gorky seemed more remarkable than that of Leningrad, Stalingrad and a thousand Karl Marx squares.

The Soviet sleaze lay low around the station, excoriated blocks of flats, potholed roads, an architecture of despair. But a bus ride up to the ramparts of the old city overlooking the Volga led to a new buzz of life. Little girls in frilly dresses, their flaxen hair tied up in frothy nylon bows, took pony rides up and down outside the old baroque theatre; people strolled along eating ice-creams. It seemed delightful until problems surfaced for me when it became obvious that the hotel opposite the theatre, recommended as being the only reasonable one in town, had been closed and shuttered for some considerable time. Its grimy door was propped to against an ineffectual lock by an unravelling wicker chair on which sat one of the usual fat-kneed '*niet*' breed of women.

The only other hotel lay on the far side of a square on a beautiful promenade high above the river, whose faded elegance had more than a whiff of the Riviera about it. The hotel would not have been out of place there either, apart from the armed Russian soldier on duty outside, nor indeed would its tariff, and I was obliged to settle into a small sordid broom cupboard on the top floor. Another armed man guarded the lift and as I came down for dinner I found an American tour group had taken over the place. No dinner was therefore forthcoming and I had to fall back on the leftovers from that morning's breakfast, which Marina had wisely insisted I might need, and a jar of solid boiled condensed milk that her kindly neighbour had contributed.

An evening stroll along the promenade did lead me to the Gardenia restaurant, an establishment in whose garishly floodlit forecourt flew the US flag. A few BMWs and Mercedes were parked in the bright light, seemingly the only cars in town. A couple of prostitutes in staggeringly high-heeled gold sandals leant nonchalantly against them. On the pavement outside the open kitchen door, two cooks were taking a breath of fresh air

and sharing a joint. A glimpse inside the door revealed a confusion
of old egg shells, scummy plastic packets, potato peelings and
spilt rice that littered indiscriminately the filthy worktops and
cracked floor.

The next morning the Americans in the hotel and the armed
guards moved on and I set out to view Nizhni Novgorod and
look for its ethnographic and history museums. The history one
was a little further along the promenade from the hotel and
turned out to be a beautiful baroque building, its blue façade
embellished with caryatids and its front door bearing the sign
'Closed. *Remont*'. This message was to become a recurring theme
on hundreds of public buildings where no repairs had actually
been, or were likely to be, carried out but where an endemic
shortage of cash and the collapse of local administration had left
them unstaffed and unmaintained.

The promenade was a mile or so long and led away from the
town, one side edged for its whole length by a decorated iron
railing above steep grassy slopes that fell away to the enormously
wide Volga far below. Large shadowy boats lay moored in the
distance, the odd steamer, tug and hydrofoil plied its way down
river.

On the other side of the promenade the big old houses stood
deserted behind railings and trees, while a few modern buildings
housed official institutes. Outside them one or two Western cars
would pull up or leave but otherwise no traffic fractured the
silence. The promenade ended abruptly at a rusty fence behind
which towered one of those sky-high ski-jumps of the sort
featured on winter sports T V programmes where tense competi-
tors zoom off into the void. To all appearances, had it been in
operation and not abandoned for many years, it would have
catapulted would-be ski-jumpers straight into the Volga.

Around this erection lay the old Muslim quarter, a slum of
wooden houses set on wide dirt paths, old women and dogs
sunning themselves on the doorsteps. A wooden mosque was
padlocked, a plaster Orthodox church was boarded up but bore
a notice 'Open 8 to 12' and then what I construed was Sunday
though the Russian words for Sunday, 'Resurrection', and Monday, 'the day after the day you rest', I somehow had not managed

to master, a loss of the linguistic skill of my youth that depressed me deeply.

My miserably basic Russian made the prospect of ordering dinner that evening alarming. The Americans having left the hotel some was available and I checked the words of the menu in my small pocket dictionary. They were almost illegible and appeared to date from when the hotel must have welcomed upper-crust Soviet bureaucrats. Still unfamiliar with the order of the Cyrillic alphabet I fumbled for some time. I found only lobster and beefsteak, neither of which would they of course actually have, but otherwise only 'splinter', 'one and a half', 'magnifying glass' and, even more alarming, 'swaddle and swathe', 'altar cloth'. I plumped finally for 'freemason (aromatic)', which turned out to be the usual piece of stringy grey meat and potatoes.

Along the river bank from the Muslim quarter the promenade led to a large square where women sat selling dahlias, dark red gladioli and wild mushrooms, flanked by a walled citadel that was the original heart of the city. Beyond it lay a pedestrianized zone that was now its centre. It was Monday but even so the little girls on ponies were joined by adults sitting in sled-like carriages pulled by small belled horses and pursued by well-fed pet dogs. People thronged up and down still licking ice creams. They sat at pavement cafés drinking Pepsi and eating hot-dogs. Girls passed in sassy swinging black minis and brief sleeveless tops, middle-aged women clattered along in high heels, past shop windows still displaying the dowdy macs and matronly brown dresses they had been used to wearing. An old Uzbek woman lay on the pavement, a small boy at her feet, wailing and howling and wiping away crocodile tears. Opposite her an old Russian woman sat dignified on a broken chair quietly holding out her hand. Another went from café to café collecting all the empty bottles left on the tables and in the bins to sell them for what she could get. The Uzbek got none of my roubles. Men balanced on scaffolding repairing the lovely old shopfronts were the only sign that it was a working day. The ethnographic museum was open.

It was actually the first floor of a modern building, above a shop and entered by a small side door. It was full of woodcarvings – lintels, window frames, shutters and doors carved with grapes and vine leaves, with mermaids and fish. Solar symbols were on everything, on laundry beaters, distaffs and gingerbread moulds. The textiles included brocaded red towels with the goddess figure and dresses from the region. Those of the Chuvash and the Finno-Ugric peoples – the Maris, the Mordvinians – were finely worked with geometric patterns, but the Udmurt and Tatar were gaudy rubbish, just patchwork and appliquéd ribbons. I eliminated the Tatars from my enquiries and prepared to leave the next day to sail down the Volga to Chuvash territory.

THE CHUVASH

✠

The Volga must once have been a mighty rolling river, but its waters were now splayed by hydroelectric schemes into turgid bulges along its low banks, disturbed only by the odd splat as the currents of the main course tumbled by. The boat stopped at little jetties of mildewed planks, sometimes with the cupolas of wooden churches visible above the trees behind them, sometimes fronting a small stone kremlin.

The landing stage of Cheboksary was beautiful in its simplicity. There was no concrete, there were no lights, there was nothing that had not always been there from time immemorial, from time in the memory of fishermen, boatmen and riverine trade. Everything was constructed of wooden planks – the landing quay, the walkways, the small green building, like an old-fashioned railway ticket office, where the timetable of two boats a day was pinned. Only a worn bollard for the ropes hurled from arriving boats and the port master's kettle and mug had not been made from the local trees. No road led from it into town, only a sand-drifted path, some duck-boards and a small bridge of loose rickety wooden steps.

The few people who got off the ferry followed this path and then began to disperse along more sandy tracks that led towards the town. I asked the way, only to be cold-shouldered, but then the people I had foolishly chosen to ask were those I had already seen littering the boat with crisp packets and egg shells. I continued to where everyone congregated at a bus stop in an open wind-swept square, in the centre of which stood an imposing peach and white theatre adorned with Corinthian columns and carved figures. A young couple beckoned, took me with them on the trolleybus and put me off at the only hotel in town, paying my fare.

Supper in the buffet was a hardboiled egg, a tomato which

the surly assistant weighed to calculate its price, a solidly hefty pasty with nothing inside but yet more pastry, and a small bottle of red wine which turned out to be sweet cherry brandy. The phone rang eerily in the middle of the night, as it was to in almost every hotel room I stayed in that actually had a phone. I put it outside on the windowsill.

Cheboksary is the capital of the Chuvash Autonomous Republic and turned out to be a town of trolleybuses and trams that plied up and down from the Volga to the centre, along streets lined with impressive municipal buildings of decayed splendour or Soviet squalor. It was a town still struggling to reconcile its present with its past. Whereas other towns had long since toppled their statues of Lenin, Cheboksary's still stood in the middle of the main street, a massive plinth on which a huge Lenin was glued, marching none the less forward, his arms behind his back, gazing from beneath his peaked cap into the future. If the city fathers – whoever they were now – were to jettison this monstrous heap, should they not be obliged, even more so, to hack up the epic group of four mounted, helmeted men staring firmly ahead, that was entitled 'Monumental Decorative Composition: March of the Chuvash Delegation to Moscow with a Petition on Voluntary Incorporation into the Moscow State'. Then there was the hilltop 'Monument of Soldier's Glory' of a soldier kneeling before the Soviet flag. Only the statue of I. Ya. Yakovlev, founder of the Chuvash alphabet, a large ponderous figure not unlike a gorilla waiting for his dinner, fitted in with the new city of dollar exchange booths and kiosks selling German apple juice and bananas. The way forward would be slow and people shuffled past the statues without a glance.

If the statues aroused no curiosity, my presence did. It seemed to amaze everyone that I was English. 'Checher,' they muttered. 'Margaret Checher.' The paucity of my Russian again frustrated me to screaming point. I couldn't explain that she'd been dumped or why, couldn't discuss their lives, couldn't communicate with museum curators, who kissed me instead. I accosted hopefully young people in English T-shirts – a blonde in 'Just Do It. Nike Air', a youth in '1527. A Glen More Castle. Scotland for Aye' – but not one ever understood a word of what they were wearing.

Wandering up the hillside into a quiet village of wooden houses, I passed old men leaning on walking sticks, women bent double trudging along under the weight of buckets, women clearing the paths with shovels. All stopped to greet me and ask where I was from. They looked shell-shocked and nudged each other. I longed to be invited into one of their homes but, if I lingered and smiled, they merely clicked their high wooden gates more firmly behind them.

So it was only in the museums that I could see how the Chuvash lived. They were a people descended from the Bulgars who settled in the Volga area in the sixth century, with an admixture from their Finno-Ugric neighbours, the Maris and Mordvinians. As a group they had become part of the Golden Horde. Then, after Ivan the Great refused to kiss the stirrup of the Khan in 1502 and finally sealed the fate of the Horde, their territory was seized by the Russians. Most of the Chuvash became Orthodox Christians though some remained Sunni Muslim but, while the churches were now being dusted down, the mosques stayed closed. Their evolvement as a separate people had been gradual. It was only in the mid eighteenth century that Yakovlev devised their alphabet – of necessity in Cyrillic script though their language was Turkic – and only in 1920 that the Chuvash Autonomous Region was created. Now they had joined – this time voluntarily – the Russian Federation.

The large map of Chuvashia that filled a wall of the ethnographic museum was, I observed on peering closely, entirely hand embroidered. So were the curtains. The old linen shifts on display were decorated with small black hooked patterns, exactly like those of Bulgaria, and hung with twist thread tassels, each thread ending in one small white bead, exactly like those of the Turkmen and Uzbek of Central Asia. The Chuvash shifts were appliquéd with red silk ribbon and embroidered each side of the neck to form a cross, as on the shifts of Razgrad in Bulgaria. They were worn with headdresses of coins – Arabic-inscribed coins of the Golden Horde, Russian ten-kopek pieces, Austro-Hungarian crowns. Some headdresses peaked in a silver-capped horn shape at the top. Some had an embroidered flap hanging down the back, like those of the Kirghiz. The traditions of the

Chuvash went back to 'hoary antiquity', the catalogue said. They
were a vital link in a chain between Central Asia and Eastern
Europe, especially Bulgaria, that I should have known about
years ago and, had I known about it, would have been saved a
great deal of travelling and trouble, wandering in error around
places like Afghanistan and Iran.

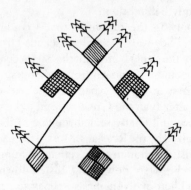

Of goddesses and triangles there was no sign, except at the
neck of an eighteenth-century man's shift. There it was, the only
one, the triangle with three pendants and embroidered black
squiggles above that turned it into the goddess emitting life-
signals. Perhaps there had been many others. But the whole
tradition had now been lost, tidied up by the Soviets into factories
and communes where 'Grand Soviet Master Craftsmen' and
'People's Painters of the Republic' turned out sterile cushion
covers and bookmarks. 'Of late in connection with the building
of the Cheboksary Hydro-Electric Power Station, new plants,
factories, Palaces of Culture and dwelling houses, monumental
and monumental-decorative art, in particular, has been greatly
developing', the catalogue proudly stated.

Would there be anything left? Would there be anything to
find through the towns and villages of the collapsing Soviet
Union? On this journey I was heading towards Central Asia –
the new republics of Turkmenistan, Uzbekistan, Kirghizstan –
then over the Tien Shan mountains into western China and
over the Karakoram to Islamabad, where I was expected to read

my paper on Islamic embroidery. Then, in the next spring or summer, I planned to return here and travel westwards.

My journeys, I reflected, when seen on a map, were in the shape of a coathanger slung from the Russian Arctic, instead of a neat and logical semi-circle from Asia to Europe. It's always here, in the middle, that those metal hangers from the dry-cleaners snap with one slight twist and in truth, if after all one eighteenth-century example in one museum was all I was going to find of my amulet amongst the Chuvash, it would be best to consider the link broken and hasten on.

I ventured that last evening to the hotel restaurant instead of the buffet for dinner. A pianist in a grey suit tried to make himself heard above the din of a pop group. A small man in jeans led a massive woman in a bright red dress on to the dance floor. All of a sudden armed soldiers burst in and pushed everyone out into the street. Some customers tried to take their meal with them, others panicked. 'Alarm,' they shouted to me. 'Killer.'

THE MID-VOLGA

✠

A barometer of the prosperity or otherwise of provincial Russian towns became the kiosks where Western goods were sold. Should there be bananas, Finnish fruit juices, Uncle Ben's Rice, Wrigley's gum, Italian lemon vodka, Snickers and Mars, then the town would be brash and buzzing. Girls in mini-skirts would walk its streets, men might wear suits – though I never saw a tie – and there would be pet dogs and shop-window displays. But where the kiosks – or worse, if there were none at all – stocked only local vodka and Mars bars, then the girls would be shabby, the women would wear cut-off gumboots, there would be deep puddles and dreary concrete buildings, the old wooden houses would be mildewed and in disrepair and the Mars past their sell-by date.

This was the Russia I journeyed through. The forgotten small towns, the supposedly unchanged countryside. Even here the 'Mafia' had encroached. As the bus waited to leave Kanash – the first miserable town where I searched for embroidery – a young man with spiky hair, his bronzed and muscled torso overspilling an Italian blue and white striped singlet, stood on the steps of the bus throwing off any ragged old women and children. The passengers he let on the bus he scowled at menacingly through mirrored sunglasses, the paper label with the designer's name still stuck on the front. When three policemen got on he merely looked the other way and then took some money from the driver before the bus moved off.

It followed a dead straight road through miles and miles of dense forest of pine and birch. Here and there at small wooden villages almost hidden in the trees women carrying orange plastic buckets filled with wild mushrooms would get on and off. The town I was heading for was Alatir, a real no-hoper.

Its centre was a desolate concrete square where Lenin's statue still stood and red hoardings proclaimed the town's 'achieve-ments'. From it little streets of sticky black mud and unchan-nelled rivulets tumbled downhill between rows of wooden houses, so decrepit they looked like nibbled gingerbread. A small park behind the hoardings had been ambitiously equipped some forty years before as a children's playground and had not been touched since. A rusty big wheel stood motionless, its ripped red plastic seats swinging gently in the rain, a small child sitting expectantly in the bottom one hoping for something to happen. Another child carefully hooked up the corroded chains along what had once been a wooden boat to ride in, two drunks walked by.

The tipping rain bounced off the buildings round the square: a pompous porticoed Palace of Culture, padlocked for many a decade, a shop with concrete façade and cracked closed door, selling only pickled cucumbers and bags of sugar, drab municipal offices, the sole café in town, which shut at six and catered for the local alcoholics and the guests of the one hotel, where the rainwater pouring through the ceiling was being attacked by bucket and mop, and where no one but me was staying.

When I left at dawn the bus shelter was bright with old women, as wide as they were tall, galoshes over their woolly stockings, their layers of clothes held by a tied apron, flowery headscarves encircling their rosy cheeks. They stood beside buckets of cucumbers, crab apples and wild mushrooms.

'Anglia?' they said in disbelief, laughing through gapped, gold-capped teeth. 'Anglia?' Then, as in Cheboksary, 'Margaret Checher President,' said one. They roared again and one was about to give me a hearty shove but, observing the thinness of my arms, thought better of it and instead picked up her buckets and shuffled away. 'Checher, Checher,' she cackled.

As the bus journeys continued southward the pine forests gave way to deciduous woods and more open country, vast rolling fields of grass, potatoes and poor short corn. Huge obsolete factories littered the landscape like massive toys dumped just anywhere by some petulant childish giant. Their idle blackened chimneys, broken windows and doors hanging off their hinges seemed to shout that they were abandoned but sometimes a few trucks and one or two men hanging around inside the rusty perimeter fence belied such hasty conclusions. There were pylons striding across the land and in the middle of towns massive pipes with corroded lagging, like exhausted batteries leaking acid, lay alongside roads and bridged urban streets. An acrid stink hung in the air, the small rivers steamed, the ponds were coated with algae, the Volga stagnated in hernial pools.

The little houses that lined the roads remained as they had always been. Constructed like log cabins, or simply of wood planking, most were built directly on the earth so that they lurched dangerously. Many had once been burnt and the scorched wood had not been replaced. They were set endways on the road, facing the passing world with three windows framed in fancy carving, and ending at the back in a scurry of decrepit outbuildings and lean-tos. The entrance was always halfway down the side, a small stepped porch hung with onions.

Each was surrounded by a picket fence enclosing vegetable patch, trees of very small apples and, rarely, a few flowers. Always the people had encroached on the wide grass verge in front of their house, tethering their cow there, stacking their winter hay, and leaving their chickens and geese to wander, watched by the old grandfather slouched on a wooden bench. Here and there stood a nursery-rhyme well, still in use, horses and wooden carts went by and sometimes a muddy tractor.

As the bus approached small towns, dreary municipal buildings and a few shoddy blocks of flats that can only have been perilously near collapse as soon as they were built intruded on the old wooden houses. In larger towns many more of such buildings, bigger in scale and greater in number, crowded out the old cottages, which none the less still stood in odd nooks and crannies and were lived in by the old. At Saransk the bus – plastered with bare-breasted pin-ups from the West and photos of Mel Gibson – was held up by a funeral, the pall open so that all could look on the face of the dead woman. It was the first corpse I had ever seen. It was also, I reflected, the first time in the whole of my lifetime that foreigners had been allowed to travel these roads. But I saw no others.

The floor of the museum of Saransk was so highly polished as to resemble glass. Not a speck of dust was visible on the display cases, as the comfortable woman in slippers lit each one as I approached and switched it into gloom again immediately I passed. The costume on display was no longer Chuvash but Mordvinian. Though the workmanship on the white linen shifts and men's shirts might be finer than the Chuvash, they were still decorated with bits of appliquéd red fabric and rows of sequins. Ornate breastplates and headgear were hung with gew-gaws – coins, cowries, buttons, bells, silk discs, metal discs, chains.

One headdress was horned, the silk needlework on the cos-tumes was like that of Afghanistan, and again there were the little black hooked motifs like Bulgarian embroidery, and the tassels of twisted threads with white beads like the Turkmen ones. But the amulets that dangled from the waist were not triangular and the red brocaded towels had no goddess motifs. Only on some large wooden pots of the eighteenth century was she carved, along with the solar patterns that were also on the women's laundry beaters.

The fat woman padded on. There was no director, no curator, no one to question. The cleaners were in charge.

Continuing southward I ambled through dozens of museums, full of stuffed ptarmigan and buzzards, plastic recreations of steppe flowers – paleolithic tulips and stunted iris – dusty dioramas of elks lurking behind birch trees, reconstructions of horned headdresses, replicas of stone goddesses from the steppes, and faded maps of the lands of the Scythians extending around the Black Sea and into Eastern Greece. All had grandiose displays in praise of Communism, which in the first days of freedom had been destined for the rubbish tip. But lack of funds and a gradual realization of their place in history had delayed their destruction so that those comrades who had deemed it an honour to have their photos enshrined in pink marble and gilt now found them-selves part of a public rogues' gallery.

It was after Penza, a town of blistering baroque architecture and umbrella repair shops, that the wooden houses ended and the steppes began. A landscape of limitless horizons, black earth, sunflowers and maize, scabbed with villages of brick, concrete and tin. The way across it was by rail and it was from Saratov – a day's journey south of Penza – that the trains left, to Uzbekistan and Siberia. And it was there that they arrived. Beggars camping in the station had thin olive skin stretched over high cheekbones, the men dressed in tall boots and thick quilted coats, *chapan*, in spite of the summer heat, the children listless and thinly clothed. Passing Russian women, poor themselves, gave them biscuits and money. Some set themselves up trying to sell Bukharan rugs nobody bought. All slept on the station floor, huddled together, surrounded by their meagre possessions.

Around them people queued and shoved and shouted and tried to buy tickets. They milled around dozens of booking offices, each with the destinations and closing times printed in Cyrillic above and each with a surly woman behind the grille. At each '*niet*' the customers disconsolately moved away and then finally succumbed to the touts hovering at their back. Only the help of a small man in a huge T-shirt labelled 'Fantastic Shirt' enabled me to discover that I had to go to Volgograd to catch a train to Turkmenistan. The departure board indicated a train to Volgograd the next day.

The first hotel I tried in Saratov – a seedy place with a lovely wrought-iron staircase – kicked me out with extraordinary viciousness. The second explained that only they were allowed to take foreigners. It was no better and ten times the price.

Saratov was a lively little town. Its main street, leading down to the Volga, was pedestrianized and thronged with people. It boasted a beautiful little Orthodox church with coloured cupolas like St Basil's in Red Square and an empty Yves Rocher shop. There were no statues of Lenin, only of thoughtful men, chin resting in cupped hand. An old-fashioned café with two rickety tables on the pavement and not enough chairs served hunks of bread and watery tea, another with bright red plastic furniture sold spit-roasted chicken and Spanish white wine by the bottle. The one was frequented by the old, the other by the young. The brutal Palace of Culture now housed only a currency-exchange office. Young women sat in the passageways selling bananas, while on the street outside an orchestra in full evening dress played oompahpah music. Girls minced by in tight shiny leggings, old women shambled along with plastic bags and knew that in the new Russia they were the losers.

The pandemonium at the station the next day was only alleviated by the discovery of Swiss chocolate and decent vodka on sale in the dark crevasses that led to the gents' hairdresser, but the train to Volgograd did not exist. There was only a night one and the scramble for tickets took hours. By the third visit – to actually catch the train – the station, the ticket women idling behind the grilles like bored zoo animals behind bars, the Uzbek beggars, the total confusion and racket were comfortingly familiar, and only the stress of finding the right platform and time – neither indicated – remained of a scenario of certain failure. So it was with considerable relief that I found myself in a compartment with a neat woman who promptly took off her clothes, displaying solid white knickers elasticated from waist to mid-thigh and a Valkyrien bra, and changed carefully into a pinafore for the journey. She folded her blouse fastidiously across her knees and placed her book on it, smoothing it ready to read. She put on her reading glasses, carefully lifting her hair to hook them around her ears, and then coughed gently into her hand. The book was a torrid romance.

The train pulled into the imposing marble station of Volgograd at 5.30 a.m. Knots of aimless people sat around but there was none of the frenzy of Saratov. Nor were any trains to Ashkhabad, capital of Turkmenistan, visible on any noticeboard.

I descended into the station underpass. The ladies' loo cost five hundred roubles, a vast sum designed to keep out station loiterers and which prompted me to make a few comments out loud. The woman in charge replied politely and in perfect English. I peered, sleepy-lidded, at this incredible creature, the first I had come across who spoke English. She was overweight, squinted and was spotty, but what a precious find. Why did she not have a much better job than just taking money for the loo? The new bosses want pretty young girls, she said, they don't care whether they speak English or German or whatever, as long as they're pretty. There was now no train to Ashkhabad, she said, after all the acrimony of the break-up of the Soviet Union it didn't exist any more. I'd have to go back to Saratov.

The ticket offices upstairs in the station of Volgograd were as at Saratov, even at that hour of the morning: crowds, queues, shoving, fierce women caged behind grilles – large blonde Russians, as all petty officials were. I asked for a ticket to Saratov. '*Niet, niet*' was snarled back. No tickets for foreigners, no tickets for foreigners to go anywhere. That was the system, and so it would stay. If foreigners had to spend the rest of their lives on Volgograd station, so be it. She would not sell me a ticket. I was unceremoniously pushed aside.

It was two months earlier that I had already tried to make this journey between Central Asia and Europe, that time in the opposite direction, starting in Tashkent. But I had not managed to get very far before being attacked twice within a few days and then collapsing, so that I had had to spend several days and nights in a hospital with no running water or medicines, having my head stitched up before being flown home. The stitching had been done with 'rope', my home doctor said, and my neck was a mess of trapped nerves and damaged bones. He provided me with a surgical collar and told me I was only to go off travelling again if I promised to wear it. This was clearly the moment.

I went downstairs again to my friend in the ladies. I took off my blue shirt and put on a yellow one. I pinned my hair up and put on the surgical collar. My friend wrote on a piece of paper in Russian: 'One ticket for tonight's train to Saratov.' I returned to the fray, sidling into the queue at another ticket office, with my back to the woman who had refused to serve me. When I reached the grille I grimaced and pointed wildly at the collar, indicating that I was unable to speak, and handed over the note and my money.

It was a sunny Sunday and down by the Volga whole families were washing their Ladas, the children hauling tin buckets of river water, the men in their underpants, the women in bikinis,

listening to pop cassettes. But Volgograd in reality was a shrine
to the battle of Stalingrad, that turning point in the war that I
remembered particularly from my childhood: a heroic defence
by the Russians, a well-deserved routing of the Germans and a
total destruction of the city. Rebuilt and thriving it now boasted
an 'Avenue of Heroes', a 'Fallen Warriors' Square' and, on the
edge of town where the worst of the fighting had taken place, a
complete hill that was now a massive memorial. Schumann's
Träumerei wafted through a huge Pantheon hung with scrolls
commemorating the names of a random seven thousand of the
one million Russians killed there.

Tape recordings of the grunts and thuds of battle eddied
around an avenue of massive stone walls, writhing with huge
arms, bayonets, faces, helmets and boots of the defenders of the
city, that led to an immense statue of Mother Russia, breasts
and arms uplifted, towering over all, conquering all. It was a
glorification of war that suddenly made it the Germans one felt
sorry for: those poor young men miles from home in an alien
clime, while the Russians at least were defending their homeland.
Just as it had been for the young Russians in Afghanistan. The
grey-haired professor of English on holiday from Hawaii was
glad to talk. He had no way of communicating with the dolly-bird
fiancée he had just found in Siberia, who walked confidently
along beside him.

In the centre of town the massive sign on top of the main post
office bearing the message 'The Ideas of V. I. Lenin Will Live
and Triumph' had been torn down and replaced by a twinkling
green digital clock and temperature display. But otherwise
Volgograd had hardly stirred: Lenin still stood on his plinth, a
fresh bouquet of red roses and a bunch of dead red gladioli at
his feet, the main street was still called Lenin Prospekt, the
restaurant opposite the station refused to serve me any food as
I didn't have an Intourist number. The city was a monument to
war and politics and its pride lay in its recent past. But not in
its distant past. Of the site of the capital of the Golden Horde,
New Sarai, which is always marked on maps on this bend of the
river, there was no sign. Though Tamerlane had sacked it at
the end of the fourteenth century, archeological excavations had
found evidence of a prosperous metropolis in the ruins he left,

so where were they? At the Intourist hotel the pretty girl behind
the desk spoke no English, nor any other language, and sat
superciliously buffing her nails. My friend at the station had by
this time gone off duty.

As the train pulled out for Saratov, the night sky was lit by a
golden moon and a sudden storm. I held my face at the window
to feel the cool rain on my burnt skin.

The scene at Saratov station was exactly as I had left it, as if
none of the crowds had ever managed to get tickets or to go
home or to depart on trains, as if none of the Uzbeks had even
rolled over on their piles of rags and none of the women had
escaped from behind their grilles. I joined battle once more until,
totally exasperated, I was driven to shout out loud, 'God, where
do they find these people?'

Behind me a voice repeated, 'Yes, God, where are they finding
these people?'

I turned to see a slim, fine-featured girl with a long blonde
ponytail, wearing heavy mountaineering boots, jeans and anorak,
and carrying a massive orange rucksack.

She held out her hand. 'I'm Alexandra,' she said.

I had a travelling companion.

TURKMENISTAN

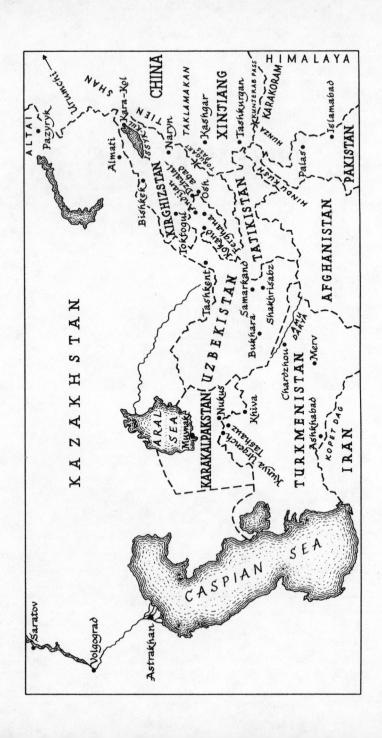

TRAIN TO TURKMENISTAN

✠

It was Lent when, in 1246, accompanied by Friar Benedict, Friar John of Plano Carpini rode into Batu's Sarai. It had taken him five weeks to reach the Volga from the Dnieper. A portly man in his sixties, this envoy of Pope Innocent IV had been given the task of finding out who these Mongols were who had laid waste to Eastern Europe, whether they might come back and from whence they came. He travelled with letters of introduction and gifts of furs, bringing greetings from Christendom and the offer of baptism. In deference to the Christian calendar, he had eaten only millet with salt and water on his way to Sarai and was almost too weak to mount his horse.

'I don't care for your stories,' said Alexandra. 'I am strong. Remember, I am German.'

'Sorry, it was just the millet that made me think of it.'

Three hours we had struggled at Saratov station to buy our tickets for the train to Ashkhabad.

'Three hours, they tell us, we must wait for a ticket,' said A. who had just spent two months studying Russian in St Petersburg. But, at the end of three hours, the woman behind the grille was still saying *niet*. Whereas on my previous attempts to buy a ticket on my own I had looked, I hoped, rather lost and forlorn and had held up my money deferentially, bleating '*billet* Ashkhabad' for hours on end and at each grille, A.'s approach was spectacularly different. She pummelled her rucksack, kicked the wall with her hefty boots, flung her passport to the ground, screamed, 'I kill these people', thumped the wall again, shouted English obscenities it was unseemly for a foreigner to know, clenched her fists and punched the grille. Neither of our techniques worked and we turned slowly away to catch a bus back to town.

'Now they tell me, now they tell me. Three hours before the train must we be here to buy the ticket.'

I began to suspect her Russian wasn't as good as we thought it was.

Alexandra had taken a year off studying to travel, though studying what wasn't quite clear. She thought she might try political sciences next but, in the meantime, had done her Russian in St Petersburg, visited the Crimea and was on her way to Kashmir, where she believed Hunza to be.

'But Hunza's a valley in the Karakoram, quite a few mountains away from Kashmir.'

She ignored me and carried on telling me her plans. From Hunza she would fly to Israel where she had already met a nice ecologist who shared her views on the planet. She hadn't been anywhere else except Israel but knew all about travel.

'I need no money,' she said. 'I am of those travellers who live with the inhabitant.'

The inhabitants milling around outside the station looked unpromising so we set off for the cheap hotel that had refused me a room several days before. A.'s scorn at my incompetence was ill-placed: they turned us both away. We headed for the only hotel that took foreigners, where A. discovered that, with all the banging and thumping she had given it, the pot of honey in the pocket of her rucksack had smashed to bits. The histrionics began again. '*Ich hasse dieses Volk. Ich hasse dieses Land.* You I kill,' she screamed at the women cowering behind the reception desk, as she scooped up masses of sticky glass. Then she calmed down, requesting water and paper to clear up the mess. The reception women raised their eyebrows and quietly gave us a room at the Russian price, a fifth of what I had had to pay before as a foreigner.

A. divided, Führer-style, our chores for the day. 'You,' she said, 'go buy your food for the train. I have. I have my millet, as I say to you and my carrot and all things. Only now not honey.'

The covered market, I found, sold acres of vodka, a bottle or two of English 'Traditional Dandelion Burdock Wine', non-alcoholic and made of chemicals, and a few poor bits of food. I walked for miles along muddy streets through districts of shabby wooden houses that tottered on earth foundations, and when I returned to the hotel found that A. had prepared a meal of millet and carrots for us both.

'I love millet,' she said, tucking in. I could hear the lively band in the street outside, playing by the café where they sold the spit-roasted chicken and the Spanish wine.

'Every day I save an animal,' said A. 'Any animal, a wasp for example. I believe in green. Aeroflot I never fly. They kill the environment. Never an insect do I kill.'

'You should be a Jain,' I said.

'What's that?'

At five the next morning, we were waiting in the dark for the first tram to the station. Everything there was the same. A. raised her clenched fists, she thumped the wall, she screamed, she kicked the steps, she snarled at the Uzbeks. To no avail. We took refuge in the buffet that served only dishwater and sat down disconsolately, A. puffing away at one of the cigarettes I carry to give to people in need.

'You have twenty dollars?' said A.

'Yes.'

'When we say for two tickets, money for two tickets and twenty dollars?'

'Good idea.' I gave her a particularly crisp clean note and off she went. Some time later she returned grinning broadly and waving two tickets.

'We just didn't understand the system' I said.

By this time my feelings towards Alexandra were ambivalent. Her arrogance annoyed me deeply, but her violence was, it had to be said, achieving much more than my patience ever had. I had never met anybody quite so extraordinary and I began to see that her features were perhaps hard rather than being just fine. But in all travelling it's usually best to go along with whatever the wind blows you and, as Alexandra had by total chance become part of my journey, I decided to stick with her and just see how things went. At least, I had to admit, she had got us on the train.

It had come from Moscow. Controllers were stationed outside
the door of each numbered coach, but not one had our number
on. Then right at the end of the platform was a scene of mayhem.
A rusty coach with missing windows and our number on it had
been tagged on to the train and was already full. Old women
were being pushed through the windows head first, their boots
and woolly stockings dangling above the platform. There was
no controller at the door, just a dense mass of people. A. went
to work with her boots and we found our places in an open
compartment with four bunks. Men lay draped on the luggage
racks like leopards lounging on tree branches, some sat on the
floor and others were piled on our bed. A. used her rucksack to
push them along. By the time the train pulled out the passengers
had, by some hefty manipulation on her part, been reduced to
those with places – the two of us, an old lady nursing toothache
in a sparkly scarf, a polite young Turkmen – and an assortment
of louche men with no tickets and dozens of boxes of smuggled
cigarettes.

We were to be on the train for three days and three nights.

'You are old,' said A. 'How old?'

'Sixty-four, sixty-five next month.'

'Exact same as my father. He is son of T. E. Lawrence,
Lawrence of Arabia.'

'What? But he was . . . I mean, wasn't he . . . wasn't there some
sort of a . . . sort of problem in Cairo? Anyway he never married,
I'm sure of that.' Scenes of Peter O'Toole being harassed by
army officers flashed through my mind.

'Yes, it was Cairo. There he had an adventure with a German
woman and there was a son. It was my father. Lawrence would
not marry my grandmother, but he tried to steal the baby.'

'How is it nobody's ever heard of all this?' I asked.

'It is possible they have. At least I have told. From here comes
my love of travel to Arabia lands. I inherit understanding of
Arabs.'

'But I thought you'd only been to Israel before this? Why did
you choose there?'

'I like kibbutz. And I was in Guadaloupe.'

'Guadaloupe? Why Guadaloupe?'

'Because my father gave me a holiday there. He is millionaire.'

'Really,' I said politely.

'Yes, in Germany. He is married six times and now looks for the seventh.'

'And your mother?'

'Half White Russian, half Austrian. She is the fourth wife. So I have many brothers and sisters, some I never know.'

'I thought you said you were German.'

'So I think of myself. Alexandra is a good name, it is any country.'

It seemed odd to think of Germany full of grandchildren of Lawrence of Arabia and I looked at her with considerable scepticism.

The train trundled on all day through golden open steppeland. At stations people sold small silvery salted fish, cucumbers, tomatoes and beer. The old lady shared her crushed hardboiled eggs. A. produced a huge bag of boiled millet, a dry loaf and a big silver knife. The men in the luggage racks leant down and helped themselves to everything. I rubbed vodka on the old lady's tooth, gave her aspirin and offered A. Savlon for the sores I had only just noticed all over her arm.

'No, no. I take no medicine. This crazy body. I have a friend. We take some stuff together. He is dead. I not. But from then, crazy body. Medicine have I never taken. Only plants.'

The train chugged on. Men on horseback rode over the steppe herding their horses and sheep. The scene had changed from Russian to Mongol.

The night was bitterly cold as the wind howled through the glassless window.

'You should think to bring your sleeping bag,' said A.

By the morning tempers were frayed. The old lady produced more hardboiled eggs, A. her millet and bread. Suddenly all hell broke loose.

'I kill him. My knife. Where is my knife? I kill who steals it.'

Boots, arms lashed out, eyes stared down. Then, plop, in all the thrashing the knife fell from the luggage rack on to the bed below.

'Give me your roubles,' A. said to me at the next station.

'They will soon be not useful. I buy food.' She returned with potato doughnuts, meat pasties and things I hate – fizzy orange, beer, cigarettes – and handed them magnanimously around, particularly to the fat-lipped luggage-rack man. 'Perhaps he learn something,' she said.

Outside on the steppe a Bactrian camel indicated another phase of the journey. The Turkmen on the train explained that it was here that the train regularly lost its windows. Kazakh men and boys, they stressed by pulling their eyes into slits – though it seemed an unnecessary refinement, given the shape their eyes already had – threw stones. A. by this time – still eating millet. 'I love millet. Crazy' – was playing snapping finger games with her admiring coterie of gold-toothed Turkmen, whose knowledge of English extended to 'I love you' and 'Dr Album'. I was inevitably dismissed as her mother, or worse – as she liked to translate – her grandmother.

By mid-morning the steppe had changed to desert. The landscape was totally empty, nothing could conceivably have been more empty, no break on the horizon, no features on the land, not a camel, not a goat, not a dog, only dry sandy earth striated by dry sandy scrub. And those relentless telegraph poles, which now seemed the only vestiges of all that once linked an endless land into a so-called loving brotherhood. The night was again cold and sleepless. We must have passed close to the Aral Sea and the old oasis town of Kunya Urgench. They were the furthest points I had reached on my journey from Tashkent a few months earlier, before I had come to grief. I closed my eyes and tried not to think of it.

We woke to the trees and towns of the Amu Darya river valley, the old Oxus that the Mongols had swept across to devastate the lands to west and east, and that the Russians had now tamed, diverted, industrialized and virtually destroyed.

The old lady had got off the train in the night at one of the bleak Soviet towns along its banks. A miserable place, she had said, and so far from her daughter in Saratov. The polite young Turkmen had helped her off while the fat-lipped thief on the rack above had grabbed her bed. He was now fast asleep.

'Some poor girl will be married off to him,' I said.

At the thought of this, A. leapt up, threw his baggage off our beds on to the floor and hid his shoes further along the coach.

At small wayside stations Turkmen women in printed *ikat* dresses sold pramloads of melons. By lunchtime we reached the cotton fields that had drained the Aral Sea – square patches of dark green flock velvet stitched with a pattern of neat irrigation channels. Around them the flat dun land was speckled with dry bushes stunted low to a camel's graze.

The train still crawled on, now waiting frequently at passing places for slow diesels to clatter by in the opposite direction. Sunflowers outlined small vegetable plots between houses of mud and thatch, brick and tin. At each station, A. set off with my roubles and returned with more food, which she dispensed generously to all the men. They crowded round her, flirted with her, gave her their phone numbers and offered themselves as guides to Merv. I munched my last carrot and smouldered.

We were due at Ashkhabad before dawn on the fourth day of the journey, just one more bitter night ahead of us. The train stopped more frequently, more and more people got off, a few got on. Strikingly they were either white-skinned blond Russian, or brown-skinned slant-eyed Turkmen, but there was never a mix of the two. It was a Turkmen who got on the train and sat opposite me. He pointed excitedly at the amulet I was still wearing.

'Good,' he said, tapping me on the knee. 'Will protect you from evil spirits, from toothache and illness, from bad people.'

I had forgotten all about it.

ASHKHABAD

✠

Ashkhabad was one of those towns that seem to drain from the memory like sand in an hourglass. It was a town of cardboard and Sellotape – flimsy, characterless, Soviet. Built on an unstable earthquake fault along the foot of the Kopet Dag mountains, it crouched low in a neat grid pattern as if cowering from the prospect of a further cataclysm. It had no centre and no heart.

I remembered afterwards the pre-dawn arrival with almost no one left on the train after the industrial conurbation of Chardzhou. I remembered the empty station, the silent streets leading nowhere, the trolleybus stand where we waited for ages in the dark with a handful of people – children in Nintendo Turtle tracksuits, squatting on the ground, spitting pumpkin seeds while their brightly dressed mothers chattered like parakeets – until the street lights went out and still it was dark and still no trolleybus had come. Of the town itself I remembered the statue of Lenin set on a plinth patterned like a Turkmen rug, a neat symbol of a downtrodden people of nomadic herders, their woolly art wiped by the conqueror's boot.

The collapse of the Soviet Union had left neither conqueror nor conquered. Nobody seemed to belong to the place. The Russians now found themselves in an alien land, though it had been their own creation. They had split the old region of Turkestan into countries based on the dominant population and language: Turkmen, Uzbek, Kirghiz, Kazakh, and promptly made them all learn Russian. Now it was they who were required to speak these petty tongues they had never bothered to learn. Otherwise they were to be left with no work, no future and no true home.

If Ashkhabad was hard to remember, Turkmenistan, as a land of deserts and oases ruled by despotic khans and peopled by brigands, was impossible to imagine. It had been seized by the throat and all life shaken out of it. Bit by bit. First the desert. It had been the home base of ruffianly nomads who raided northern Persia to supply slaves to the khanates of Khiva and Bukhara but, as the desert had become yet more arid and the wind had rolled its sands over yet more fertile ground, the nomads had moved on and settled around its edges – along the banks of the Amu Darya, in the oasis of Merv and below the foothills of the Kopet Dag – so forming a loop of settlements around an empty heart that the Caspian Sea closed to a circle in the west.

Then the Russians had come towards the end of the nineteenth century, building a railway that followed this loop and brought northern settlers and cotton seeds. This pale encroachment from the north diluted the population even more dramatically from 1928 on, when the Soviets introduced collectivization and hundreds of thousands of Turkmen fled to Afghanistan. And finally in 1954 they constructed the Grand Canal, bleeding the Aral Sea and irrigating millions of acres so that cotton fields and market gardens crept up to the walls of oasis towns like Khiva and all sense of their history of camel trains, doomed Russian raiding parties and lone horseback travellers, struggling across formidable deserts to reach them, had been lost for ever. The sharp contrast between aridity and moisture, between sand and trees, between bleached clarity and brilliant turquoise, challenge and refuge, between silence and the buzz of people, had been buried under an endless blanket of cotton pods and Soviet squalor.

As we walked past we could see that the Botanical Garden of Ashkhabad had been abandoned for some considerable time. Its heavy old wrought-iron gates were firmly padlocked, its rusty fencing enclosed what looked like a secret garden, weeds rampant, unkempt branches lying where they had fallen.

'Your fucking guide-book,' shouted Alexandra, hurling it after me. 'This fucking Englishman is only staying at home.'

As dawn had broken we had finally caught a taxi to the rather remote hotel the guide-book recommended, only to find it would not take guests unless they were invited by the management.

From all I could see, the author of the guide-book, an old Etonian it said, had manfully tramped these streets before us and in any case it was the only post-Soviet guide available.

'I hate it, your guide-book,' screamed A. 'I hate this country. I hate these people. I go back to Russia.'

'You haven't been here two minutes,' I gently pointed out, wondering why I bothered to dissuade her.

Mercifully, and utterly by chance, we came across a hotel just beyond the Botanical Garden.

'You see,' shouted A., 'your Englishman says nothing of this hotel. He was only at home.' She protested at the price, bellowed at the tightly crimped scowling woman at reception, kicked the desk with her boots and finally got the room for twenty dollars. 'I've fucking had enough,' she yelled. 'Hurry or I shit in the lift.'

We rushed past the Russian floor lady offering us tea, but A. didn't make it.

'I know the story of another friar who visited the Mongols. William of Rubruck. He went a few years after Carpini and hated them,' I said. I read from my book: *If they were seized by an urge to void their bowels, they moved away from us no further than one could toss a bean – in fact, they would do their filthiness next to us while talking to one another. And they did a great deal more that was excessively tiresome.* I stressed the last sentence. A. glowered at me.

'I can't eat this,' said A. as we sat down with new-made friends to a Muslim dinner laid on the floor, 'I'm vegetarian. Normal,' she added, as her protest met with only incomprehension. It was a wonderful spread of spicy food and bottles of vodka, offered in celebration of the tenth birthday of a fat boy who looked vaguely like a Japanese Genghis Khan, his narrow eyes embedded in flesh. More and more dishes were brought in from the kitchen by a crippled girl who was thirteen but looked forty and had the pinched face of a Murillo waif. It was a new disease, they explained, not polio. Children are born with it and if you massage them continuously it can be cured, though they never really grow. Was it from pollution? They didn't know. The pollution, like the vodka, had been foisted on them by the Russians and both were now intrinsic to their lives.

Among the camels' knee-bands in the Ashkhabad museum – in patchwork from the Tekke Turkmen tribe, dense *kesdi* ladder stitch from the Ersar and tufted carpeting from the Yomut – were triangular amulets to hang on their trappings, not with tassels, but with pendants made of snippets of fabric, still in the odd numbers of three, five and seven. Pinned above the door was a goat's skull wrapped in bright rags and hung with a triangular amulet, this time with five pendants of string. The women attendants in the museum were all busy embroidering. I was in seventh heaven and A. had gone to the market.

In the prehistory room, a vase from 3000 BC was decorated with a horned animal in a style that was distinctly Cypriote, while stone goddesses from the local excavations at Nisa, a spectacular walled Parthian town dating from 250 BC, looked nothing other than Minoan. All dragged me westward but I had to continue to the east first of all. I had told A. that my destination was Islamabad.

'I come with you. I come too.'

'Instead of a nice neat route beginning in the Himalaya and heading west to Karpathos,' I explained to her, 'circumstances have thrown me into a more muddled itinerary beginning in Russia and going east, then returning to the central Volga and going west.'

'Normal,' said A. 'I come also.'

'Fucking embroidery,' she screamed as, lost in a carpet of textiles and jewellery laid on the sand, we missed the camels at the Sunday market. On the Monday, to compensate, while I went into the homes of women – Yath Bibi, Dolon and Aman Goezel wearing amulets and cowries round their necks – and watched them working *jehek* and *alimgash* edgings, A. called on the camel family in their garden.

'Animals I so love.' As she caressed the baby, the father flared his nostrils and turned to kick her. 'Normal,' she said.

'You notice even the camel's wearing the amulet,' I pointed out.

She looked at it carefully. 'Possibly it is OK, this work that you do.' She bought a pair of baggy embroidered trousers from the women, who frowned at her jeans and gave her a long skirt to wear over them. From that day on she wore the trousers and skirt together all the time and boasted to everyone of the quality of the embroidery.

Both so attired, we attended a Turkmen wedding, deafened by a raucous band to which men danced in couples and where there was no sign of the bride and groom. We had crossed completely from the Orthodox world to the Muslim.

We left Ashkhabad on a night train to the tinkling of glass as several of the windows fell out.

KARAKALPAKSTAN

✠

We were travelling only a short distance east to the old oasis of Merv and so not returning past the Aral Sea and through the territory of Karakalpakstan – a country I had never heard of until I had found myself in it a few months before – but I could not help but recall it as the breezy night air through the train windows prevented sleep.

'Land of the Black Hats', the name meant. A nomadic people of Kazakh stock, the Karakalpaks had come from the lower reaches of the Syr Darya and had settled around the south of the Aral Sea in the early eighteenth century. Their territory had been an autonomous Soviet republic and now was part of the new Uzbekistan but, though the population was heavily diluted with Uzbeks and Russians, they aspired to independence. Only there was no money to pay for it.

I had begun, on my previous visit, at the town of Nukus, a Soviet wasteland intersected by massive rusting pipes wrapped in peeling aluminium foil that flanked the cracked concrete roads at ground level and then crossed them, raised to the height of a triumphal arch above the traffic. From there I had caught a bus to the Aral Sea, in a soft cold drizzle that merely licked the parched salty sand where rusting hulks of fishing boats lay marooned, tilted to the skew in which the water had been sucked away, sucked until the small town of Muynak lay now more than sixty miles from where its men used to catch their fish. Its Scandinavian-style houses of flaking slatted green wood stood deserted behind worn brushwood palings. As I walked along the empty sandy lanes, fishing nets, scrumpled into forgotten cobwebby humps between rotting rowboats, blocked my way.

For a packet of gum two boys led me out of the town and over a desolate expanse of mud, criss-crossed with more gigantic rusting pipes, to the abandoned fish factory that marked the old

coastline and beyond it to the rolling land that once had lain
beneath the sea. The salty sand had been blown into a dry
mockery of a green landscape, roughed up into hillocks here,
left flat there, corrugated between. An occasional plant had
anchored itself into the barren ground.

The drizzle turned to rain. In the town everything was closed
down, the fishermen had long ago drifted away to look for work
and to escape from the salt and sand and poisons that the frequent
duststorms blew into their throats and lungs. Karakalpakstan,
with the Soviet irrigation programme diverting the waters of
the Amu Darya and Syr Darya away from the Aral Sea and into
the cottonfields of Turkmenistan and Uzbekistan, had become
a poisonous salty bog, and now, after the fall of Communism,
people had discovered that there had long been a nuclear testing
plant on an island near the centre of the sea. One in every
hundred children died before reaching the age of one. Then
there were children born without a hand or leg, or with deformed
skulls and intestines.

'I've worked here for twenty-three years,' said the doctor,
'and it was never like this before.'

The steamed-up evening bus had crawled from Muynak
back into Nukus, past rows and rows of crumbling flats with
boarded-up windows. In the hotel restaurant I was served the
left-over mutton broth from a wedding party of the night before.
Two young men eyed me up and down and then grabbed me.
They were viciously cuffed by the fat blonde manageress, while
the waiter sat calmly by adding up my bill on an abacus.

When I went up to my room a note had been left on the bed:

You have to come to Ministry of Internal Affairs to
registrate your passport at 17.05, room 11 or 13. I'll be wait
you. Inspector of registration service (Murat). P.S. If you
going to be here more than 3 days.

Murat found me the next morning in the town museum, as I
was stepping around the tin buckets that caught only some of
the relentless rain pouring through the mouldering fungus of
the ceiling, deeply reverent before forgotten treasures of thirties
Russian art: abstracts, landscapes, portraits of wistful women in

bonnets and aprons, their gentle profiles belying the toil their peasant hands betrayed. A few modern paintings that were too highly coloured, or where the perspective was not quite right, had been put aside in another room and were being sold in aid of the removal of the buckets and a possible investigation of the disaster of the roof and the effects of sixty years of neglect. And there beside them was a glass case full of amulets for sale. They were all neat triangles of fabric with three tasselled pendants, embroidered with horns.

'They're protective amulets,' the curator said. 'No, nothing inside. Texts from the Koran? Writings by the mullah? Certainly not. We have no mullah. We are only finding our way back to Islam.'

I paid an exorbitant seven dollars for one of the amulets, hung it round my neck and removed the Afghan one I was wearing.

'You are here, I see,' said Murat, 'already more than three days. Twenty dollars you give me to registrate your passport.'

I scrabbled around in my bag.

'You can get me visa to England? I learn English only because it is an escape. Perhaps it is an escape that you can help me? You truly are here only for these cottons?' He took twenty dollars with alacrity, stamped some meaningless piece of paper and smiled sweetly. I had ensured his bread and vodka for the next month.

In retrospect, the events of the next few days that led to my finding myself badly gashed in the head, lying semi-conscious in a hospital that had no running water, let alone any medicines, and being flown back to England, pass as if in a fractured sequence of dreams.

Odd people flit through my memory: the customer in the Nukus café, depositing on my table a wad of notes that represented the amount he'd seen me being overcharged for my breakfast; the only Westerner I came across, an American arranging auctions of factories, real estate and businesses for Price Waterhouse and the Peace Corps, telling me that 'yes, sure they work together'; the floor lady stealing the empty plastic gin bottles I kept to fill with vodka and water.

Then the image of my bleeding hand and torn bag as I
retreated from the bus ticket office, where a small hole in the
wood fascia was the only place to offer money for the ticket I
was trying to buy to leave Nukus. I was so ruthlessly manhandled
by those pushing behind me that the fittings were ripped from
my high tech American bag and the back of my hand was badly
cut. But of the crowd pummelling and pushing me, no one
got on the bus that crossed the frontier from Uzbekistan to
Turkmenistan.

If anything stood out as a dream rather than a nightmare in the
blur of those last days it was Kunya Urgench. It should, of course,
have been Khiva. Khiva, the only silk road oasis town still to
be preserved within its high mud walls: gems of turquoise
architecture – soaring *iwan*, porticoes, domes and minarets –
rising above a huddle of adobe, all perfectly set as in aspic, all
just as it had been for the hundreds of years that merchants had
rested in its caravanserai, unburdened their camels and traded
in its bazaars before setting off again on the long journey east
or west across desert, steppe and mountain.

In point of fact, it was no longer set in any desert at all
but in cottonfields sprayed with pesticides. A dreary town of
sandblown streets spread right up to the walls and to the town
gate, where buses dropped off tourists and a café advertised real
coffee when it had no such thing.

It was not the hum of bazaar life that had saved Khiva, but
Soviet restoration. It had been manicured into a surfeit of blue,
green and turquoise tiles, in front of which dozens of wedding
parties endlessly photographed themselves. Only the cool forest
of the ancient wooden pillars of the Djuma mosque, flickering
with sunlight, through which a group of white-turbaned priests
moved teasingly like fireflies, gave any real feeling of what Khiva
must once have been. The similarity alone with the forest of
pillars of the mosque of Cordoba seemed to string Khiva onto
a necklace of the powerful cities of Islam and convey what was
once its rightful place in the world.

The streets that lay inside the walls and surrounded the
prettified heart of Khiva straggled in poverty. Dogs lay asleep
in the sun on top of each other, children dressed only in vests

sat in crumbling doorways and boys threw stones at the city walls that, though they presented a majestic photogenic fortress on the outside, on the inside were riven with crevasses and slipping banks.

Kunya Urgench was different. Once also an important oasis town on the silk road, the capital of the Seljuks, it had been sacked by the Mongols and then abandoned in favour of Khiva. Its site was flat and open, the minaret of Kutluk Timur clearly visible in the distance, above the rooftops of the nearby small town. I had struck out across open country. At first I had supposed there had been heavy rain but as I struggled on, ankle deep in wet marsh, I realized it was rising saline groundwater. I had jumped rivulets, waded through streams, sunk in the marsh until I reached a firm gravel path that led to the minaret and way beyond it to the ruins of mosques and mausoleums. They lay at such a distance from each other that the vast extent of the original town – the buildings, the bazaars, the life that once thronged on what was now an empty bog studded only with small scrubby thorns – was still palpable.

Outside a small stone mausoleum topped by a beautiful conical dome with remnants of turquoise tiling, a group of pilgrims sat on the ground listening to the mullah. Only birdsong disturbed the peace. Further away, the Turabeg Khanym palace soared on high arches, its cupola only half-covered in blue tiling and surrounded by abandoned scaffolding. Inside, the unrestored dome rose into a deep blue heaven painted with golden stars.

From there a road, by which I should have come, led to the town. Old men in wild black hats, seemingly made of dreadlocks on an acid trip, walked along beside me, stooping as if under the weight of all that uncontrollable fur. Their striped *chapan*, worn over high black boots, were tied like dressing gowns around them, their sticks assertively prodded each step ahead.

It was now late afternoon, I remember when I think of those last few days, and I had walked since dawn with nothing at all to eat or drink. I had investigated roads in the modern village of Kunya Urgench where people came towards me with shopping bags, but had found nothing. I had accosted a young man and asked him to change five dollars into Turkmen *manat*, but still I had found no food to buy. It was time to move on.

The bus stand was ankle deep in water, so two large stones had been strategically placed in front of the ticket office for people to stand on. It was the same system as in Nukus of a small hole in the wood fascia being the only place to offer money for a ticket. So poised, holding out my blood-stained hand – right arm bandaged, face scarred and chest bruised and aching from being mugged in Bukhara a few days before – hungry and thirsty and politely asking for a ticket to Tashauz, I suddenly found myself attacked from behind, thrown to the ground and kicked out of the way by eight or ten men trying to buy tickets.

It was only much later that I discovered there is such a desperate shortage of fuel that tickets for the bus are only sold when it has petrol in its tank and is ready to go. The men did not consider they were assaulting me, I was simply in the way. I was picked up by two young men who took me in a taxi to Tashauz. I had no strength to cross the road to the hotel where they left me and crashed to the ground, splitting my head open. I was soon dimly aware of the flashing light of an ambulance.

'When we've seen Merv,' I said to Alexandra, as the train pulled into the station in the early light of dawn, 'we'll go straight on to Bukhara. You wouldn't like Karakalpakstan. Not your cup of tea.'

'I hate everything here, Karakalpak too. And we have not cup of tea and that silly way of talking in Germany.' She kicked the train as it drew away from the platform. 'What is Merv, in any case?'

MERV

✠

The scene on our arrival was inauspicious for a site as ancient
and significant as Merv. Cities had been founded there since the
Bronze Age, tumbling ever westward until they culminated in
the town of Mary, the grim Russian excrescence of empty
concrete spaces and gaunt buildings in which we now found
ourselves. There was the station, the bus station and one hotel.
No coffee or food was forthcoming at any of them and A. pushed
and shoved her way to the front of the bus queue to buy tickets
to move on. It took a couple of hours before all the options had
been sorted out: bus tickets onward to Bukhara were non-
existent, in fact the bus had ceased to run since Turkmenistan
and Uzbekistan had become separate countries; the hotel was
too expensive for us; the price I had managed to negotiate for
a taxi to the ruins was extremely favourable and that was where
I was going.

'Perfect,' said A. 'I come, too.'

Merv was no clear impress of a destroyed settlement on which
one or two buildings still stood, like Kunya Urgench, nor was
it the obvious compact ruin of an old walled city. It was a jumble
of mounds, wells, bits of walls, piles of stones, destroyed buildings,
mausoleums and rusting Unesco Heritage notices, spread over
a huge area.

The driver took us first to the Kys Kala. 'Six century. House
for Girls,' he intoned.

We entered the open ruins of a castle and were somewhat
surprised to see an Englishman standing there. At least it was
clear to me that he was English. He wore the travellers' clothing
obtainable in Kensington High Street – easy-care Rohan stuff
with multitudes of pockets – and he clutched a shiny blue
aluminium Sigg water bottle, sold in the same establishment.
Where, in fact, I had bought my clothes for Palas.

He was gazing intently at a collapsed plaster wall of the castle while a young woman with a lovely figure recounted its history.

'Built in the sixth century by the Sassanids, it is famous because Sultan Sanjar used it six centuries later for intimate parties where the guests were all men and young women slaves.'

The Englishman, stooping slightly so as not to miss her words, nodded politely. He tried first to ignore us but then glanced in our direction.

'You must be English,' I said, somewhat elated at the prospect of talking to a compatriot for the first time for ages.

He tried to disguise his discontent at this intrusion, but then held out his hand. 'Indeed. Hugo. From London. SW7 I'm afraid, not 1 or 3. How do you do?'

A. tossed her long blonde hair at him and smiled sweetly. 'Alexandra. I am German, but also a little English. My grandfather was Lawrence of Arabia.'

'Oh, really?' said Hugo quizzically, after a second or so's hesitation. He looked at her carefully. 'Perhaps you would both care to join me and my guide?'

'Yes,' said A. and immediately followed as the young woman walked on, her white T-shirt 'Rotel Tours' bobbing ahead.

The main edifice of Merv still standing was the mausoleum of Sultan Sanjar. The three of us stood dutifully under its dome in a small group around the guide.

'This building alone is left of the Seljuk city and was complete in 1140, so is older than Moscow.'

'What city?' said A.

The guide ignored her. 'Notice the double dome. One time tiled on the outside and you see beautiful on the inside. But when the Mongols attacked, Merv was a very rich city and they think treasures hidden in the two layers of the dome. So they break but nothing there.'

'Shit,' said A. Hugo raised his eyebrows slightly.

'This is a very clever building,' the guide continued. 'Very deep foundations, so it moves in earthquake but doesn't fall down. Also below is a system against water and also moves air around the building. This,' she said, pointing down a hole, 'we think was a well, but it is not a well. It is a pipe for air.'

'Perfect,' said A.

'Are there any more such ventilation shafts?' asked Hugo.

'Eight more outside,' the guide answered.

'Really?' said Hugo.

We continued around the vast site.

'This place had a city, Margiana, built by the Seleucids from northern Syria three hundred BC, but there is a wall older, maybe six hundred BC. Then each city built further west. This one of Seljuks where we stand is eleventh century. Very famous for mosques and big library of one hundred and fifty thousand books.'

'Really?' said Hugo. 'How interesting.'

'Normal,' said A.

We drove on to some recent archaeological excavations.

'All of the cities here were because of water of the Murgab river,' the guide began her spiel again. 'After Seleucids came Sassanids from Iran – the ones who built the party castle – then Arabs, then Seljuks till Mongols destroyed and killed all people.'

'Shit,' said A.

We looked at abandoned digs of the most ancient cities while the guide waved her hand westward.

'More cities built there by Timurids, Persians and Turkmen. End of Merv 1785 when attacked by Khan of Bukhara and dam of Murgab river broken.'

'Most interesting,' said Hugo. 'When I passed through a few years ago, I was not aware of any archaeological work being undertaken.'

The guide looked at him with new respect and A. scowled.

The holy saxaul trees surrounding the Mohammed Ibn Said mausoleum were said to be hung with white rags bearing wishes and prayers. It was important for me to see them, just in case any of them were triangular, or embroidered, or red instead of white.

'Amulets? Embroidery? Really?' said Hugo. 'How interesting. My wife has an interest in porcelain but has never thought it necessary to travel further afield than France.'

The rags were mostly just plain white, hung there by people praying for sons. Just a few coloured ones stood out for the odd daughter, but none were embroidered.

'Shit,' said A.

Would there be anything left, I wondered, of the old superstitions of the Tekke Turkmen of Merv, mentioned by O'Donovan, who stayed there a hundred years ago? They hung smoke-dried lamb and goatskins inside out – of mysterious importance, he had said – and placed pockets of calico cloth outside the doors of their tents and buildings to receive the bounties of wandering spirits. Such strange practices were the remnants of some old pre-Islamic worship they'd inherited from their Scythian forebears, he claimed.

'Scythians are too soon for Merv,' said the guide. 'Seleucids the first here.'

The tour was over and we strolled in the hot sunshine back to the cars. When we reached them ours had a large wasp flying frantically against the rear windscreen, trying to get out. I tapped across the glass hoping to edge it towards the open door.

'You stupid woman,' shrieked A. 'You I kill. You're a stupid old woman. You make it scared. I already tell you I save one animal every day, even the wasp.' She stamped her feet, kicked the bumper, waved her fist at me, swore at the top of her voice and then leant inside the car and blew gently on the wasp until it flew out. Though somewhat shaken, for we had just agreed it would be sensible to keep our taxi and continue together into Uzbekistan, Hugo took charge. He pointed out that we would have first to return to Mary for, though we had our bags with us, his were at the hotel. Also he had to collect the champagne he had left in the hotel fridge. Cheered by such a prospect, and A. with the additional satisfaction of her life-saving success for the day, we returned to Mary in readiness for our journey on to Bukhara together.

The landscape was bleak and unmemorable, and the taxi driver would only agree to taking us as far as Chardzhou, the last town on the Turkmen side of the border. There the hiring of another taxi proved far more difficult and expensive than we had imagined. A small, rather cowed, driver of a blue vehicle – though this came later to be hotly disputed, some of us remembering it as yellow or white – agreed to take us on.

We crossed the wide bed of the Amu Darya over a pontoon bridge of huge iron slats that jostled together and bucked up and down as the weight of lorries raised and lowered them. The river there was still powerful and thrashing, with many miles to go before it splatted out into its shrinking delta south of the Aral. On the other side we drove into a scrubby desert of sand and tamarisk, a half-hidden canal edging it on the south and so to our right. Did a camel or two pass by? If they didn't we felt their presence anyway: we were now fair and square on the silk route and should reach Bukhara by early evening.

At the border of Uzbekistan a man sat on a rickety wooden chair, smoking. He noted the registration number of our taxi in the book on the table in front of him and waved us into the checkpoint building. The events that then ensued lasted four hours and are almost too painful to recall.

First, the quaking taxi driver was grabbed by the scruff of the neck and fined one thousand new Uzbek *som* for bringing us into the country. Only Hugo had Uzbek money and then just one hundred and five. This they took in settlement. They then drove us a mile or so up the road to a second checkpoint, siphoning off the petrol to do so from the taxi driver's tank.

Here the grilling began again. None of us had Uzbek visas – impossible to get, we explained, as Uzbekistan had no consulates in Europe and we had come by road. Hugo had a letter promising him a visa when he got to Bukhara, I had an out-of-date one from my previous visit, A. had nothing.

We were then taken to the first border post again but as we had no Turkmen visas either we could not be sent back. The taxi driver was smoking heavily, the sun was setting. Hugo produced his letter again. They viewed it with scorn. I knew I had a letter of invitation that would get me in, perhaps I could guarantee the others. I fetched my document case from my bag in the taxi and produced the letter. They read it and agreed to let me go on.

A. exploded in a way I'd never seen before – the incidents of the guide-book, the train tickets, the lost knife and the wasp were as nothing compared to the fury she now vented on me. She screamed and bellowed, 'You screw me up. So you, you can go. It's all right for you but me you kill.' Four-letter words followed fast and thick and with every reproach she kicked the taxi, the table, the wall, pummelled the air and punched the passports and ledgers.

'Steady on,' said Hugo. 'Either we all three go in together or none of us does.'

That's it. I shall offload this young woman. I should have done so ages ago, I thought, not for the first time. I replaced my letter in my document case and went to put it back in my travel bag but the taxi driver had locked the boot while the argument was going on, and so I put the case on the floor in the front of the taxi where I had been sitting. That much I later recalled. I sat and watched the sun set while Hugo and Alexandra continued to argue with the guards. After another couple of hours of interrogation they were each fined twenty dollars and we were allowed to proceed.

It was pitch dark when we arrived in Bukhara and it soon became clear that the Chardzhou taxi driver had never been there before. He drove round and round neat suburban streets, never passing the landmark of a minaret or *madrasa* familiar to me. I searched in vain for the Laub-i-Khauz, the pool at the heart of town where old men play chess in the sun and near which I knew we would find shelter. Finally in the gloom I thought I recognized a mosque and some steps and leapt out. Having found my bearings I returned to the taxi and ferreted around in my bag for cigarettes to give the driver. It was only as we waved him goodbye and he sped off back to Turkmenistan that I remembered the document case. All my papers, all my notes on amulets and embroideries, all my work for the past two months. I sat on the pavement, my head in my hands.

'Normal,' said A. 'It has happened also to my grandfather. He wrote again all *The Seven Pillars of Wisdom*. He remembered all. You will, too. I know it.'

I thought of the Reading station of seventy-five years ago: the cheerful porters and capped stationmaster, the ponderous trains, the flyblown buffet, the lost property office, the honest passengers. And I thought of Lawrence's manuscript lying on a shiny brown

GWR seat, a neat bundle that even in that homely, friendly place vanished for ever.

And I thought, with misery more and more abject, of my own packet of papers enclosed in a black document case on the dark dirty mat beside a frightened taxi driver heading back through the night along an unlit potholed highway, past, he fervently hoped, those rapacious officers in their dim-bulbed frontier kiosk, past the queueing Iranian lorries, through an empty no-man's-land, to the next snarling border where even his own bureaucrats were nothing but bullies. Then the slow lurching drive over the chained irons of the long makeshift bridge that crossed the Amu Darya, and finally the last stretch home to a shoddy little Soviet flat, to his wife's castigations and whatever was left in the cupboard for supper.

The next morning he would be back in the taxi rank at Chardzhou bus station, never looking on the floor of his taxi, just anxious to pick up a good number of local fares and forget the horror of his venturing into Uzbekistan.

There was no hope.

UZBEKISTAN

BUKHARA

✠

The still, almost stagnant, pool of Laub-i-Khauz lies at the heart of Bukhara. An ancient mulberry tree where storks once nested stands gaunt and twisted like a modern sculpture at one corner. Steps on either side of the pool lead to an imposing Islamic building, on the one hand a former *madrasa* where now-faded *ikat* coats and tourist souvenirs are sold, on the other a mosque whose tiled façade of sun symbols and tigers has been heavily restored. Below them are two open-fronted tea-houses, *chai-khana*, swirled around by the smoke and steam of their wood fires and boiling cauldrons. One has a few tables and chairs alongside the pool, the other groups of huge wooden seats, *karavod*, like giant beds, each a territory unto itself, balustraded at head and foot, covered in dirty cloths, and set with a small table in the middle. Here old men while away the day, drinking tea, eating bowls of rice or noodles, playing chess, chatting. They wear embroidered caps, *chapan* and high boots and roll themselves cigarettes out of torn-off old newspaper, sticking them between their gold teeth and chewing them before lighting up. A few women in flowery dresses and slippers walk round collecting bits of leftover food from the plates.

The pollution had driven the storks away and the pool was no longer the water supply for the town, the young and the Jews were leaving . . . well, they had already left in their droves, the Jews, an old man said, now that there was no money and only bread to eat. Left, not just from Bukhara but from the whole of the former Soviet Union, though in Bukhara they were particularly missed. The capmakers' bazaar had too many empty stalls, dust gathering in the chinks of their padlocked wooden shutters and there just wasn't the trading done around this old pool that there used to be.

It was the Laub-i-Khauz that I had been looking for in the pitch dark to find somewhere for Hugo and Alexandra and myself to stay. For close by was the beautiful traditional old Bukhara home of Mubinjon where I had stayed on my previous visit. Mubinjon was a proud and defiant man who was determined to open his home to foreigners and, thus finding himself on the fringe of official tourism, was constantly harassed by petty officials.

He was tall and strong, a born actor with a craggy Tajik face and expressive hands. His long dark hair was combed back behind his ears and flicked into grey-tinged curls at the nape of his neck. He had once been the 100-metre sprint champion of Central Asia and always brought out to show his guests a dog-eared black and white photo of himself with a chestful of medals. And another standing beside his diminutive late mother and an equally tiny aunt.

On my previous visit to Bukhara I moved into lodgings with Mubinjon – following a chance encounter at the Laub-i-Khauz with a young Englishman who recommended his place – under rather unhappy circumstances. I decided to leave my hotel as I had been disturbed by officials coming to my room at midnight to tell me it was impossible to get a visa for Turkmenistan, and by a man trying to break in during the small hours, against whom the wooden chest-of-drawers propped behind the door had held. Then in the morning I had been the victim of an unfortunate incident of mugging, so that I arrived at Mubinjon's heavily bandaged and accompanied by a policeman in a tracksuit carrying my travel bag.

My wounds had been attended to at the medical centre of the Intourist hotel, the only one in town that accepted foreigners, by a tense, compact little doctor called Damir. He was on holiday from Tashkent and was an iridologist studying acupuncture under Dr Park Jo of South Korea, whom he felt sure I should know. He ran his hands around me, transmitting biological energy, he explained – and I have to say I felt a distinct tingling – while the nursing sister he was visiting dabbed iodine on the wounds. He then peered into the irises of my eyes to tell what internal damage had been done and what my general state of health was. 'Heart good. Liver good. One of the tough kind,' was his verdict. 'You'll live to be a hundred, unless people keep knocking you down in the street.'

The police then took charge of me and led me to Mubinjon's so that they would know exactly where I was, should they need me for questioning. The house lay in the age-old labyrinth of narrow lanes close to the Laub-i-Khauz. We walked from the Intourist hotel, the policeman and I, across cracked stones and over manholes without covers. We passed the odd butcher's stall with goats' heads thrown in the corner, stray dogs, a waterseller ringing his bell, and women in bright print *ikat* dresses sitting in doorways. Above us the electricity and phone lines slung from roof to roof were bizarrely hung with little pebbles on string. Small boys, it seemed, hurled them up to try to knock down their flimsy paper kites caught in the wires.

The heavy wooden door below Mubinjon's painted sign 'Welcome to House Museum. Come and take green tea' led into a paved courtyard. To the left of us was a high verandah, the shallow canopy that shaded it supported by three massive wooden pillars tapered at the top and then broadening near their base to a carved husk that encircled a ball resting on their sober pedestals. The shape was like an acorn upside down. In the centre of the courtyard steps led down to a lower level, where an Alsatian lay always chained and sleeping by its bowl, and a mulberry tree grew. Here were the cool rooms where Mubinjon kept his vodka and made his own wine. The other three sides of the courtyard were raised and around them was set the single-storey house, its windows shuttered in pale wood.

The main reception room occupied one side of the courtyard. Its floor was of the same paving stones partly covered by a carpet on which a quilt and pillow had been laid for my bed. The room had an immensely high ceiling of stout carved beams fringed by plaster flutes, the star-shaped end of each one painted bright royal blue. One fretted white lamp hung down with two doves perched on it. The white plaster walls were lined with little niches of blue and red edged with white frills like doilies and displaying Gardner porcelain, red in the blue, blue in the red. Every other inch of the room was painted with bright flowers, like a child's summer frock.

*

I spent the day, on that occasion, feeling rather beaten up and
sitting on the one *karavod* in the courtyard. Mubinjon, who
usually went about the work of looking after his guest-house
dressed in a T-shirt, put on all his embroidered and brocaded
Uzbek costumes to show me and entertained me handsomely,
though he spoke no English.

As evening drew on he made me a bowl of *laghman*, a herby
broth full of noodles and meat, and sat down to eat with me. He
then climbed up on the roof of the house to feed his flock of
pink and white doves and released them in the air. In the warm
night the only sounds were the crackled rustle of the parched
leaves of the mulberry tree and the muffled beating of the birds'
wings as they circled above. I felt gently healed.

And now I had returned to Mubinjon's and brought Hugo and
Alexandra with me.

We were not welcome. It was late, very late. Then Hugo
and Alexandra had arrived without the visas Mubinjon had
immediately asked for. To make matters worse, they then went
off around the police stations of Bukhara to try to get our taxi
stopped at the border. Dejected, I had said it was hopeless and
had given up, but, tired as they must have been, they insisted
on trying. Mubinjon told them they wouldn't be able to stay, he
was too scared to phone the police about the visas.

Then he snarled at his wife. He was tired of her. 'She thinks
only of money and herself. When she is old like you she will
not be here any more.'

There were now written rules for guests: shoes must be taken
off indoors, there must be no noise after dark. He had had enough
of Italians and French, he said, chopping the air with his hands.
England, America, Switzerland, Germany, Canada OK. The
other guests staying were actually French, gentle honeymooners,
he thin and pale, working for the charity Solidarité, which takes
food into Afghanistan, Bosnia, Rwanda, she for Christian Action
Against Torture.

They sat with me in the courtyard on the one *karavod* while
I waited for Hugo and Alexandra to return. The quivering leaves
of the mulberry tree became more and more translucent against
the night sky, there was distant music of accordions and voices

from a marriage, the doves were in the pigeonloft for the night, and the couple slipped quietly into their room, light and soft sounds escaping from the chinks in their shutters. It was a long time before Hugo and A. returned, and we sat and ate melons but the night air was cool and much had changed.

The next morning Hugo flew to Tashkent to join his new wife. She wouldn't have liked places like Mubinjon's, he pointed out, so he had taken an extra week's holiday on his own before meeting up with her. I set out to show Alexandra the sights of Bukhara.

I didn't want to see Stoddart and Conolly again, I told her. I had wept.

'Wept?'

'Yes. And thrown money down.'

'Thrown money? What is this Stoddart and Conolly?'

It was part of the Great Game. On 17 December 1838 Lieutenant-Colonel Charles Stoddart rode into Bukhara, a British officer in full uniform, emissary of the East India Company, with the intention of trying to form an alliance with Emir Nasrullah against the Russians. And one of the problems was that he had ridden. He had not dismounted in deference to Nasrullah, the savage, despotic ruler of Bukhara, and so had been thrown down a 22-foot deep, lightless well in the prison of Nasrullah's palace citadel, the Ark. Full of lice and rats and scorpions and fleas, its only access by rope, it was known as the Bug Pit. For nearly two years Stoddart endured a slow verminous torture, but was let out of the pit for a while when he converted to Islam, though still held captive. Then in November 1841 another British officer rode into Bukhara – Captain Arthur Conolly – on a one-man mission to rescue Stoddart. But he displeased the Emir who took him for another spy and the two were thrown together down the Bug Pit again. When Conolly refused to convert to Islam, and Queen Victoria, whose empire Nasrullah took to be no more powerful than his own, had not replied personally to a letter he had addressed to her, they were taken out into the square in front of the Ark and, one morning in June 1842, were beheaded.

*

We set off together to walk to the Ark, I to its museum, A. to the prison, the Zindan, which lay nearby. Bukhara was beautiful. Perhaps it lacked the cool elegance of Samarkand but made up for it in a gutsy earthiness, a golden glow of adobe and sun-baked brick, flashed here and there with turquoise. Its domes were humped rather than soaring.

We strolled through the deserted capmakers' bazaar. It huddled in warm curves over the crossroads where routes east to west and north to south once met, so that travellers were ensnared at the merchants' booths, like modern traffic gelled into immobility at traffic lights. An easy prey.

'For selling newspapers and washing windscreens,' said A.

But then for trading silk and porcelain in exchange for gold-work caps.

We walked on to the magnificent cluster of *madrasa* and mausoleums, turquoise domes and honeycomb-incised minarets that once had risen sheer from the desert as Chartres rises from the plain of Beauce but now sat in a building site, a tip of rubble, abandoned wooden pallets, dumped concrete slabs and wind-blown sand. The old walls skirting our way stacked slender hand-wrought bricks of pale buff in perspectives that were never straight. They curved horizontally into bastions and vertically sloped giddily skyward, leading the eye to towering façades and *iwan* behind them that tapered their rich blue-green mosaic into the clear blue sky. As the churches of Tuscany they seemed to cheat with pediments that were backless, a prima donna window-dressing that is the antithesis of a solid Norman tower. Monument after monument was of the same beautiful slender buff brick, tricked out here and there with Koranic calligraphy and green tiles and even notices in Uzbek and Russian as to what they were. Still the eye could not ignore the rubbish around them – 'Bolshevik' rubbish, everyone said, bluff concrete walls that hid builders' diggings begun years ago and clearly never to be finished.

We wandered through a park to a small mausoleum, that of the Samanids, made of the same buff bricks, small, flat and pale. They consisted of clay and egg and camel's milk, a man said, and were intricately set into a woven pattern, the work of bread and basketmakers. A young woman carrying a baby walked slowly round the mausoleum, touching the bricks with the baby's hand, holding on to its fingers to stroke her own temple and then caressing the bricks again.

I escorted A. to the Ark, where we were to split, she to the Zindan, I to the museum where she would join me.

The Ark was both citadel and palace and dominated the open square. It was approached by cobbled ramps to the famous open audience chamber where suppliants crawled on all fours before the Emir and withdrew backwards in the same manner and where Stoddart had ridden in caparisoned and swaggering military style. Now, it was delightful to see, the ladies who manned this establishment passed their time embroidering. Narrow bands for the cuffs of trousers, patterns of roses worked in cross stitch that they sold for a dollar or so. The collections on display in the Ark included some lovely textiles: *ikat* robes and gold embroidered coats of the Emir that took five years for the women to make.

'Did you have a good morning?' I asked A.

'No. What is it to change to Islam? The fuss that silly man Stoddart made. Then Conolly he could just do it instead of they have their heads cut off. A German would.'

'Well, I just couldn't bear it,' I said. 'I know it was naff, those two stuffed models at the bottom of a gloomy well, but at least they were made of a grey sort of cotton and dressed in rags, not pink plastic Disney-type things. They look eaten to bits by bugs themselves, just imagine what it must have been like for those two young English soldiers, I couldn't bear it.'

'Normal,' said A. 'You're English,' she added in somewhat scathing tones.

'Then,' I said, 'there are all those other prisoners in the room by the side of the Bug Pit. Made of grey cotton too and disintegrating. Shackled. Only allowed out on Fridays to beg for their food for the week.'

'For God's sake,' said A. 'They're all just dolls. Germans don't weep. And you threw money?' she continued.

'Everyone had thrown money,' I said. 'It's ridiculous, I know. I've always thought throwing money into fountains and down wells and things like that was ridiculous.'

But everyone had done it. All the display cabinets for the Emir's instruments of torture were full of money too. When I was there it was only Uzbek coupons, the rubbish that was issued as an interim measure before they introduced a proper new currency, the *som*, just as worthless.

'Perhaps people threw them down to show what a pig life is.'

'It's a bugger,' said A.

We were standing in the museum in front of a triangular amulet, this time in silver with eleven pendants. I viewed it with some misgiving. I had been wearing the Afghan version on my previous visit when mugged and it had failed to protect me. Then the Nukus museum example was round my neck when I was finally felled a couple of days later. 'Souvenir,' someone had astutely commented when I queried why it had not saved me. And displayed here, incongruous among the baubles of Soviet propaganda, were also huge mountain-goat horns wrapped in rags, the same shape as the horns embroidered on my Nukus amulet.

'Ah,' said the attendant, 'these are hung in a holy place to ask for a wish. If your wish is granted you give money to the poor. This is the idea of Islam. They are no older than Islam, these horns. Nor is the amulet.'

'Bullshit,' said A.

DOLLARS AND DOCUMENTS

✠

The back end of Bukhara, south of the Laub-i-Khauz and the lanes of the old town, must originally have been reclaimed from the desert by the irrigation system that had now resolved itself into a few stinking culverts where frogs croaked and hopped. Between them beds of roses had been laid out and the excreta of Soviet administration had been built – a mini-skyscraper that housed the Communist party headquarters, the bleak multi-storey Intourist hotel and the National Bank. We had needed money as soon as we arrived and had headed for the bank. It was a shabby building with no sign or name on it, situated just behind a very smart new hotel built by a Bombay company, complete to the last balcony but locked and empty, as the government of Uzbekistan would not, or could not, pay for it.

The exchange office was at the side of the bank, guarded by an armed policeman. We went in but were immediately pushed out again, an incident that triggered A.'s usual histrionics. She became uncontrollable when they didn't want German marks and, though her invective was as usual turned on me, the guard fingered his gun nervously. We set off to look for another bank, but when the same story was repeated I left her and returned to Mubinjon's.

Some time later A. appeared, flushed, and handed me a few Uzbek *som*. 'These are for the dollars I owe you.'

It wasn't enough.

'The rate for dollars was bad at the bank I found, but I go there because they like Deutschmark.'

My resolve to split with her deepened.

She took off her long narrow money belt. 'Here I keep my money. I don't throw it down holes at stuffed people.'

'Alexandra, you should never show anyone where you keep your money.' If the atmosphere was bad then, it got worse.

'I took your pen from your bag while you were sleeping,' she boasted. Then later, 'I am missing a fifty-Deutschmark note, only you know where I keep my money.'

I sat impassively on the floor of our room. She looked at me and launched into her usual tantrum. I ignored her.

Then, 'Him I kill. He who took my money, him I kill.' She stressed the gender as a way out of her gaffe, and started to put her money back. 'My money is not enough. I know it now. The inhabitants' welcome is lacking and hotels are expensive.' She looked at me carefully. 'You have American Express card?'

'Yes.'

'When we get to Tashkent you cash three hundred dollars and lend them to me.'

'You can't draw money anywhere in Central Asia, not till Urumchi. You have to have everything you need in dollars in cash with you. That's why travellers get attacked.'

'If you can't get three hundred dollars for me then you lend me one hundred dollars.'

'Alexandra, you have some things to learn about travelling. Firstly don't take so much stuff with you. You don't need bottles of olive oil, bottles of ink, that honey that broke and all that millet and cheese.'

'What about your vodka?' she interrupted.

'That's different,' I snapped. 'What you must take plenty of is money. Dollars, dollars and only dollars. No one's interested in anything else, not even German marks, and they've never even heard of Swiss francs. But be very careful of hundred-dollar notes. If they're dated before 1990 people won't take them, though they're perfectly OK. I was told it was because Iraq seized billions of dollars in the Gulf War so the US Federal Bank have invalidated pre-1990 notes. But really it's because they're easily faked. The later ones have a metal strip.'

'Then you must always take small notes because no one will ever give you change in dollars, only in the local currency, so if a room's fifteen dollars you must have exactly that to give.'

She didn't take kindly to criticism and could see her chances of getting hold of more money seemed slim. She looked crestfallen.

'All right, I'll lend you a hundred dollars.' It was foolish I know but in spite of everything I had a gut feeling that this girl was OK. I handed her one hundred dollars in small notes.

From that day on, through the rest of my travels, I worried about my hundred dollars and the more I worried about them, the more I felt their safe return was inextricably linked with the truth of whether or not Lawrence of Arabia had an affair in Cairo in 1929.

The new flag of Uzbekistan hung outside the post office, at the back end of Bukhara. It depicted the crescent moon of Islam, twelve stars for each of the months, a blue stripe at the top for the sky, a green one at the bottom for the earth and in between white for heart and life.

'We've had enough of red,' Kurban said.

We had no idea who he was. He had simply picked us up in town and had invited me for an Uzbek dinner at his home in the suburbs that night.

Alexandra would already have left for Samarkand but I was staying on. At Mubinjon's the situation had become intolerable. She just had to go. He was terrified at keeping someone who had no visa and seemed to be making no effort to get one. He had already been threatened with a fine for letting her stay. She must move that very day to Samarkand, he insisted. Then Kurban's invitation gave her an alternative.

'I will come with you and stay some nights at Kurban.'

With first Hugo and now Alexandra out of the way, Mubinjon reverted to his old hospitable self and snapped only at his wife.

Kurban lived in the Soviet satellite town of shoddy flats a mile or two out. Buses had run between there and the city when the tarmac roads had first been laid out but now there was no fuel and so no buses and little hope of a lift. We walked. The road was cracked and potholed, and Kurban had difficulty carrying A.'s pack. One half-dead tree brightened the concrete wasteland, the staircase to the flat was littered with cigarette ends, lumps of concrete and mouldering rubbish, the walls were peeling, the wiring and piping exposed. Kurban, along with other workers, had always lived there rent-free but when the Russians departed he had suddenly found himself the owner of this property he had always hated.

'The Russians just went away, back to Russia, and abandoned the flats,' Kurban said. 'We shall leave them to rot.'

Inside, the flat was furnished half in Muslim style with cushions on the floor and a carpet on the wall, and half in Russian with a table, a sofa and a sideboard displaying bottles of Chinese oil and Saudi perfumes.

Two small boys stared at us, the elder thin and pale. He'd always had problems, Kurban said, anaemia, kidneys, one thing after another, they didn't know why except that usually that sort of thing came from the pesticides used in the cottonfields. Children had to take a couple of months off school every year to help pick the cotton, so things weren't going to get any better.

Alexandra made herself at home. She ate all the bunches of grapes laid out on a big dish on the floor, she announced that she was a vegetarian and that Kurban's pretty young second wife would have to make the traditional steamed *manti* without meat, she unpacked all her belongings and tipped some ink on the tablecloth.

When it came for me to say goodbye and return to the city, she insisted that she still wanted to accompany me as far as Hunza and that we should meet in Samarkand. She would wait for me. She would leave a message at the Intourist hotel there to tell me where she was. I agreed on condition that we split every time either of us had had enough of the other, a situation I envisaged would occur very soon. Kurban walked me back in the dark without her, along deserted streets that were threatening and creepy.

The next morning on my usual trail around police stations trying to trace my document case, a familiar figure with a large orange rucksack came striding up. 'How are things at Kurban's?'

'Perfect. But he says he is going away and I can't stay. Also he says it is very dangerous to travel alone. We must go together. You must come now to Samarkand.'

I refused to move from Bukhara until I had found my papers and she caught the bus alone.

Niyazov Bahodyr was a police officer in the customs division. A slim young man, with a lively intelligent face, he took considerable pride in his appearance and on that particular morning was sitting in his shabby office wearing neatly pressed slacks and a soft red silk shirt. Reports had come through from the police stations around town that an Englishwoman, who had shared a taxi with two other people travelling from Chardzhou to Bukhara, had left a file of papers in it that she was anxious to get back. She had haunted the police stations for days, asking for information. The woman concerned, the police said, was small and fair, a babushka, a grandmother.

Niyazov pondered this latest disturbance to his routine work. He recalled that a couple of months previously an English babushka travelling alone, also small and fair, had been attacked in the street as she was taking photographs, in broad daylight in the centre of Bukhara. A man on a bicycle had gathered up speed on a downhill slope and had grabbed her bag and camera. Unfortunately the woman had held tightly on to them, not letting them go, and so had been dragged along the street and rather severely bruised and gashed. The medical centre at the Intourist hotel had taken care of her and the police had tried their best to make a few enquiries though as nothing had actually been stolen they had not pursued the matter too assiduously.

They had, however, pointed out that she was obliged to accompany a policeman round the town to help identify her assailant and the two had accosted every man with a bicycle they came across, but to no avail. The woman herself had not been much help. She had been unable to describe her attacker, beyond the fact that he had black hair and gold teeth, as did almost every man in Bukhara. As to what he was wearing, she had described his shirt and trousers, but indicated that he wore something over the shirt. Glancing about her own clothes in order to help with the description she had seemed unable to find anything similar and had merely looked at the interrogating officer and bleated, 'Baa, baa.' It was at this point that the police had given up their enquiries.

Niyazov lit a cigarette and thought. Had she been a tourist with a group that incident would never have happened. Such tour groups came frequently through Bukhara, keeping together like flocks of bewildered goats shepherded too close to the dangers of the main highway. Then they got the odd youngster with hiking boots and rucksack, but a granny alone they never saw. And this one again was English. Could it be the same woman? If it was, Niyazov resolved that she would leave Bukhara this time with happier memories.

'A car will come for you tomorrow morning, as soon as we can find some petrol, to take you to the border,' Niyazov assured me with a kind, friendly smile. 'I will take you there myself.'

The wail of the dawn muezzin had been a long-forgotten sound until Bukhara. I woke now to the memories it always brought of other distant Muslim mornings and the emotions the all-pervasiveness of Islam inevitably aroused. Two pink doves perched on the carved white lamp above my bed of cushions on Mubinjon's floor peered down at me over its rim. At breakfast two young American couples had arrived, aid workers from Tashkent, and a message had come through from the police. Niyazov had a car but was unable to find any petrol. It would be lunchtime before we could leave.

The summer palace of the Emir was guarded by stone lions, backed by a stagnant pool and surrounded by parkland. Now a museum, its attendants stood around cracking pumpkin seeds in their teeth and scowling at me, the only visitor, as I passed the morning there. It was full of the beautiful goldwork costumes the Emirs wore, which took years to make and were reputedly the work of men, as it was claimed that women's hands tarnished the gold, though it was actually women who embroidered them in the seclusion of their homes. And *suzani*, those dowry textiles made of strips of cotton stitched together into bedcovers and hangings and embroidered in rich floral and astral patterns in all shades of reds, pinks, coppers and oranges. They were worked in couching, except those from Shakhrisabz, which were in cross stitch. I would have to go there. An attendant blew bubble-gum in my face.

The message at Mubinjon's on my return was that we would be leaving at one to try to find my document case. At twelve-fifteen Raisa, a neatly dressed woman responsible for visas, called to collect my passport. As the border guards had kept my letter of invitation, a visa was proving difficult, she explained. I pointed out that I was about to go to the border and would need my passport. It would be ready for Mubinjon to bring back by one, she said. It wasn't, of course. But by one Niyazov was there, dressed today in a grey pinstripe suit, a grey striped tie and a white shirt of too big a collar size. On his feet he wore pink and black co-respondents' shoes, somewhat down-at-heel. With him was an interpreter, Angelica, who worked for the Bombay construction company that had built the mothballed hotel, and spoke perfect English. It was two-thirty by the time we had cruised round Bukhara searching for petrol and had fought for it in massive queues at a dump of tanks on the edge of town. We headed for the border.

The guards at the first checkpoint denied ever having seen my letter of invitation. They had recorded a blue car coming through from Turkmenistan and returning at night, but the timing was wrong.

'What colour was the car?' Niyazov asked me.

'Bright yellow,' I said.

At the second checkpoint, close to the border, they had recorded a white car passing through at six and returning at midnight. Its registration number and the name of the driver had been written down by the man sitting on the wooden chair.

Hadn't the police from Bukhara phoned, as Hugo and Alexandra had gone to such pains to ask them to, and told the guards not to let the taxi back into Turkmenistan without keeping the document case?

'Phone? We have no phone.'

By this time it had become clear that Niyazov and Angelica were in love. He slipped his hand gently over the back of the seat for her to caress, she powdered her nose frequently when he wasn't looking in the rear mirror. In the ensuing debate – should we continue to Chardzhou when I had no passport, let alone visas for either Turkmenistan or Uzbekistan? Was it worth the seventy dollars the driver, mumbling about problems problems, was asking? – they were happy to continue. It was a long and tedious journey. The car kept stalling and jerking – no doubt the petrol was laced with water – and the driver was forever opening the bonnet and tinkering with screwdrivers. Heavy lorries and tractors passed us. Finally we clanked over the pontoon bridge and into Chardzhou.

Niyazov toured round police stations for information while Angelica and I waited for hours sitting in the back of the car. The driver looked at us with curiosity.

'That amulet you're wearing,' he suddenly said to me, 'Turkmen and Karakalpaks wear them like that, outside for people to see. We Uzbeks hide them inside our clothes.' They were usually embroidered, he continued, but not necessarily with horns as mine was. Different patterns could be used. He had one in the car, a prayer in Arabic from the Koran, especially for drivers and people who work on the roads, but uncovered, just a piece of paper folded into a triangle. But then he was wearing one too, a triangle of pink and orange fabric enclosing a prayer. It hung round his neck inside his shirt by a loop and had an extra loop stitched on the bottom edge that protected him specifically from the evil eye. They were a Muslim tradition, he was sure.

By ten o'clock the taxi driver's address had been found but he was out. His wife confirmed that he drove to Bukhara on that particular night but she didn't know whether he had taken foreigners or what had happened to any document case. We would have to wait.

'We can't phone,' said Niyazov. 'We have to telex the police, then they have to go to the driver's house. This isn't Europe,' he added.

I assured him that the registration number and the name of the driver of every car crossing a border in Europe would never be recorded. He preened himself slightly and went back into the police station.

At midnight he came out again, accompanied by a policeman. There was still no news. The policeman, Ura, took us to his flat for dinner, where dishes of chicken, liver, egg, potato, bread and salad, with small glasses of tea and large ones of vodka, were laid out ready for us. With no phone Ura must have walked home while we were waiting outside the police station and alerted his wife. It was splendid hospitality at such a late hour and we sat ourselves down. Niyazov, by this time, was looking very dishevelled. His tie was askew; he had taken off his jacket and shoes, revealing socks of vivid turquoise, green and blue stripes. Angelica still looked matt-faced, neat and smiling.

The flat was furnished in Russian rather than Muslim style,

with chairs and a table, though the shelves displayed cans of Fanta, Pepsi and Czech beer – just as the Emir's palace had displays of empty champagne bottles – and a photo of Ura when young. Slim and good-looking. Now his paunch strained between the buttons of his blue shirt, like a string of pink sausages. Ura's son, a lad of sixteen, stood quietly in the background and served us.

The driver refused the vodka. 'Machine,' he explained.

At two a.m. we returned to the police station and Niyazov and the driver went in. Within a split second the driver ran out again, very excited, hands in the air, shouting, '*Yest, yest.*'

My papers had been found.

'It's the amulet,' he said.

We drove the thirty miles to the village where they were, the car now going noticeably faster. There in the police station was my document case. I hugged and kissed all the policemen and, having nothing else, distributed all the London bookmarks in it. They looked flushed with pride and offered to share their supper, a huge enamel bowl of cold congealed fat, meat and potato with hunks of bread to dip into it. Ura wiped it clean as a dog's bowl, as if he hadn't eaten for days, and I wondered what had made him throw away his slim youth.

As we drove back, the crescent moon faded and dawn broke over the desert, tipped into reflected pink in the canal. While Angelica slept I slipped the silver bracelet off my wrist and slid it into her make-up bag. Bukhara was just awakening when we reached it, the children setting off for school, the old ladies laying out their freshly baked bread for sale.

Mubinjon had been terribly concerned. He had dashed around in taxis all night looking for me, he said. He was responsible for his guests but it was all a great worry. He was doing his best for Uzbekistan, but it would be another ten years before things really worked and meanwhile there was the police. They were always at his throat.

It was only an hour or so after our return that Raisa, the visa lady, still dressed in her black shoulder-padded suit, called to discuss what she referred to as 'the escapade'. I was to write out two letters, one stating that it was me who asked the police to help, the other saying what I had paid. They were to be separate.

She wouldn't say what they were for. She handed me a visa covering the whole of Uzbekistan. I was free to move on.

That evening Hugo walked into Mubinjon's, accompanied by his wife, Angélique, a young Frenchwoman expensively dressed for a vacation on the Riviera, and with them Dickie, his wife's neighbour in Paris. Hugo was showing them where he had stayed, having now returned to Bukhara and found a place with hot water and showers. Not as beautiful as Mubinjon's but Angélique wouldn't have liked the room full of dusty whisky bottles that he had had, and the primitive washing arrangements. I paid Mubinjon five dollars for a bottle of his mother's home-brewed wine to offer them. Dickie and Angélique winced at its taste and put it aside, Hugo gallantly accepted more.

'What colour was the car we came to Bukhara in?' I asked him.

'Blue,' he said. He had enjoyed travelling with us and didn't care whether Alexandra repaid him the twenty dollars he'd lent her at the border, or not.

'What about Lawrence of Arabia?' I asked.

'I reserve judgment,' he said. He was a barrister.

SAMARKAND

✤

It was as if the sparks of turquoise amid the golden bricks of Bukhara had flared to Samarkand to explode in cluster-bombs of blues, turquoises, greens. Spattered around a mundane city was this azure fall-out. It was at its most beautiful in the narrow lanes of tombs of the Shah-i-Zinda, set on a hill above the Stairway to Heaven, in the bony, scaffolded ruins of the Bibi Khanym mosque, in the mausoleum of Tamerlane himself, hidden in the leafy avenues of old Uzbek suburbs, and in the frigid square of the Registan.

Fall-out in Samarkand was not just azure. Selenium rectifiers, dimmers, voltage stabilizers, transformers – all were produced there, a book of Soviet propaganda recounted with pride. 'Mingle with the happy throng of well-dressed passers-by in any Soviet city and you will notice their lovely brightly coloured silk clothes' – all also made in Samarkand. While azure domes and golden roads merited hardly a mention, the rugs, wine bottles, tinned fruit, tea packets, cigarette packs, shoe leather, suit pockets, knitted jackets and research establishments were eulogized. The beauty of Samarkand is savagely flawed. It is a city of run-down historic renown overlaid by Soviet sleaze. Even the azure fall-out on closer inspection turned out to be more coldly celadon and aquamarine.

The heart of Tamerlane's city is the Registan, a vast empty square of cobbles laid on sand and blood, the site until early this century of beheadings and bazaars, faced on three sides by *madrasa* of arrestingly noble architecture. A small park separated the square from a cracked main road clouded with spewed black exhaust.

Tiered plastic seats embedded in concrete, built no doubt for *son et lumière* presentations for tired workers from East Germany, were set before it as if before a theatre stage. These too were empty. Though the eye was entranced by the play of light on the greens and blues – at ground level shading into marine intensity, at sky level brightening into spindrift – it was impossible not to notice that the Uleg Beg, the oldest of the three *madrasa*, was shored up by wooden poles. Just a few years after restoration, rising saline groundwater and pollution were destroying the buildings again, just as surely as neglect had done.

Then, within a few minutes, it was just as impossible not to notice that the whole place was tottering and was nothing but a coldly restored theatrical façade. Behind the wings formed by the high *iwan* of the Uleg Beg and the facing Sher Dor was a litter of courtyards and quarters, like dusty abandoned dressing rooms. Those at the back of the Uleg Beg were locked and unused, but enough fragments of sapphire tiles lay around to shock the senses with a vision of how beautiful Samarkand must once have been.

The courtyard rooms of the Sher Dor, and of the Tilla Kari that was the stage backdrop, housed a number of textile dealers, not to speak of dealers in whatever commodity might conceivably bring in hard currency. One claimed to hail from Shakhrisabz, where he would happily take me. We discoursed for hours on cross stitch, *suzani*, amulets, fertility goddesses and horns, but when I went back the next day he had disappeared and the men in the tourist stall next door shrugged their shoulders and purported to know nothing about him.

Even the decoration of the Registan's central mosque turned out to be only illusion. Its inner dome of gold leaves floating down from deep blue night sky and blown into a burning gold mihrab, like autumn leaves swept into a bonfire, was actually a flat ceiling cleverly painted in distorting perspective and a mihrab too heavily daubed in new gold leaf.

Perhaps a different play of light at night would change the production, enhance the theatricality. I returned. The empty square, now floodlit, spread in low humped cobbles beyond the flimsy silhouetted trees of the park. The Uleg Beg stood almost in darkness, while the tigers and profane suns with human faces on the *iwan* of the Sher Dor opposite were caught in a glow of light. In the background the gold and turquoise of the Tilla Kari shimmered only slightly, fuzzed against the empty black of the night sky, while along the façade of the *madrasa* the floodlight torched with silver the balconies of the students' rooms and their rows of worn brown wooden doors.

Walking away through mud and into unlit potholes I was accosted by a Russian policeman. Papers? Visa? Group? I was English, alone, papers buried under my clothes, and the Registan was beautiful under the shroud of night. There had been no one else there, I said. He shook me by the hand and escorted me back to my hotel.

On first arriving in Samarkand I had tried the Zerafshan Hotel. It looked solid and old-fashioned from the outside and beyond the carved wooden doorway I could see an encouraging latticed plasterwork wall. Reception was manned by a large woman dressed in black polyester with a diving *decolletée* edged in red. She glowered at me through curtains of black eye-makeup. 'Go away, go away,' she shrieked. 'No foreigners. Only change dollars.'

I stood my ground and requested tea.

'No tea. Go away.'

I enquired about food and she indicated a restaurant round the corner and flounced off there herself. They refused to let me in and I went back to reception to wait for her return.

In a small side room the hotel barber was working. He had discarded his electric razor and the plug was dangling in a bucket of water that also caught the drips from the mildewed ceiling. He was attending to a customer, plastering his hair over the bald patch on top. He was Israeli, he said, and hoped to leave for Israel. 'Terrible people here,' he said. 'You must fight. A room is only one dollar and since the new laws they have no right to turn away foreigners.' He insisted on sharing his lunch with me, cold cabbage leaves stuffed with spicy rice.

When the woman returned I jumped into the fight again, but after two hours had to admit defeat. I found in the end, at thirty-five times the price, a room in some old Russian officers' quarters, hung with chandeliers and ruched pink curtains and decorated in pink and white flock paper adorned with gilded curlicues. The plumbing was antediluvian.

Humbly conceding that it was just as ridiculous to be in a

city of such renowned beauty looking for an embroidered triangle
as it was to go there to manufacture selenium rectifiers, I set off
again to be saturated by blue, by Madonna blue, marine blue,
aquamarine, by turquoise, green, jade and celadon, gold and
even violet. Ignoring the stinking smirch that almost engulfed
the divine, I visited the wonders of Samarkand beyond the
Registan. This was the tourist circuit, though there were no
tourists, the East German workers being now in Marienbad, and
the Western tour groups perhaps frightened off by the fighting
in nearby Tajikistan and the incidences of mugging and theft.

Emotive words were the basis of this trade. 'The Silk Road'
evoking sheen, cut purple, luxury and boudoir lingerie and
relating not one whit to the appalling rigours endured by the
merchants, nor to the fact that it was along several routes between
China and the West that they worked in relays, nor to the
religions, ivory, horses and patterns traded by the same routes.
Then 'Samarkand', a name that had always glistered in the
remote distance of unknown Asia and of romantic imagination.
Reality now had overtaken. The voltage stabilizers and knitted
jackets, so to speak, had won – considerably aided by the lingering
Soviet attitude to foreigners – and the tourist trail was deserted.

The streets that led to the mosques and mausoleums, away
from the choked main roads, were surprisingly if anaesthetically
delightful. They too had been restored by the heavy clout of
Soviet socialism. Quiet wide avenues, with sometimes a horse
and carriage trotting along, were lined by low façades of gently
carved pale wood.

The 'happy throng', though basically miserable, was, it had
to be said, colourfully dressed. The women wore bright printed
rayon dresses that faked the beautiful old *ikat* of Uzbekistan.
Heartbreaking in truth to think of that prized technique of
weaving, and the exquisite robes that all dignitaries wore – and
that were presented to foreign emissaries as a token of esteem
– now reduced to garish factory cloths. Tinselled scarves swathed
every woman's head, old men wore boots, *chapan* and fur hats.

Teahouses served small glasses of hot sweet tea and bits of
fried doughnut, shops were empty, market stalls sold wares
infinitely more drab than the customers. A dear old man in a
turban gave me a pot of honey. A swift shot of guilt flashed

through my mind. I had so far done nothing to locate Alexandra.

I continued my sightseeing with the Shah-i-Zinda. It lies in the corner of the archaeological site of Afrasiab, the earliest settlement of Samarkand, watered by the Zerafshan river flowing from the mountains to the south and mentioned by Alexander the Great in 329 BC as being even more beautiful than he could have imagined. And that was a thousand years before Tamerlane brought the finest artisans from his conquered lands to glorify the city.

From the entrance of the Shah-i-Zinda thirty-six steps – pilgrims are consigned to hell if they miscount – lead up to the narrow alleyway of truly exquisite tiny mausoleums of tassellated turquoise, studded with gold, blue, green, violet. Domes, apses, niches hold the eye to ever more beautiful pattern, so that even the word 'pattern', its sense lost in the West, is inadequate to carry the discipline of repetition, the abstraction of line and angle that represents art almost beyond anything that figurative motifs could achieve.

And yet, in all this dignity of line and form, my triangle, my amulet, was nowhere to be seen. Chinese cloud patterns, Iznik flowerheads serried in repetition, held sway. I left dismayed that in this historic and venerable settlement of mankind, my own particular link with history, magic and our origins was missing.

On then to the second azure explosion, the Bibi Khanym mosque. The scale of this mosque is of skyscraper dimensions, both vertical and horizontal. Like the Registan its blues and turquoises tower over the everyday city. Cracked, falling into disrepair even within the lifetime of Tamerlane, it has stood faltering – though with Unesco Heritage benefaction – for some considerable time so that its scaffolding and cranes have become an integral part of the skyline of Samarkand. A giant marble Koran-rest is reported to guarantee fertility to barren women who crawl under it. A woman custodian in an apron showed me there and demanded dollars. I protested, and she moved on to try other more serious swindling devices but forgot to ask for the tuppence entrance fee.

The last wonder of the blue history of Samarkand was the Gur Emir mausoleum shaded in the tree-lined avenues of the back streets, where a wedding party, the bride in effervescent white nylon clutching a Cellophane-wrapped bouquet of red roses, was making its way down the street.

The mausoleum was approached by leaping across a low wall onto stones, across builders' bricks and conservators' markers. Hip-hopping through this debris of long-abandoned restoration, I found myself within the dome of the mausoleum that Tamerlane had built for his grandson, but in which he was buried himself – ostensibly under a jade cenotaph, black in all normal light and only glowing with a greenish tinge when the setting sun struck the cenotaph through the westerly window. The patterns were curled, no possible link with triangles and amulets, none the less I wandered through, exercised by how little of its history I knew and how there was no one to ask. Only when I was leaving was I approached by a guard in uniform sitting on a chair.

'You want to see the real tomb of Tamerlane? Never for a group, never for a tour, but for you alone, I show. Woman alone? Yes, I show.'

I followed him down a short steep ramp into a dark crypt, its stone vaulting oppressively low and heavy. He shone a torch on the grave of Tamerlane, a low tomb under a marble slab incised with tendrils of Arabic script that traced a mythical descent from Genghis Khan. I gazed at it, not so much reflecting on Tamerlane's conquests of the lands of the Golden Horde as worrying whether I should tip the guard or not.

'No, no. No money. Those we want to show, those who come alone to see, we show.'

Before leaving Samarkand, and remembering my promise to Alexandra, I went along to the Intourist hotel, the usual bleak Soviet mini-skyscraper, and asked the surly woman at reception if there was a message for me.

'We don't take messages,' she snarled, and walked away.

'How helpful,' I called after her retreating back, in a tone that might have been mistaken for sarcasm.

Boy in Bar Paro,
Palas Valley,
Pakistan.

The 'Afghan
Amulet' motif on
an embroidered
shawl from Palas.

Church of the Transfiguration,
detail, Khizi, Northern Russia.

Street scene, Nizhni Novgorod,
Volga, Central Russia.

Ruins of old Nisa, Parthian
royal city, Turkmenistan.

Ashkabad
market.

Woman selling ikat fabric,
Khiva, Uzbekistan.

Samanid mausoleum, Bukhara.

Registan, Samarkand

Valentin with his pony and trap,
Kara-Kol, Khirgizstan.

Felts in market, Kashgar,
Western China.

Woman selling amulets
in market, Kashgar.

Woman in embroidered
cap, Tashkurgan.

Diveyevo monastery,
Central Russia.

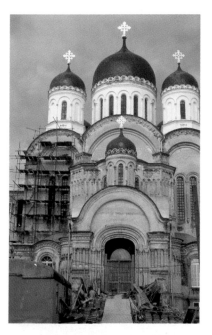

Woman in waistcoat, embroidered
with goddess motif. Kosmach,
Carpathians, Ukraine.

View towards the village of Olymbos, Karpathos, Greece.

House interior with draped pillar representing the head of the family, Olymbos.

Amulet on altar behind iconostasis, Olymbos.

SHAKHRISABZ

✠

Tamerlane was born in 1336 to a noble Mongol-Turkic family in the quiet little town of Shakhrisabz, from where he embarked on a trail of conquest and butchery beyond anything even Genghis Khan had perpetrated. He began by subjugating the lands around him that belonged to the Jagatai Khanate and by 1369 had made nearby Samarkand his capital. It was from then on, as he made each conquest, that he was to bring back to Samarkand the best craftsmen he could find. From Persia, overcome by 1385, he brought the workers in stone and stucco of Isfahan, and those in mosaic from Shiraz. From India, where Delhi fell to him in 1398, he acquired the most skilled stonemasons and even elephants to help with the construction of his capital. From his conquest of Syria in 1404 came the weavers, potters and glass blowers of Damascus. But, in the lands of the Golden Horde, conquered in 1395, Tamerlane seems to have found no skilled artisans worth bringing back to Samarkand.

It was as he embarked on a campaign to China in 1405 that he died and was then buried in the Gur Emir, the Ruler's Tomb. And when his grave was opened in 1941 he was indeed found to have been Timur the Lame: one leg was shorter than the other.

'Also, it's a load of nonsense that no one is allowed to see the actual tomb', said the English tour group having lunch in Shakhrisabz, 'you just have to tip the guard.'

Shakhrisabz lies a short bus ride away from Samarkand, to the south over the Zerafshan mountains, which unfurl in dry rolling hills and rocky outcrops rather than peaks. Behind me a small boy was being very sick and ignored by his mother as the rickety bus lurched round bends. An old woman with a very Mongol face, a bright Uzbek print dress and a shopping bag, got off at every stop and back on again. Her headscarf was embroidered in cross stitch rectangular patterns and bordered with the motif of my amulet. Attempts at conversation were thwarted both by language problems and the interruption at each stop. As there seemed to be no obvious reason for her getting off so frequently I had reluctantly to conclude that she disliked being questioned about triangles with pendants, prayers from mullahs and the incidence of sickness in her life. No amount of simulated retching, or of vague waving of hands to indicate pattern and prayer, can replace the ability to converse with vocabulary and grammar.

The hotel staff flexed their muscles. Single room thirty-five dollars. If I wanted to see the embroidery factory that would be ten dollars and I had to use their guide. A. would never have agreed, I knew. I narrowed my eyes and prepared for battle. The gloomy single room became a gloomy double one for twenty-five and the English-speaking guide beckoned me to follow her down the street.

'No money,' she said. 'No one wants to see the embroidery factory usually.'

It had been installed by the Soviets, no doubt at the same time as the industrial works in Samarkand, trading on the traditional *suzani* of the region by reproducing them by machine. As the motifs are floral or solar, but in any case not geometric, chain stitch machines can easily copy them, cheaply and crudely, but still with appeal for tourists. The very fact that the motifs were curved and that the rhythm of chain stitch machines is circular meant that there was no hope of finding the amulet motif surviving on these embroideries, nor historically had I ever known it to exist on the *suzani* of the Uzbeks, only on their woven braids. And how much it was worn here as an actual amulet and why was still unanswered.

Two thousand women worked in the factory and the din was appalling, row after row of machines clattered on. Only there where the young woman working it had collapsed fast asleep over it, was the machine silent. Three floors of these sewing machines whizzed away and on the dirty concrete staircase a woman stood breastfeeding her baby.

'What about hand embroidery?' I asked.

A few women made bags and caps in their homes, but it was mostly the machined cloths that sold. The little factory shop had stacks of them, piles and piles as hardly any tourists came now, but they had almost nothing that was hand-worked.

'And the old cross stitch *suzani?*'

'Never made now.'

'Why were they in cross stitch while everywhere else in Uzbekistan the technique used was couching?'

The women looked tired and didn't know.

'How old are you?' one suddenly asked. 'Old then, but you're beautiful. Hair so fine and pretty, back straight, eyes looking ahead. We are bent, we have no teeth, no hair under our scarves.'

'They have a hard life,' said the guide.

'We used to get five or six tour groups a day – Russians, Germans, Czechs – now we're lucky if it's one a week,' the guide continued. 'Of course it's the Timurid monuments they come to see, not the embroidery factory. The Ak-Saray 1340 to 1405, Tamerlane's magnificent palace, collapsed two hundred years ago. The Kok Gumbaz mosque 1435 to 1436 built by his grandson Ulug Beg, famous astrologer whose *madrasa* is in Samarkand. Beside it Dorus Tilavat mausoleum 1438 and nearby Jehangir's tomb.' She droned on.

'And the English group having lunch?'

'They don't stay. No one stays now. They just come for the day from Samarkand.'

The small-town main street of Shakhrisabz ran in an almost straight line from the massively high pillars of the Ak-Saray that once supported its main entrance arch, down past the old domed bazaar to a group of gentle turquoise mosques and mausoleums. The street was quiet. The odd bus belched down it, a small crippled boy pushed an even more disabled boy along in a wheelchair, a man bicycled past pulling a huge trailer. At a teahouse of high carved wooden posts old men sat and played chess. Opposite, a pavement fridge was stocked with expensive Cokes.

At the cluster of mosques and mausoleums workmen idled among the strewn white bricks and stones of intended and long-delayed restoration. One stood balanced precariously on a ladder draped in white rags, painting part of Ulug Beg's blue-domed mosque. Across the sunlit paving and scattered bricks, the blue and white tiling of the two small mausoleums glinted softly. Bureaucracy had ensured that the bricks were ordered but the workmen not paid. The scene was thus of timeless tranquillity.

Around the corner, along a dusty street, the remains of the giant mausoleum built by Tamerlane for himself – though he was buried in the Gur Emir – and his favourite son Jehangir stood in an overgrown plot of waste land. Topped by a bizarre conical dome like a Kurdish hat, a few bits of tile cladding still clinging to it, it had an air of stark abandon. A group of boys playing by it threw stones at me by way of greeting.

Marauding youths pinched my bottom as I wandered in the evening light around the site of the Ak-Saray. Its paired pillars, massively out of scale with everything around, were still covered in intricate tilework, the last outburst of turquoise Islamic decoration I expected to see on my travels. Where once the vast palace stood, there was now a municipal car park empty of cars, and a small park. It was here that the local old people brought their sheep for an evening's promenade and free dinner. A thick-set woman in frayed *ikat* dress and jazzy headscarf pulled down the tree branches for her flock of three white and three black sheep to eat, an old man in boots, *chapan* and embroidered cap shuffled by leading his one mouldering ewe on a string. The youths made a grab at my camera.

That night I was the only person staying at the hotel. At dinner I sent back the stale bread and the cook walked out of the kitchen to my table.

'England? Husband? Children? Alone?' He replaced the bread with something delicious. 'Uzbek,' he said. 'I make it for myself.'

What about the fine local wines Chirine and Vassarga, featured on a decorative panel of grapes and vines in the foyer of the hotel?

'We return to Islam,' he said. 'You see why. You have an amulet from the Koran, a *tomar*, that is why boys cannot get your camera.'

In the middle of the night, yet again, the phone rang several times and the door was rattled. I lay brooding. It may well be that the pillars of the Ak-Saray entrance arch – as all that remains of it – are splendiferous and God knows how many feet high and once led to acres of gold leaf and Mongol swimming pools and that turquoise tiles cloven with sprouting grass, ruined and wrecked as they might be, are still indescribably beautiful, nevertheless their appeal withers under the onslaught of doors shaken in the middle of the night, phones that ring inexplicably somewhat before and again somewhat afterwards. There comes a time when the sordid circumstances of travel cannot be compensated for by any beauty, let alone when even that is wrinkled and jinxed. I prepared to move on.

'*Niet, niet*' was spat at me again from behind the grille of the bus station for Tashkent. A pocket dictionary and a curious onlooker confirmed that the bus was full. I caught the local one and went a mile or two up the road to the bus junction of Kitab. There by the small stand for buses to Samarkand dozens of hopeful passengers lurked on the thin line between the kerb and the asphalt road.

'From England?' a smart young man said. 'The plane, how many dollars?' I was branded instantly as rich, my general scruffiness notwithstanding.

A man at a small stall across the square, fronted by cans of orange fizz broiling in the sun, concocted some fry-up over a wood fire. 'Come,' he beckoned, and gave me some. It was delicious. 'Forget the bus,' he said. 'Take a shared taxi straight over the mountains. It's too steep for the buses, but much shorter. Then a bus to Tashkent.'

I looked at the taxis and it was only then that I noticed they all had my amulet dangling from the rear-view mirror. Some were hung with bits of fishjaw, others with cloves, nails, cardamom. I negotiated a deal for a little gold one sporting chains of cloves, included in the price the journey to Samarkand. At the top of the mountains the engine boiled, the taxi broke down.

'It's the amulet,' the driver said, piercing me with his glance. I offered to return it, but he shrugged his shoulders. 'You had it in the taxi anyway.'

Water from a small waterfall was thrown over the engine. Everyone got out and pushed. The descent was alongside a tumbling river, past small patches of tobacco plants, then large fields of more tobacco, then vineyards and orchards right up to the suburbs of Samarkand where the driver got lost in streets busy with schoolchildren, market vendors and stray dogs.

I caught the bus on to Tashkent with a minute to spare. On its rear-view mirror hung a purple velvet triangular amulet, embroidered with sequins and a golden flower. Inside was a prayer from the Koran, the driver said, so the bus didn't crash or run out of petrol.

An eighteen-year-old youth sat beside me. 'From England? How much is a kilo of bananas there? You have cocaine?'

TASHKENT

✠

Damir remembered healing my wounds some months previously, and diagnosing me as OK to live to a hundred. The
other patients he saw in the hotel medical centre at Bukhara all
had cancer from the cotton-field pesticides.

'And our cotton is poor, very poor,' he explained over a Russian
dinner of marinated herrings and potatoes at his Tashkent flat.
'Our women grow old and our children sick picking it and only
the Japanese buy it and then just to use as cheap wrapping.'
Things were very bad in Uzbekistan, he continued. 'Benzine
was as a glass of water, now it is very expensive.' Everyone was
leaving – Jews, doctors, engineers, everyone. 'All go to where
they can become dollars. Now America becomes the golden
brains for nothing.'

He and his wife were both Tatars from Kazan, she a comfort-
ably built woman, if not to say fat for the wife of a world expert
– as he assured me – in alternative medicine and bio-energized
health. They too would like to go back to Russia, but it was
impossible to sell property and they had a spacious flat in central
Tashkent, heavily furnished in fifties style, the motheaten skin
of a wild boar and the mounted head of a large curly-horned
animal on the wall adding to the general stuffiness. Still, there
had been a few improvements. They could now see English life,
films on television, Mister Poirot. His son was able to study
Spanish, where Western languages had been more or less taboo
before. He was working on it very seriously as his intention was
to go to Mexico and then slip over the border into America.
The pimply youth smiled proudly.

'If over the border big problems, no?' asked his worried father.

As he took me to the door Damir clasped my arm. 'You
bring next year to Siberia ten or twenty ill people, best with
back problems. I am there with doctor friend. We cure with

bio-energy.' Over the door hung a bunch of dried plants. 'To keep out the demons,' he explained.

Tashkent was a tedious city, rebuilt after the earthquake of 1966. There were noticeably more Russians walking around its streets than there were in the smaller towns. Men in shabby suits, white couples pushing white babies in prams, Junoesque women – yellow hair tightly frizzed, sweaty armpits oozing from tight polyester dresses, puffy feet in fur slippers. Considering the Russians had been there for some hundred and fifty years there was surprisingly little mingling.

'We want them all to go back to Russia,' said Andrei, who had come to Tashauz hospital on my previous visit to rescue me and put me on a plane back to hospital in England, and had now made it his duty to look after me again. He was very tall with piercing icy blue eyes, a doctor specializing in bone fractures but happy to do any work with foreigners that actually brought in some money.

'And you, you consider yourself Uzbek or Russian?'

'Russian. It was my great-grandfather who came here as an officer with the army, but now four generations born in Tashkent.'

'And Sonia?' His wife, dressed in pale pink and blue, masses of blue-rose lipstick, snazzy sunglasses and down-at-heel white shoes, was as blonde as he.

'Her parents were sent here in 1941. Her brother and sisters all have a life here and want to stay. We want to go, but we don't know where. We belong nowhere.'

The museums of Tashkent displayed, without distinguishing them, beautiful old *suzani* alongside modern machine copies, fabulous gold-embroidered robes of the Emirs of Bukhara, and a few bits of heavy silver jewellery dripping with triangular amulets. The real jewellery museum had been moved into the old Lenin Museum and was closed, the History of Socialism Museum was now that of the History of Uzbekistan. A forlorn building approached by a staircase of Aztec proportions, its doors were dusty and padlocked, its dry fountain of slabs of pink marble had flaked off, exposing dabs of concrete like bathroom grouting, the grass around it was overgrown with weeds and uncut rose bushes.

'Soviet style,' said Andrei.

My hotel was a tottering skyscraper overlooking an old stadium, the ceiling of the room sagging to the floor in one corner from a downpour of some years before. The café on the ground floor had sugar but no coffee or tea, that on the fifth floor tea but no sugar. The phone did not ring in the night as there wasn't one, but the door was rattled as usual.

Escaping from the city and moving on eastward, even with Andrei's help, was a nightmare. The easy option was a fifteen-hour bus ride to Bishkek, capital of Kirghizstan, along the main highway through Central Asia that skirts the north of the Tien Shan mountains, and then on to Almati and Kazakhstan. But it was not the way I wanted to go.

It was time to take stock. I sat down on a peeling slatted bench next to an old woman. She flashed her gold teeth at me and proudly produced a photo of her grandson that her daughter had sent from America. He was standing in a supermarket in a Batman T-shirt and baseball cap, leaning on a laden trolley in front of a shelf piled high with an obscene choice of varieties of pasta.

'Lovely,' I said and moved on to a deserted bench.

Islamabad lay due south-east over two forbidding mountain ranges. The slides and the abstract of the paper I was to present at the Festival there – a brief survey of Islamic embroidery embracing the Maghreb, the Middle East, Yemen and West Africa, followed by a serious dissertation on each region of Pakistan – that I had sent on ahead should by now have arrived. But the Festival was still a month or more away and there was time to wander. There were rumours in Tashkent that it was now possible to get over the Torugart Pass from Kirghizstan straight to Kashgar and from there over the well-worn Karakoram track to Islamabad. This would mean arriving somewhat too early. So why not wander around Kirghizstan? What might I find there?

For the Turkmen and Uzbeks the amulet was clearly a protective device against illness, happily purloined by Islam along with cloves, cowries, garlic and nails, much as the Christian Church had purloined the rites of the winter solstice and trapped them in a manger. But the Kirghiz? They were a different people, semi-nomadic herders of the mountains, felt makers, *yurt* dwellers – what amulets would they use?

'*Niet*,' said the very Chinese-looking man in the small shabby office that stood stead as a makeshift Kirghiz consulate. 'No visa. Only in Bishkek. Also, you can't go through the Ferghana valley. You have to go straight to Bishkek on the bus.' Nevertheless he gave me a small piece of paper that declared I had tried to get a visa and that I promised to do my best to have one within three days of arriving in Kirghizstan. It felt good at last to have a piece of paper to brandish.

The approach to Kirghizstan through the Ferghana valley was over a spit of land that was now part of Tajikistan, a country at war. Such convoluted territorial rights had never been imagined by the Russians when they had divided the land more or less according to linguistic groups, which only in any case formed part of the happy union of Soviets.

No one was allowed on the bus that crossed Tajikistan, albeit without stopping, unless they had a special permit. The police office at the bus station was up on the first floor behind the hairdresser and the watch repairer. It was closed. After several hours of missed buses, abortive conversations with uniformed men and kindly instructions on how to wind up the Soviet military watch I had bought in Petrozavodsk and never quite mastered, the door of the police office was finally unbolted. My permit to cross Tajikistan, undertaking not to get off the bus for any reason whatsoever, was finally delivered with great pomp and circumstance by a plump policeman who smelt of lily-of-the-valley. I signed the permit and he pocketed my pen.

The bus crawled along past miles and miles of dreary dark green cotton fields that extended way beyond the horizon. A few women were bent picking. At the border we were greeted by an array of Kalashnikovs. The bus picked up speed and rattled through a few vineyards that sadly would never be used to produce wine, then back again into endless cotton fields, which this time hunched up to a low range of bare mountains. The fields, ever diminishing in size, were segmented by lines of low trees, giving way to small patches of cabbages and cows, before reverting again to vast cotton fields.

The bus drew into Kokand and I was filled with alarm. Everything I had seen about this place was written X O X A H D. And now the huge letters on the bus station, one or two skew-whiff, the name on the buses themselves, on buildings and signs everywhere was X Y X O D. It was a mystery I never solved but it was indeed Kokand I had come to and everything seemed all right.

Newspaper reports were dire: sons roasted to death with blow-lamps and then discarded in ditches, guns shipped in their thousands from Afghanistan, Marxists waging war against Islamic fundamentalists, America shipping in relief cherry pie – such was the scenario a few miles to the south in Tajikistan.

'But they're different from us,' said the young mother as we sat waiting for three puppets on a small Punch-and-Judy stage to do something. 'Persian-speaking while the rest of us are Turkic.'

The little park was otherwise deserted, the children's play-ground empty, the Ferris wheel rusted, the old train tracks overgrown with grass, the tree-lined avenues quiet apart from one tree alive with the twittering of small birds. A grounded Aeroflot plane with flat tyres sat where a war memorial might have been. Behind it the Khan of Kokand's immense nineteenth-century palace, a folly approached by an impressive flight of steps and now propped up by iron bars, extended over acres. It was grandiose in a jolly sort of way, its bright ceilings like Christmas crackers laid edge to edge, its walls of garishly painted plaster hung with beautiful Bukhara *suzanis*. One or two stuffed wolves and wild boar skulked around glass cases of Ferghana embroidered caps. I dawdled round with a few sightseers. Old women in huge white Muslim headscarves, younger ones in short bright print dresses, only a few conceding to Islam by wearing trousers under them and scarves covering their heads.

Kokand was a pleasant little town of wide avenues, where a few men swept and burnt autumn leaves, and of small parks and kiosks selling candy bars and cigarettes. It struck me that I had seen none selling bananas, no bananas anywhere, since leaving Saratov where they were just about the only thing to buy.

The road on to Andijan, the industrial centre of east Ferghana, was long and dreary, through more and more miles of cotton fields. The small towns looked more prosperous and busy, a few men wore suits and ties and some women were completely veiled. Andijan's bazaar was a disappointment, selling sheep's heads rather than embroideries. The policeman at the bus station changed ten dollars into Kirghiz *som* for me, shortchanged me and asked for a present for his son before returning my bag. I climbed on another rickety bus and headed for Osh in Kirghizstan.

THE TIEN SHAN

KIRGHIZSTAN

✠

Osh is the back door into Kirghizstan, a border town where the Ferghana valley cuts into the Tien Shan, the Heavenly Mountains. Geographically part of Uzbekistan, it is politically Kirghiz and ethnically an explosive mix. The scene of fierce rioting in 1990, it had settled down into a bland characterless town, giving no hint of its long history as a centre of the silk route trade. Here were no proud buildings, no artistic patronage of despotic khans, only the promise ahead of an unspoilt remote mountain land, of woods of juniper and walnut, of glacial lakes and wandering herdsmen.

The *tarbaza* at Osh, the guide-book insisted, was just the place to stay. Nobody had ever heard of it and I was pushed in a most friendly way from taxi to bus to taxi again until deposited at the bottom of a steep path beside a very high steel fence topped with barbed wire. I climbed up through fields of fruit trees to a group of shacks full of students. It was the wrong *tarbaza*. Two very Chinese-looking girls picked peaches off the trees for me, took my bag and escorted me back down to the bus stop.

'How old are you?'

I told them and then asked, 'And you, how old are you?'

'Teacher, I am teacher of English.'

'Where are you from?'

'I am eighteen.'

The second *tarbaza* was marginally more crummy than the first. It was a weird place of rundown wooden numbered shacks set among trees, and appeared to be an abandoned Soviet workers' camp, taken over by strolling musicians and fathers walking their families around. I began to wonder whether Alexandra had been right about the guide-book and vaguely mused on where she might be now and whether we might bump into one another again.

It was, in fact, a young couple I bumped into, the first Europeans I had seen for a very long time. They were riding around
Kirghizstan, trekking on horses, wearing good boots, speaking
fluent Russian. They had been sick the day before. Mostly
a hangover, they explained, from having to drink too many
toasts in vodka in the little village they'd just left. And also from
eating a whole sheep, slaughtered in their honour. A child had
slit its throat and the whole thing had been devoured, the
head cleft in two and everything of it eaten. Only cracked bones
left.

'And we're vegetarian,' said Shivaun.

'Flexible,' added Serge.

He was half-Swiss and half-Egyptian, bearded with soft, rather
droopy eyes. He had served in the Swiss Navy with Basel as its
home port. 'It isn't a joke,' he said. Then he had finally quit after
violent storms in the North Atlantic had meant that the sailors
all shared each other's soup. 'You just took a spoonful from
each dish as it slid up and down the table and passed in front
of you. That's when I decided enough was enough.' Now he
would like to be a journalist or work as a broker on the Baltic
Exchange.

Shivaun was Irish, dark hair, fair skin, light blue eyes. Her
career was mapped out. She was going to be a solicitor, first
taking articles and then working as a lawyer in both London and
Moscow. She was concerned about ecology and the environment
and they had spent a month working on a nature reserve near
Nizhni Novgorod but weren't sure how useful they'd been, or
indeed could be. They had little flurries of bickering when Serge
tried to assert his point of view, but generally these were quickly
over.

We were staying in the same block, a rough chalet of rooms
leading off a fractured wooden corridor, most of them without
locks. The musicians, performing at some gathering, were there
too. Eighteen people in all, sharing the worst loo I have ever
seen. Small windows in my room looked out over the trees and
were impossible to close. We went for supper to the teahouse
nearby, where beds under the trees looked over a rushing river.
The meal was a particularly greasy *plov* – that national dish of
rice, mutton and yellow carrot – partaken in the company of

two Uzbek men and two very obvious prostitutes, one accompanied by a small boy.

The men scooped the women into the crotch of their trousers, stroking their hair and nibbling their ears. Serge and Shivaun had also only chosen this place because of the guide-book. The author must have taken leave of his wits, fallen in love perhaps, I suggested, stars in his eyes, hadn't noticed the prostitutes. Or could it all have changed so dramatically in the space of a year?

'Ha,' said one of the men, 'you're wearing an amulet. Only a souvenir,' he added, but he was worried that I had it. Nobody should sell it to me, especially as I wasn't a Muslim. They were made by the mother when pregnant, he continued, and she prayed for particular qualities: courage, intelligence, health (wealth he considered a quality too), and the stitches and patterns were associated with that. No, he couldn't say whether cross stitch meant health, or chain stitch intelligence, it wasn't that simple, but then inside the embroidery she would put a piece from the Koran or a prayer that the mullah had written and blessed. Then when the baby was born, he would wear it all his life and be buried with it. And a girl? Oh, no, the mother would put the amulet away until the next baby. Girls were not wanted but if they survived then as women they would wear the amulet for festive occasions in their hair or between their breasts. It could be triangular, or rectangular or round.

He couldn't understand why three corners, why the trinity, why three pendants. Two was the duality of the breasts, life for the newborn baby, but three he didn't know. In any case, even if only a souvenir, mine would protect me from danger and horrors. No, he didn't wear one. And the prostitute leaning on his trousers? No, she didn't have one either. It could, of course, protect from divorce. 'Here, in Kirghizstan, we have 23 per cent divorce,' he said. Even though as Muslims they had to spend forty days' honeymoon secluded in the house. 'Can't go out, can't leave each other's sight, parents bring food. Even so,' he sighed, 'we have much divorce.'

Back at the chalet three policemen arrived and banged on our doors to see why we had eaten at the teahouse and not at the restaurant that belonged to the complex.

In the night, someone crept in with a torch and shook the door.

In the morning a group of bare-torsoed soldiers jogged past the window. The teahouse was deserted, apart from a man raking over the embers of the night before. The restaurant was closed.

If nothing else, the door shaken in the night induced me to move on. Serge and Shivaun couldn't. The police had come searching in the mountains for them because they had no visa. They had been nowhere near Bishkek, the only place it was possible to get one, but still they had to report at the police station in Osh that morning.

We walked down into town together to look for breakfast. All around were Kirghiz men – thin faces, Chinese eyes – wearing wonderful high white hats of four pieces of white felt joined at a point on the crown and folded back around the brim, which was often lined with black velvet. A black tassel swung from the point and small bizarre horn and plant-like motifs were embroidered on each section. No one could tell me what they represented, or even understand my curiosity.

Serge and Shivaun said goodbye to me at the bus stop and went to sit, yet again, on the doorstep of the police station.

A woman waiting for a bus accosted me. 'Big problems, big problems we have,' she said, 'since the break-up of the Soviet Union. Kirghizstan has cotton, silk, gold, tobacco, very small amounts of gas. But no fuel, no fuel for buses. The airport is closed. No fuel for planes. Only hydroelectric power do we have to sell and who of our neighbours can pay for it?'

On the bus to Dzhalalabad I was allocated a seat near the front, but no sooner had I settled into it than a fat man in a dirty grey suit came up to me.

'*Aufstehen!*' he bawled, spitting bits of white curd all over me. '*Vous me compris, mademoiselle. Heraus!*'

I was manhandled by his friends into a seat at the back, where he followed me and stood chatting politely in bad French about where my husband was and how many sons I had. The bus crawled through a landscape of dry foothills and yet more cotton, relieved only by a few fields of maize. The man finally returned to what had been my seat, taking leave of me with an '*excusez-moi*'.

Dzhalalabad turned out to be a sleepy place of traffic-less

avenues, distinctly cleaner and brighter than anything I had seen for a long time. A silver statue of Lenin, somewhat pocked and seated in the guise of Rodin's *The Thinker*, dominated the small town square.

It was a town of little single-storey peasant houses set slightly crooked to the road and shaded by trees, as in so many villages of Eastern Europe. The bazaar lay away from the modest centre, past a disused children's playground and over some railway tracks. It was alive with traders shouting, with piles of tomatoes, women sitting on the ground behind boxes of herbs, small boys chasing around. I bought food for the journey ahead and tried to find a taxi driver. I needed to negotiate a deal to be taken to the bus station for five the next morning. It was an ungodly hour, they said, and most refused. One driver scraped his foot back and forward on the loose earth and then agreed to be at the hotel by four-thirty.

Away from the bazaar there was a tranquillity about Dzhalala-bad that I hadn't felt since Mubinjon's. The hotel room was papered in peach-coloured flowers, the odd mosquito squatting on a petal here and there. The price was only three dollars, the lights didn't work. The balcony looked over a wide empty tree-lined avenue that led down into the town from the desert foothills around.

The restaurant was across the road, an aquarium-like deserted room decorated in pale green, flicked here and there with pink paint. Pink roses were set on each table, bluish psychedelic patterns covered the wall behind the huge platform for the dance band that used to play every night for crowds of holidaying Soviet workers and now still on a few evenings played to empty tables. The food was the same as in Uzbekistan – *laghman*, that soup of meat and noodles, black tea and bread, but the bread was different. It was still a disc but slightly leavened, dry and unsalted with a hard crust, rather like the bread of Umbria.

Moving on to Toktogul over the mountains was going to be difficult. The only bus left at five, but if there was no fuel – and Kirghizstan's national airport at Bishkek had indeed closed down because of lack of fuel for planes – then it might take several days to get there. I spent the evening preparing, sorting out my bag which seemed to have got rather heavy. I'd bought embroideries – a Kirghiz hat, a Turkmen child's bib and tunic, a man's wedding sash, one or two bits more – another kilo or so on top of the five I'd set off with. But then the presents I had brought had mostly been given away. I'd read and torn up page by page through Russia *War and Peace* and was now doing the same to *Road to Oxiana*, but then I'd bought pears, apples and Turkish biscuits for the journey ahead. And there was only a quarter of a litre of vodka left, with none to be found in Dzhalalabad. A smidgen only then, on the balcony.

The one street lamp was lit, blackening the trees and bathing the simple architecture – the steep pitched roofs and sash windows – of the little peasant houses in ambered glow. Birdsong flittered the twilight, soft music fuzzed the restaurant across the avenue – a gentle orchestral piece of pizzicato violins counterpointed by mellow saxes, the whizz of crickets and a few muffled voices of passers-by. The hush reminded me that, apart from Alexandra and Hugo, Serge and Shivaun, and the distant protected passage of the odd tour group in Bukhara, Samarkand and Tashkent, I had seen not a single tourist since leaving the pilgrims at the quayside of St Petersburg. It was a honeyed thought.

The pre-dawn muezzin woke me, the first I had heard for a while and no doubt the explanation for the shortage of vodka. The bus finally left at seven-thirty, old, rattling, overloaded with men in Kirghiz hats, women in short, bright, shiny dresses, kids in garish clothes sporting words in bad English, ICE CREA. All were laden with heavy sacks of potatoes and apples and the bus stopped every few yards to pick up more.

I was unprepared for the beauty of the landscape. The bus ground uphill into the mountains. There was nothing steely grey or glacial white about them, they were dun-coloured, tawny, buff, here speckled like potato skins, there striated like the bark of trees. Occasionally an intrusive rock formation pleated itself across them like the underside of a pale mushroom. They were empty and parched; no conifer tree line or snow cap defined their surface. They were reflected, as a thin trembling of their majestic solidity, in lakes that were deeply turquoise, while the sky above them was so drained of blue that it was as if they were a litmus through which the sky bled down into the water.

The bus shared the road with herders, wild fearsome men dressed in felt and fur, mounted on high horses with lambs draped across their saddles, driving cattle, goats and sheep down from the high mountains to winter pastures. The bus edged slowly past the herds and by evening approached the dammed lake of Kara-Kul where a flock of turkeys blocked a main bridge. On the shore a shoddy abandoned concrete factory, its broken windows scattering what was left of the evening light, its chimney violating the flow of form and colour, stood as a grotesque relic of Soviet rule, painted with red stars and with the date 1970. That was when the lake had been created and along with it the small town of Toktogul, buried in trees as if it were in northern Finland.

The trees shrouded the town in silence: groves of birch, avenues of prim poplars, abandoned orchards of fruit trees. It was laid out in a grid of split concrete roads, too wide and too far apart, segmented by unmade earth streets. The houses were small, single storey and of brick, with high-pitched tin roofs in whose open gables tobacco was dried and hay stored. Each was set behind an enclosing wall, overshadowed by trees. Only in a very few places were there Soviet blocks of flats, red flags still flying. A rusty metal tower painted with red hammer and sickle seemed once to have been a part of some engineering works, now abandoned. The unemployed youth of the town hung around the bazaar, a mean place selling only meat, onions, peppers, a few apples and grapes, the odd fifties dress and voluminous bras. What seemed to have been shops were all padlocked and the lines of kiosks destined to stock coveted goods from the West were closed. There was not a Russian in sight.

The hotel must have been built for the construction workers. The rooms were 'residential': huge, furnished with tables and chairs, cupboards and wardrobes, coatstands and bookshelves, their balconies shrouded by trees. Sheep were busy munching the marigold beds outside. In the restaurant, there was nothing to eat. The man at reception was very apologetic and suggested the bazaar. For the first time my Russian visa was not required. He waved it away, almost threw it back at me. 'We are Kirghiz,' he said. But that I had no Kirghiz visa didn't bother him. Nor did he want my dollars. Just the equivalent of three in *som*. 'Welcome'.

The bus had arrived at the town's little bus station set in woodland. 'Buy your ticket now for Bishkek,' the driver had said. 'It's only a small van and it leaves at five in the morning.' He waited while I did so and then drove me in his bus to the hotel. Now at four-thirty the next morning I walked in pitch dark below the rustling trees, only vaguely remembering the way, until my trepidation was calmed by a glow of lit windows from the tiny bus station, like the house of the seven dwarfs deep in the forest.

BISHKEK

✠

It was easy to understand how the Mongol hordes so terrified medieval Europe as thirteen of their descendants crammed into the small van, pushing me onto a space on the floor. In the dim light their faces pressed around me. One man – taut parchment skin over high cheekbones, cold almond eyes set in a long thin face – stared without expression. He was just like the mummified man from Pazyryk in the basement of the Hermitage. Another had the wide face of an Eskimo, others in the wan glow of pre-dawn were ghosts in yellow flesh. One woman with gold teeth was sick before the 'bus' even started.

Dawn broke to reveal a countryside of rolling grassy moorland, of round felt *yurt* and of yet more horsemen herding their cattle, horses and sheep, ready to move down to lower pastures. Was this the region where the Karakalpak came from? For instead of white felt Kirghiz hats the horsemen wore caps of black wool and fur.

The van climbed, grating and grinding, more people being sick through their gold teeth, over a high mountain pass, whipped with chill wind and flurries of snow, through a long deep tunnel, then, scraping past herds and horsemen, alongside a view of hydro-electric pylons, down, down, then up again over another pass until by the afternoon it drew into the neat suburban approaches to Bishkek.

The first tune the band played that night at the hotel sounded vaguely like 'The Girl from Ipanema', the second was a gargling Asian dirge rasped out by a young woman swathed in gold lamé. Two men got up from their table and began to dance together. There were only five tables occupied in the restaurant – an affair of dusty chandeliers, smeared gilded mirrors and faded carpeting – three by men only and two by women only.

Waitresses in woolly socks were bringing two-litre bottles of vodka to the tables, but spoken requests, gesticulating and pointing excitedly brought me only black tea. At least with sugar.

The following night, only one other table was occupied. By three Finns. 'Salad or National Salad?' they were asked. Both appeared to be cucumber and tomato with a flourish of dill. The dance band duly appeared at 8.05 and turned on the flashing lights. The Finns disputed their bill and left. The singer, tonight in plum velvet and gold, flounced off and I danced the night away alone with the band.

'We used to have a hundred people here every night, groups from Czechoslovakia, Germany, Bulgaria. Now no one.'

Rather as tripping on a small pile of newly dug earth alerts one to a warren of mole tunnels underground, so the meeting with a heavily funded American aid worker, with nothing to do and anxious to latch on to my embroidery studies as suitable 'wimmin's' work, brought to my attention a whole network of young people devoting years of their lives to help pick up the pieces of the old Soviet Union. They came from all over Europe, from the States and Canada, and worked tirelessly for a multitude of acronyms.

Full of admiration for them, but nevertheless managing to gently deter the young American woman from joining me, I continued my quest. Through parks and along avenues of chestnuts – Bishkek was almost as wooded as Toktogul – past draughty Soviet town squares and cracked pavements that ended in ditches, I walked to the Fine Arts Museum. They knew the amulet well, they said. *Tomar* they called it – as the Turkmen did. It was made by the mother who put a lock of the baby's hair inside, or a prayer by the mullah or something from the Koran. Then she gently laid it on the baby's chest inside his clothes and tied the cord round his neck, and so he would wear it all his life. It would protect him from illness and evil spirits.

'And a girl?'

'No. Only a boy do we preserve.' But they mostly knew of leather amulets and not embroidered ones.

'And the three or five pendants or tassels?'

'No, such bristles we know not. But yes a triangle, why we know not. And if of silver it is only empty.'

They had recently had an exhibition of the textile art of Kirghizstan and a few of the souvenirs they had had for sale were left over. 'Here,' they said. 'This is your amulet. But it won't protect you. It's only a souvenir.'

It was of white felt, hung with only two red tassels and not three. In the centre, embroidered in blue, was a diagonal cross, a small dot in each of the four spaces. The motif of the fertile field.

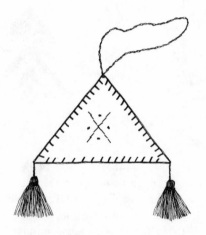

Childbirth for most of us is urgent, messy, invasive. Public when we wish most intensely to be private. For some it is a celebration, the zenith of woman, 'goddess of creation, in splendor and strength of majesty, spreading wide tissues that burn with sacred fire'. Never having viewed the whole disturbing business from such an elevated point of view, I had completely missed in all my embroidery research the symbols of birth and the fertile field. To my shame I had not recognized them or even noticed they existed.

'You can see it is a symbol of fertility,' the young saleswoman at the museum said scathingly. 'We have it on many of our textiles.'

It was, in fact, only another version of the goddess that I would later have to go westward to seek.

I showed my purchase of the triangular amulet embroidered with the fertile field to a young Kirghiz woman.

'My grandmother always wore such an amulet, a triangle with tassels so embroidered, like all old people in the countryside,' she said. 'She came from the mountains south-east of Bishkek, but naturally she sold all her amulets and jewellery during the war to buy flour.'

'Which war?'

'The Great Patriotic War. But the people who bought the amulets must still have them. They are not something you can just throw away.'

It was surprising to discover in Bishkek a considerable German population. It transpired that Stalin's forcible moving in the early forties of whole populations to Central Asia to punish them for not assisting him in the defence of Russia – the Tatars of Crimea, the Kalmuk, the Chechen, for example – had included settling large numbers of Germans from the Volga in Bishkek. A monthly newspaper with a print run of two thousand was published for them, raising hopes of emigration to Germany or, at the very least, brotherly handouts. Its reporters had surnames like 'Tichonava-Gorzen' or 'Saposhnikava-Mann', and it discussed matters such as the fact that people living in towns with electricity, whose lights were left on all night, grew physically bigger than country folk.

But the greatest concern was to try to stop the flow of applicants wanting to leave for Germany. They were not wanted in Germany, they were needed in Kirghizstan. A committee had been founded to assist those who had stayed, mainly the elderly and infirm. It could deal with their papers, help them with medicine and heating, translate and type letters for them, even simply find them someone to talk to.

Switzerland was also helping economically. It had chosen Kirghizstan as its centre of activity in Central Asia as 'reform was further advanced here than elsewhere' and human rights were better observed. President Akajen had stressed that he wanted help with agriculture and so Swiss francs were being put into milk marketing and forest administration. But still everyone wanted to leave.

A peeling silver snow leopard mounted on a plinth by the roadside at the entrance to the gorge announced that the way out of Bishkek to the east would be as turbulent as the approach to it was from the south. But, once through the gorge, and as the view flattened out into the depression that holds Lake Issyk-Kul, the land was tamed. Enclosures of maize, grazed meadows, a few clipped vines, a gentle calm into which slipped a few quiet settlements, first a small house or two, then, as the intense blue of the lake sparkled on our right, over the shoulder of the man spitting pumpkin seeds, a long line of simple houses along its northern shore. They were low and gabled in carved wood under steeply sloping tin roofs, strung along the unmade road, utterly Russian. Low fences guarded little orchards of apple trees, red chillies strung like hammocks between them to dry, and wispy country flowers laced the long grass around them. Old women sat on benches, geese around their feet. Horses were everywhere, sniffling in groups or galloping round and round fields that began neatly defined on the edge of the houses but opened into grassland space towards the mountains behind.

The bus followed the shoreline – villages to the left, and to the right, sloping down to the lake, maize fields and meadows piled with stacks of hay – the Ala-Too mountains all around. Those to the north beyond the villages, 'the sunny ones', were bare and low, though a few clouds powdered the clarity of their rolling outline. The 'shady ones' on the southern shore were craggy and snow-capped. Beyond them lay the Tien Shan that I would eventually have to cross or circumvent. Their epithet of 'heavenly' was easy to understand in the profound calm of pristine lake and mountain. Nothing had changed, the small villages had dribbled in a hundred years ago, the gentle intrusion of a handful of settlers from Siberia and the heartland of Russia. The Soviets had built a few concrete health spas, invisible from the bus, and had closed the whole area entirely to foreigners. Now a few stirrings of the new order slightly ruffled the old civic and religious establishment. One or two women wore headscarves that were black and not flowered, a small shiny new mosque intruded its minarets into a roofscape of gables, and cracked stone graves covered with horns leant against upright ones decorated with crescents.

All day the bus followed the lake, stopping at each small village and wayside halt until by evening it drew into the small town of Kara-Kol, previously known as Przhevalsk.

KARA-KOL

✝

Przhevalski's ass, *Equus caballus Przhewalskii*, stood stuffed in the local museum. The Russian explorer's name had been given not only to that now rather mangy beast he had been the first to discover, but also to the quiet garrison town the Russians had founded in 1864 at the eastern end of Lake Issyk-Kul. It was rumoured that on his explorations there Przhevalski had reported back to Moscow that the land was fertile and the region delightful, but inhabited only by syphilitic savages, so the Russians should move in. The custom of droit de seigneur was reputed to have existed here then and as the tribal chief was indeed riddled with syphilis it became the regal marriage gift to every young couple. Whether truth, legend or excuse, the Russians moved in and established their garrison, evicting the Kirghiz, most of whom died on the high passes of the Tien Shan.

More froze to death there again in 1916, victims of Russian retaliation after the Kirghiz killed two thousand of their number. The Kirghiz feared that the Bolshevik rebellion against the Tsars, which had already seared Ferghana, would spread and that the Russians farming around the lake would soon take over the Kirghiz mountain pastures too. Whether the piles of bones travellers were said to stumble across from time to time in the passes of the Tien Shan were those of Kirghiz fleeing from the first Russian settlement or the uprising more than fifty years later was hardly taken into account. In local folklore Przhevalski's report to the Tsars was held to blame for all the deaths and, as soon as Russian rule ended, the town of Przhevalsk reverted to its old name of Kara-Kol.

The hotel café was a nautical affair hung with nets, decorated in wallpaper of waves and bubbles, and furnished with padded green plastic chairs. Cooking smells and Hawaiian music wafted

through it under hot fluorescent lights to which the two frilly
goldfish in a dirty tank had almost succumbed. I was the only
person eating there.

I was about to try it again for breakfast when a small grey-
haired woman seized my arm and bustled me off to her flat
giving me tea, cognac, and bread with home-made honey and
jam like gooseberry. Introducing herself as Lena, she then sped
me round the town, telling me she was sixty-two and her teeth
were all still her own. She cleaned them with raw garlic.

She took me first to the Orthodox church where sheep grazed
at the foot of carved wooden walls, then to the mosque, smart
and very Chinese in style. On then to the market square, a dry
dusty place where a few tomatoes were laid out on rags and the
shops around were fronted by old wooden colonnades. We
climbed up the rickety stairs to a bookshop. On to the museum,
where we looked at lovely felts embroidered in the same way
as the Pazyryk ones, and at chain stitch hangings for walls and
coloured felts for floors.

Through all this I had no idea at all who Lena was. She had
simply scooped me up and whisked me off in a proprietorial
way and, though I had understood about the garlic because she
showed me, I had to admit, when she took me back to her flat
and tried to lock me in till three, that I had no notion of what
was going on. She waved hospitably at tea and bread and was
persuaded to hand the key to me when she left.

Lena's kitchen had no water. There was just one cold tap over
the bath and a loo that didn't flush. She cooked on a slow electric
hotplate that stood on the floor. All the food she had in her
kitchen was what she had offered me: old tea, bread, jam, honey,
fish she caught herself. I touched nothing, locked the door and
set off on a more leisurely tour of the town.

Kara-Kol was no tight defensive garrison town piled on itself
for protection, it spread with a lordly feeling of space. Its tentacles
of wide avenues, unmade and tree-shaded, their pretty wooden
houses set behind fences in large rough gardens where cows and
sheep were kept rather than flowers grown, radiated from the
centre towards the foothills of the Ala-Too.

Lena's flat and the hotel lay at the heart of the town, on a
small square hemmed by large stone administrative buildings

wearing big red labels in Russian and Kirghiz like buttonhole poppies. The Soviets had no doubt intended the square to be imposing, but had succeeded only in making it bleak. Lenin still stood on his plinth, striding out in his ill-fitting suit, right arm raised. But the two massive red-bordered panels in the square, topped by hammer and sickle, that once had held faded photographs of honoured Soviet factory workers, now were only a mesh of square holes through which the wind from the mountains blew keenly. Behind them the War Memorial Park was laid out with a small avenue of carved busts. The names on them were all Russian.

The small park beside it was littered with stone stelae brought from the steppes. Fertility goddesses I was sure, until I noticed that they all had curly moustaches and held what looked like a phial in their left hand raised across their chest. They were statues of the sixth to eighth centuries, erected across the steppes by the Tatars in honour of their dead, facing eastward and holding a cup in their hand.

Wandering further, I passed a large old floor felt, patterned with horns and solar symbols, hanging over a gate to dry. As I photographed it the family rushed out and dragged me off to their uncle who, they said, had a much better one. His house

had virtually no furniture, only carpets and felts on the floor
and walls – his felt was newer and not nearly as interesting. We
took our shoes off and they plied me with fermented mare's
milk, explaining proudly how the felt was made. The whole
family used to gather round, rolling the sodden wool to and fro,
but now it was only the old women who embroidered and made
felt. The Kirghiz hats are all made in factories.

'Valentin will come,' said Lena, as we walked back in the late
afternoon from the dealer in old silver who had sold me a Kirghiz
amulet, a version in heavy silver of my embroidered one. Sasha
had no idea of any meaning but weighed it carefully, showing
me his collection of coins, many ripped off old embroidered
headdresses. 'Some can be worth eight hundred dollars and
others that look the same only four dollars.'

'Valentin,' whispered Lena, as a man on a horse galloped
towards us down the dusty road, like a Mongol from the East.
He stopped by us, a fine, strongly built man, wearing a baseball
cap, his horse beaded with sweat. He had taken four trekkers
into the mountains, the horse was exhausted, he would look
after it first. Lena, he explained, was his mother-in-law and I
was her responsibility. She would want very little money. He
would find me at her flat that evening and give me advice on
crossing the Tien Shan into China. He rather considered himself
in charge of tourism in Kara-Kol. There was no one else.

Kashgar, where I was to pick up the Karakoram Highway to
Islamabad, lay due south, as the crow flies not much further
away than Bishkek, but between lay a land of eagles and not
crows. The immense mass of the Tien Shan mountain range
divides the Kazakh steppelands from the Tarim basin in China
in a range one and a half thousand miles long. Range upon range
of mountains, rising to peaks thousands of feet high, stencil the
skyline of the south shore of Lake Issyk-Kul and veer southward
to the hub of Pik Pobeida at 4,650 feet, almost within spitting
distance south-east of the lake.

But it wasn't the mountains that were the main barrier to
crossing south directly into China, it was the bureaucracy.
Because of the political sensitivity of the border zone with China,
the mountains had long been out of bounds even to the Kirghiz,

but had recently been opened. On the Chinese side, however, there was still a military zone, so that, though it was possible to hitch by road to the frontier at the Torugart pass, travellers were turned back by Chinese border guards unless they had prearranged to be met by a Chinese jeep. But it could be done, Valentin felt. One of his trekkers, a journalist, had tried. We could talk to him.

The journalist from Hong Kong was wearing only his blue underpants and hanging out his shirts and all his other clothes on lines of string across his room, when Valentin took me back to my hotel to meet him. He had a nervously mobile face and spoke with expansive gestures. Yes, he had tried Torugart last year but from the other direction. He had got to the border all right but was turned back by the Kirghiz. He had had huge problems because a packet of cigarettes had fallen from his pocket, he said, and the guards claimed he had 'thrown' it at them, and only an abject letter of apology written out then and there had persuaded them to let him back into China.

'Well, I think it's OK now,' said Valentin. 'A car to the border costs a hundred and twenty dollars, so it's better to get a bus to Naryn and ask. You might have problems there, but once you get to the border you can now walk across no-man's land, it's less than five kilometres and you can probably pick up transport there.'

'Don't go,' Sasha the silver dealer had said, adding facetiously, 'even with this amulet you've bought. It's a bone-shaking seven hundred kilometres on the bus and you won't get across.'

The alternative was a bone-shaking five hours by bus to Almati, then twenty-four hours east to Urumchi and then thirty-six back again to Kashgar. I stuck with my decision to try the Torugart. It was said to be wild and dramatic and, most of all, a challenge, if only a bureaucratic one.

Lena whipped me off first for a good scrub. A beautiful resort in the mountains, Valentin had said, lovely clear air, hot thermal baths, pine forests. The whole place will soon be invested in as a tourist resort. I imagined some sort of Swiss spa, albeit poorer, as the borrowed car groaned uphill past yet another silver snow leopard on a plinth and a proletariat worker with his muscled wife. We progressed through a gorge cut by a rushing river and a huge corroded pipeline wrapped in aluminium insulated with yellow fluff that seeped through here and there.

The resort itself consisted of a couple of simple neglected buildings like the old halts along disused railway tracks in the French Vosges. A horse was tethered outside but there was no one about. Lena busied herself and found a robust Russian woman who led us into a small room where there were two old tin bath tubs, a tangle of rusty pipes and a bowl of salt.

'Watch your heart pumping,' said Lena, 'and don't stay in too long.' She waited outside while the woman filled the bath with scalding water and ordered me in. I emerged soon after, emeried with salt, flushed and weak, and staggered to the café where we sat alone to the meal of cabbage soup and rissoles that awaited us.

On our return to Kara-Kol, Valentin drove up – still in the same yellow baseball cap, dirty jeans and heavy miner's boots – in a pony-trap. Its roof was looped with fretted wood, it was painted a glowing red and had rows of seats. Valentin sat at the front holding the pony's reins. 'No fuel for car, so horse is good,' he said.

The man had style, I thought.

'I take you to Tungan for amulet.'

The Tungan are an ethnic minority of Kara-Kol, considerable in number, in outward appearance Chinese, though they claim not to be. The pony-trap rattled up to a house that looked much like any other behind its iron gate. A young man was shovelling coal in the driveway. Inside, the main room was almost filled by a low carpeted platform on which the family slept and ate, warmed by a system of pipes underneath fed by an old stove. It was the home of an extended family: the parents, one son, his wife and child, three daughters and then a number of children and young men who were presumably families and husbands of these.

Sophian was the embroiderer and she had laid out all her work to show me. It was modern Chinese, garish cloths of flowers, peacocks and winged fish worked from patterns and threads brought from China by relatives who went there regularly. I felt a strong whiff of the next stage of my journey. More embroideries were brought out, finer and older and even more Chinese: a pair of slippers made by an aunt forty years before, some trouser cuffs encircled by fine flowers and multi-coloured birds.

The amulet hidden under my shirt seemed entirely of another culture, its primitive design of horns, its symbolism at odds with the Chinese iconography of peonies and lotus, mandarin ducks and cranes exquisitely stitched in silks. Nevertheless, it was for the amulet that Valentin had brought me here and I diffidently produced it.

The family crowded round. Yes, yes. They knew it. Not exactly with those horns but usually in textile and usually embroidered. It was very common among Muslims. The grand-mother, or some old woman, made it for the child who wore it from the age of one until it was five.

'Why wasn't it worn until the child was one?'

'Because we keep the child hidden away, out of sight, so that it is safe. Then at one year old others see it, so that is when it can be attacked by the evil eye, by bad spirits or by illness.'

After five the amulet was kept and worn again when there was any threat of danger or illness. If it was still good when its owner died he would pass it on to one of his children.

'Anything inside?'

'Yes, a prayer from the mullah.'

Heartened to find these people still placing their innocent trust in the amulet, I was considerably shaken by their next remark.

'Usually we do feasts for tourists, crisp pasta in honey, noodles, that sort of thing.' They brought out a visitors' book signed by dozens of Cambridge students, tourists from Spain, Germany and no doubt many other countries. I took my leave of them and prepared to move on the next day.

But first I visited Przhevalski's museum. It lay in a memorial park on a spur overlooking the lake and walking round it were the Hong Kong journalist and a large jolly Austrian named Rudolph, accompanied by a German interpreter. The guide recounted the journeys of Przhevalski through Siberia, Xinjiang and northern Tibet from the 1860s to the early 1880s, illustrated

by exhibits of maps, accounts, beautiful sketches of the local
people he encountered, stuffed animals, including the ass named
after him, and all his equipment. 'But someone has stolen his
gun.' The guide looked crestfallen. It had been in his charge,
cherished as everything here.

We walked out along a small path between apple trees to
Przhevalski's memorial stone and grave. A whip-round among
the intelligentsia of St Petersburg had paid for it, as the Kirghiz
were not prepared to, but it was cared for and a bunch of red
gladioli lay fading on its tablet. Rudolph walked straight past
and looked proudly at the lake. There were two boats moored
there, two grey cutters. 'I've bought them. They're mine.' He
owned a travel company in Austria that specialized in hunting
and fishing holidays, and produced a visiting card decorated
with bears and huskies. They took people to Canada to fish
salmon, to Kamchatka to shoot bear, now they would fish here.
He was spending a hundred thousand Deutschmark refitting the
boats and would charge a thousand dollars each for the trip
round the lake, stopping here and there for trekking. It was
crystal clear down to fifteen metres, he said, no motor boats
were allowed and the whole area was unknown and unspoilt.
Germans would certainly come.

As I packed that evening to leave I went to throw away the
pages of the guide-book that covered Kara-Kol, to lighten my
load, when a sentence caught my eye: 'Moored beneath Przhevalski's memorial by the beach road are the two grey cutters that
constitute the Kirghiz navy.'

The small whitewashed houses along the southern shore of Lake
Issyk-Kul wrapped themselves around in picket fences like
mufflers as if in protection from the majestic awe of the scenery
around them. They were quietly domestic, their tin roofs glinting
like mica in the sun, their window frames cobalt blue, the trees
of their overgrown gardens laden with red apples, their wooden
gates snapped to. But after a mile or so this taming of the wilder
shore of the lake was abandoned, a half-hearted lick at the hem
of a massive wilderness. Schist, dry grassland, wild lavender and
bushes aflame with autumn lay between the shore of boulders,
grass promontories and empty beaches on one side and the

towering shadow of the distant mountains on the other. A small group of people worked by the roadside constructing a *yurt*, a token outpost of conquest.

From Balichki, at the western end of the lake, buses went south to Naryn, towards the Chinese border. I climbed on one and squashed between laughing, chattering olive-skinned people in bright clothes and heavy boots. They passed round a bowl of fizzy lemonade and offered it to me. They asked if I were going to China and expressed no surprise or misgivings when I said I was. This was encouraging I felt. The driver collected the fares and then drove round to find petrol to spend them on.

The bus first lumbered up a broad, flat grassy valley between low barren hills to the west, and jagged, cloud and snow-capped peaks to the east and south. It then entered a narrow, meandering defile climbing up to the Dolon pass at nearly two thousand feet and then down again through grasslands studded with *yurt*, horses, cattle and sheep. Finally it descended into Naryn, a dismal blemish strung along the whipped-up Naryn river and enclosed by mountains. The bleakness of people's lives lay heavily on it like a river mist. The hotel was predictably seedy, the buffet closed, the restaurant out of service.

Lena's gifts had almost immobilized me: a book on Kirghiz felt, picture postcards of the joyous Sovietization of Kirghizia, a woven belt, a chromium phial in the form of Manas – a hero of epic tales – apples, tomatoes, a jar of honey and a bigger jar of slightly soured but very good cream.

'There is nothing in Naryn,' she had said. She was right.

Throughout the night a mournful chanting blanketed the town. By five-thirty the chanting had stopped and an icy drizzle scratched my face as I walked the dark and empty streets looking for the shared taxi the bad-tempered woman at the hotel had said left at six for Torugart. Daylight sifted into a dense fog sagging over Naryn, blocking out the mountains completely, and the drizzle had turned to freezing sleet, but I had still found nothing. As the deserted bus station roused into life – its broken door unpadlocked, its ticket office opened – I asked about Torugart. Nothing. Certainly no buses and no one knew of anything else. There was a bus for Bishkek, why didn't I catch that? There wasn't anywhere else to go. I let it leave and sat down on the icy pavement to think.

Against crossing the Torugart was the fact that it was a direct route south, so that I would arrive in Islamabad too early, unless I dallied in the small villages along the Karakoram, but they were already well known to me. Then with the thick fog, I would see nothing of the pass. Would it perhaps not be more useful to go further east?

While the amulet from Karpathos had been the most westerly sent to me, I had also been presented with a temple bag of the Bai people of South-West China hung with three triangular amulets. They were embroidered in soft pink silks, delicately unpagan, with small figures and flowers. So, while so far east was at the moment beyond the brief I had assigned myself, perhaps a flurry into western China might disclose more than the fog-enshrouded mountains, albeit beautiful when visible, could reveal. The detour would entail following the barrier of the Tien Shan along their northern slopes and then returning along the southern. About a week's journey.

The pavement was cold, a dog padded by, its fur frosted, the men at the bus station shouted at me, 'Bus leaving now for Bishkek, come, come.'

I took it. Mountains that yesterday had been blurred opaline washes of watercolour delicacy now were blotted out by soupy fog. Four hours later the bus had broken down three times and the sky had cleared. I stood waiting for it to be mended seething with regret. I kicked a stone across the road. Heftily. On the way to Naryn I had seen only spectacular valleys and defiles. Now, in a recalcitrant frame of mind, I saw only the stupid bus stops. Made of cheap mosaic they whimsically depicted muscular Soviet workers and Kirghiz herders sitting down to tea. Then there were more of the bizarre sculptures, like the silver snow leopards that had graced the approaches to wild country further north, and now also families of tame deer, and, on boulder outcrops, wobbly chipped plastic renderings of Soviet women hikers, hands shielding their eyes, gazing ahead. Inside the bus, there were no stones to kick.

*

My revised route entailed a return to Bishkek and the Hotel Ala-Too. The band had been fired and Shivaun and Serge were there, still hounded by visa problems. I left them Lena's honey.

Fugitive images of the glacial beauty of the Torugart pass crowding my mind, what I actually saw was the sordid reality of Bishkek bus terminal shortly after dawn. Men and women in bright Fair Isle stockings were cleaning its littered ground with witches' broomsticks. A woman busily picked the roses in the grass patches around the terminal and bunched them into five to sell. Kiosks offering pasties, cognac and champagne had not yet opened. The seven o'clock bus to Almati no longer existed, the eight o'clock wasn't running as there was no fuel. There could be one at nine. A hole-in-the-wall, which when peered into revealed a steaming windowless kitchen of women boiling kettles and rolling pastry, served jam jars of tea and doughy pasties that the small resident dog much enjoyed.

'It's a miserable day.' I was addressed by a medical student wishing to practise his English and somewhat perplexed by the phrases concerning the weather that he had had to learn. 'Not too bad today. Turned out all right, after all. Can't complain.'

The bus arrived, ran for half an hour and then broke down, entailing three hours' wait at the roadside. It flashed through my mind that it was perhaps fortunate that Alexandra was no longer with me. The small houses of Bishkek ended abruptly at an insignificant little river to give way to pale green steppelands of wispy grass, rolling into endless horizons. The road ahead lay dead straight following the line of the Tien Shan mountains to the south, whose covering cloud gradually focused into yet more mountains. The odd lone horseman and his drove of cattle and sheep blocked our path. We passed an occasional village of utilitarian homesteads marked by trees and the odd field of maize, otherwise the steppe obliterated all until we hit the city of Almati, capital of Kazakhstan and tucked into its south-east corner.

DETOUR

✞

Wheeler-dealers from Korea, oil technologists from the West, men in suits – even ties – smart cars parked outside the scabrous blocks of flats, hotels at hundreds of dollars a night, Almati is the boom town of Central Asia.

'You must get out now!' yelled the receptionist at the huge, gloomy hotel by the Medeo speed-skating rink in the hills above town. 'Foreigners only one night.'

No one else was there and there was no breakfast, not even coffee or tea. The road back down to town led past woodlands of leaves crackled by early autumn, past small shuttered houses with wild gardens behind high fences. They smelt of wood fires and cooking. Behind, the Tien Shan mountains rose in an icy curtain.

The receptionist at the next hotel, sniffing and blowing her nose, could only be approached across a pool of water. The ceiling above it was mouldy, the smell dank, the room twelve dollars. Wandering through the hotel looking for the usual spartan buffet I found that one whole wing nine storeys high had been closed down. The ceilings had all collapsed under the weight of leaking water.

The avenues of Almati were too wide and too long, the bronze warrior statues too pompous, the buildings too massive, but the museums were rich with Scythian animal art, with stone goddesses from the steppes – and the Tatar phial-clasping statues – with Kazakh textiles and jewellery, with old musical instruments and portraits of the last masters to play them.

It was walking in the evening that I bumped into the Hong Kong journalist again, on his way down to Shaggies Burger Bar. As we strolled along together, he listed all the events he had to cover for his work, which month he would be where and why.

He thought while he was here he would first do an article on the nuclear capability Kazakhstan had been left with on the withdrawal of the Soviets. It was said to be the fourth nuclear power in the world, he pointed out. Then there was the Russian insensitivity to the steppes and to the nomadic lifestyle they had supported. Not just the collectivization plans of the thirties that had led the Kazakhs to slaughter millions of their livestock rather than hand them over to the Russians, but also the Virgin Lands scheme of the late fifties when the Russians had ploughed up millions of hectares of steppe only to find it was too arid to grow wheat. And now the Kazakhs themselves were selling off their heritage of gold and oil. He'd go up country to investigate all that. Then back to Bishkek for the tourism conference. Then finally he would have to go to the States as he needed new shoes and socks. 'Can't get good socks anywhere else.'

The bus for the twenty-five-hour journey to China and Urumchi left just after dawn and broke down almost immediately. The driver tinkered round the back with a screwdriver and it lurched off again. Outside the small houses, blurred in the morning mist, rows of tobacco leaves were hung out to dry. Women and horses pulled handcarts, sheep and cattle wandered along the tracks scoured parallel to the road edge, where innumerable others had passed before them. A large plastic bear – like the snow leopards, deer and jolly women hikers of earlier roads – presumably indicated the type of terrain to expect. Some villages were entirely enclosed by high metal fencing. Was that collectivization? Had they been hustled into one compact unit? The maize fields beside them then ended as abruptly as the irrigation that sustained them, and gave way to plateau after plateau, some fertile enough to support a small town and some so barren as to be home only to one flock of sheep in several square miles.

By the time we reached the frontier the landscape had petered out into a vast arid plain and only half a dozen people were left on the bus. Rows of pigeons squatted on the huge Customs building. 'Forbidden to take out of Kazakhstan', the notice said, 'sewing machines for life conditions, knitting machines for life conditions, bicycles, mechanical watches, children's clothes till

size 42 and shoes till size 35.' A few yards further on at the
Chinese border I had to sign a form declaring that I was not
suffering from diarrhoea, Aids or a sore throat.

It was a travesty to be in a country as rich, as important, of
so ancient a civilization as China, simply as an unwanted detour
on a rather esoteric journey, but I had to acknowledge that it
was only a small corner I was cutting across and that it was in
any case Turkic Uyghur territory and not Han Chinese and
therefore not truly China.

We crossed the border and, in a matter of seconds, the scene
exploded into life and colour. The drab shroud of Communism
metamorphosed into a blaze of brilliant textiles hung along
roadside stalls, the inertia of recalcitrant bureaucrats, of massive
Russian women wielding a smidgen of power behind their ticket
windows evaporated into a whirl of busy people: men and women
building houses, scraping the road, filling potholes, bicycling
past on rickshaws, playing serious billiards on green-baized
tables that lined the road as seeping, terminally sick piping had
done up to now.

The buildings were single storey, of natural brick with flat
roofs, but confidently decorated with bright graphics. More
people bicycled past, washed the bus windows, carried their
babies upright in baskets on their backs, called to each other.
The ludicrous kiosks of suspect vodka, Western candies and
bananas had vanished. The scene inexorably cleared my eyes
of the scabrous rubbish I had come to expect. But the horses
and carts were still there.

Along the poplar-lined street garlic lay out to dry on rush
matting. The flat land behind was golden with maize and sunflowers and patched with green ponds. The bus stopped at a
wayside café, where men twisted thick strands of noodles in fast
loops above their heads like skipping ropes, and turkeys pecked
around in the dust. Supper was included in the fare.

In the early evening sun the bus climbed into the pass
beyond Korgas, following the river that here thrashed through
boulders in a narrow crevice and there crawled over a flat
stony bed. The homes of the mountain herders were like wig-
wams rather than *yurt*, and along the roadside whole families
living in tents beside their wooden beehives laid out their pots of

honey for sale, like the nougat vendors along the road through Montélimar.

Lorries belched and wheezed and broke down, the road steepened. Tall dense pines, the shape of their own ashen silver cones with no trunks visible, twisted their roots into the thin skin of earth clinging to the rock face. They grew denser and denser until the road finally veered away from the river and snaked up into the mountains and into moon-stroked darkness.

However skilfully the art of sleeping on a small hard bus seat with no head rest is mastered, morning inevitably strikes early and limbs and neck take a while to unfold. I craned gradually to see a wide plain cultivated yet again with sunflowers and maize and dotted with wispy saplings, the distant ones delicate as sugar dust. By six, there were people everywhere – building brick houses, bicycling to work, selling food at roadside stalls. Finally, the bus pulled into the 'International Second Class Port Urumchi Xinjiang China' and missed the Kashgar connection by one hour.

The province of Xinjiang had been closed to foreigners when I tried to enter before, because of rioting, a not-uncommon event. There had been bloody rebellions throughout the nineteenth century and conflict still erupted between the Muslim Uyghurs and their Chinese overlords. This time it was quiet but the hold of the Han Chinese over this desolate distant province is flimsy and resented. It is the home of a dozen or so minority groups whose embroidered costumes, neglected and unlabelled, filled the Museum of National Minorities.

A fancy pagoda sat on a hill above the park, the market sold frilly goldfish and plastic buddhas, but Urumchi didn't feel particularly Chinese. It just felt buzzing and modern, seething with all the qualities missing in the old Soviet Central Asia: initiative, involvement, risk-taking. It was a refreshing city of entrepreneurs rather than bureaucrats. The hotel TV showed Marilyn Monroe dubbed in Chinese. And it worked. And in colour.

Not far from Urumchi, carved on the rocks of the Tien Shan, were prehistoric cult goddesses with hourglass figures and

shapely legs. There was no sign of triangles as skirts nor of
pendants. All, however, were horned, horned with small antennae
rather like Martians, excrescences that symbolized plant life and
fertility.

It was impossible to get to see them but the Museum of
National Minorities and History sold postcards of them. It was
there too that the embroidered costumes of the dozen or so
minority groups whose home is Xinjiang gathered dust in the
glass display cases. No triangles, no goddesses, no horned headdresses. But in a dimly lit room lay a group of mummified
corpses: women who lived about four thousand years ago and
whose hair was rolled up into plumed felt caps ending in two
horns. Two horns like the women of Eastern Europe and of the
high valleys of the Hindu Kush, not one as on the petroglyphs
of that woodland clearing in northern Russia, which now seemed
so far away. One woman had been buried with a straw basket
and rams' horns at her side, another had the skin each side of

her nose scarified with horns. It was evident that the powerful talisman here was not the triangle but horns.

The bus from Urumchi to Kashgar skirts the northern edge of the Taklamakan desert in the lee of the Tien Shan for thirty-six hours. It has no seats but narrow metal bunks stacked on top of each other like dinners on an aircraft trolley. Reclining on them were four hulky self-satisfied males, bearded and hippy, wearing Myanmar T-shirts; a Swiss hiking, mountain-bike-club pair dressed to match in purple and turquoise and a Japanese girl with a huge rucksack. They were on their way from Beijing to the Karakoram. I had hit the tourist trail.

It took an hour and a half to clear Urumchi's traffic jams: lorries, buses, donkey carts piled with boxes, pedal rickshaws smothered under loads of farm greenery, horse-drawn carts laden with severed goats' heads sticky with blood, women bent under shoulder yokes, jeeps, smart cars, ramshackle cars. An infernal din.

The travellers on the top bunks could see nothing at all of the landscape, only the jolting bus roof as we travelled all day through a silent wasteland of stony desert, followed by stark granite mountains and then stony desert again. At first a few settlements of adobe and mud-brick roofed in thatch, then a small brick town or two were all that impinged on the void. We stopped here and there for meals, always the same bowl of noodles.

The desolation of the fringes of the Taklamakan cut bone dry into the senses as we followed the old silk route. Lunar screes of shiny mica-schist lapped against bare mountain slopes, which then levelled down to yet more glistening mica and yet more desolation.

'Not like Japan,' said the Japanese girl. 'Japan wet, very wet air.'

The discomfort of the bus travellers, recumbent on their hard bunks one above the other, brought home the feeling of what it must have been like to traverse these deserts on camel for months on end and then arrive at some welcoming oasis, a feeling lost on the silk route further west where irrigation, cotton fields, industrialization and market gardens have crept to the gates of what was the only fertile land, to leave the distinction utterly blurred.

Now there was not a camel to be seen, no life bar the blue lorries overloaded with coal that we passed here and there. They were always at a standstill, jacked up on three wheels with the driver fiddling around under the fourth, or with the bonnet open spewing smoke and steam. They were all that peppered the void.

All day, all night, all day again we lay mesmerized until ponds, trees and donkey carts signalled the approach to Kashgar. The detour had been almost one and a half thousand miles.

KASHGAR

✠

Han domination of the Uyghur town of Kashgar asserted itself in the neat red jackets and cheongsam of the hotel staff and the complete lack of dinner. The place was forcibly on Beijing time, some two hours out of sync with the surroundings and the sun. It might be eight o'clock but in Beijing it was ten and dinner was over.

The Chinese had been early settlers here, probably just after the Scythians, but had abandoned the town and from the ninth century it had been settled by Uyghurs. It had been one of Genghis Khan's earliest conquests, around 1206, and, too far east to be part of Batu's Golden Horde, it had passed to Genghis's son Chagatai. When the Chinese had returned in 1755 they had been heartily resented and still were. It had been Uyghur Muslim uprisings against the Chinese that had closed the city when I first tried to come here in 1991.

Kashgar was always the hub of the silk routes, an oasis for shattered travellers after surmounting on yak and pack-horse the rigours of the mountains to the west, north and south, or negotiating on camels the trails along the Taklamakan to the east. Now it drew other travellers arriving by plane or coach.

They came always for the Sunday market and polluted it. Where donkeys were being trotted round and their teeth bared to prospective purchasers, an obese Frenchman, his stomach hanging down to the hem of his shorts, stood and sneered. Where old men lifted the sheep's fat tails and felt underneath them, a pale woman carrying a souvenir meat chopper and wearing a mask to protect her from the smells nevertheless peered inquisitively. Where an unsuspecting old man piled up his tomatoes, a photographer set up his tripod under his nose. While the animals were arranged by species – here the horses and donkeys, there the sheep and cattle, at the back the tethered camels – and the fur caps and onions were carefully segregated, the tourists roamed everywhere. Peering through lenses, hung with yet more lenses and expensive equipment, they walked along snapping remorselessly, down the roads lined with piled-up vegetables, past the donkey carts, the people carrying chickens, the droves of sheep and goats. Nothing escaped their sharp focus or their wobbly camcorders. There were the young, mainly in couples, eating melons and dressed for hiking. There were the Scandinavians, heads above the crowd, following a flag. There were even Chinese padding along behind a sign 'Big China Tours'. Most eventually went adrift in the pandemonium: hissing tea-kettles, steaming dumplings, boiling mutton, braying animals, warning bells and shouts, goats pulled on a string, people pushing and shoving, horses rolling in the dust and – the purpose of it all – old gnarled brown hands counting wads of dirty torn money, the women stuffing theirs into their knee-length woolly knickers.

The painted sign 'Kashgar International Market of Western and Central Asia' was no exaggeration. In the lanes behind it lay the covered walkways of the more permanent market. Stall after stall of brilliant shimmering fabrics, embroidered caps, shoes and babies' crocheted helmets. On again and piles of brightly painted lac cradles, shiny brass chests, amulets for horses and new wooden carts.

And then I saw her. A little woman with a face like a russet apple, wearing dark woolly stockings and sandals, an old dress and cardigan and a wisp of dirty white scarf over her head. She held on a wooden rod dozens of brightly coloured amulets. They were all triangles of plastic hung from beads and decorated with a coloured tassel at each corner. The women who thronged around to buy were, I noted, all Muslim. Their heads were covered with thick scarves of brown cotton which they drew over their faces when they thought they were being observed. My questions sank without reply into a sea of brown cloth.

On Monday most of the tourists moved on and Kashgar returned to normal: a dusty little town of mud walls, small adobe houses, balconies of potted plants and the odd mosque in a peaceful garden of trees. The bustle and trade of the Sunday market simply moved back into the streets. Old men and boys sat hammering copper, turning wood, sharpening knives, stitching fur, beating caps over wooden moulds, chopping melons, selling embroideries: men's hip shawls tasselled with gold, Kirghiz bonnets of white cotton, shaped like helmets and finely worked over lappets that covered the ears and the woman's long plait.

A rickshaw ride away, down a wide avenue of poplars, a last glimpse of the shimmering green and blue of Central Asia, all the more beautiful because of its isolation, lay the Abakh Khoja mausoleum. Tiles of mint and emerald glinted in the sun, the tracery of blue and white patterned ones beside them ruffled between sun and shade. Boys chanted in the Koranic school, leaves floated on the pool, bits of cloth hung on a window frame – white, blue or black to pray for a boy, a few flowered or red for a girl.

In town the Pakistani dealers prepared to leave for home. They piled bale upon bale of silk and velvet along the pathways of what was left of Catherine Macartney's old garden of the British Residency, now part of a multi-storey modern hotel. The bus left from here, its axle sinking as the Pakistanis loaded their stuff on the roof. The journey would take two days with a night stopover in Tashkurgan. More and more bales were brought. The other three foreigners hung around waiting. Camille and Eva, a young couple from Poland, had never travelled before. Things were getting good, for the first time ever the future was in your own hands and even the young could earn enough to travel. Still, they were worried about Russia and the stranglehold of the Mafia. Everything was imported and nothing was made in Russia. The shops were terrible, the butcher's stank so much you couldn't even go in.

Bruno smiled. He was a pathologist from Chicago, well used to travelling. 'You have to be careful, and not just with meat,' he said. He himself never ate, for fear of illness. Just apples washed three times in soap. He carried a large drum of antiseptic wipes for his private parts, he said. He couldn't avoid respiratory problems, but he survived by caution, though he had already lost eight pounds. In answer to his close questioning about my own health concerns, I pointed out that I was lucky. I had innards of old rope, I had built up a natural immunity to hepatitis and insects hated me.

'But that still leaves salmonella and brucellosis,' he pointed out, 'and you know there's bubonic plague in India now. It's said to be either smallpox or bubonic plague, but they're very different. One's a virus and the other's a bacterium. It's most likely bubonic plague.'

We stood waiting while more and more packs were loaded onto the roof of the bus, Bruno sweltering in the heat.

'I always wear layers of clothing for every eventuality,' he said.

KARAKORAM HIGHWAY

✠

The bus skirted the maize fields of the oasis of Kashgar, past brick factories, along poplar-lined roads, then out into the desert and through more small oases of the same kind. They were watered by *karez* and divided into small cultivated patches by low mud walls. Then back into the desert and suddenly into the embrace of the mountains, at first sheer cliffs of stone, then the wide, flat stony valley of a meandering river flanked by mountains, then more and more mountains piled in snow-covered ranks behind. Up over a high pass and onto a plateau. Every little patch of grass supported a stone enclosure, a small hut, a few yaks and sheep, a Bactrian camel or two, a horse and a family.

The plateau widened out, mountains on every horizon, still lakes reflecting the sky. Then more pasturage that now was almost marshy, with yaks everywhere that fled at the sound of the bus, fur flying. We stopped for lunch, Bruno waiting patiently in the road outside. Then again at a Chinese control post, where most people bought hard-boiled eggs and Bruno stood by telling us about equine strains of Aids.

Vaccination will probably never be possible for Aids, he said, but many diseases have no vaccination. Cholera, for example. vaccine is only effective for one month and viruses change all the time. 'I guess you guys had a jab before you came,' he added, 'but that probably protects you for the sort of cholera they get in Turkey. Here, you're unprotected.'

The bus wheezed on through more stony desert, past more snow-capped mountains, then down a long straight wooded valley into Tashkurgan. The scenery had been magnificent but the bus had arrived too late for the hotel to provide a proper dinner. Bruno glowered at the rice, chips, Chinese leaf and chillies they had mustered up.

'Considering all the yaks and lambs we've driven past, they're not much in evidence at the table,' he remarked.

I had somehow imagined him to be vegetarian. In any case, he ate nothing of the dinner and explained that he had taken an antibiotic for his respiratory condition at six and would take another at nine. He had travelled from Islamabad to Kashgar up the Karakoram Highway and was now returning. He had already sent cards to his family from Kashgar to tell them how much he was dreading the harrowing journey back. His wife didn't come travelling with him, he said. She didn't enjoy that sort of thing.

Tashkurgan was the staging post for buses going both north and south along the Karakoram Highway. They arrived at night and left in the morning, emptying the small town of travellers and so the trade they brought. Days there were thus peaceful and quiet, except for the piped music relayed from loudspeakers in the trees along the town's one main avenue. Wide and dusty, it led gradually downhill, low brick and adobe buildings on each side, to an old stone fort and the broad riverbed where women washed their clothes in irrigation channels.

The people were Tajik. The women all wore hats of a flat pillbox shape like those of Hunza further south, heavily embroidered in cross stitch. Across their foreheads orange and red patterns of rosettes, triangles and crosses glowed against a deep brown background and touches of Lurex sparkled in the sun, but the tops and backs of the caps were hidden under scarves. I decided to stay and investigate them and waved goodbye to the bus.

'You'll regret it,' said Bruno. 'You'll be exposed to all kinds of things here.'

The women were happy to show me their caps. The backs and crowns were thickly padded – 'Winters are cold here,' they explained – and solidly embroidered with flowers or triangles. I was unsure of the ethics but the small local museum even sold me one from their display. Down the side streets young women walked, their hair braided and hung with coins, dirty small boys wore triangular amulets of leather round their necks. 'To keep them well', though a thorough wash would no doubt have done more good.

A handful of tourists passed through during the day: two cheerful young people on a tandem – four months on the road from England, they said – and a small tour group of white-haired Americans who had come from Beijing. They didn't remember where they'd been, but they had it all written down. But the evening bus from Kashgar didn't come.

Television whiled away the long evening, as it had in Urumchi. Instead of the set being broken down or emitting only a jazzy black and white stew – if indeed there had been a TV in the room at all, as I had become used to – here Placido Domingo sang with pure clarity, shampoos were advertised in glorious Technicolor, while white subtitles in Chinese sailed across the bottom of the screen like swans on a lake. It was strange that this remote corner of China was far more in touch with the world than the regions of the old Soviet Union I had travelled through where nothing worked, there was no knowledge of other countries and time had stood still in the poverty of more than half a century ago.

At five the next morning I found a Pakistani brewing tea in the yard. Yes, the bus had finally arrived in the middle of the night and would leave later in the morning for Pakistan. And, yes, there was a spare seat on it. Next to two Australian women, he knew, because none of the men had wanted to sit there: they were all Pakistani and Muslim.

The bus was not allowed to pick up passengers *en route*. It had a manifest of people and baggage from Kashgar and that was what was allowed over the border. The driver and the officer from the bus company were adamant.

After a while there was a slight weakening. If I paid the whole fare from Kashgar again they might consider it. Once I had done this they changed their minds again. They were emphatic. I must get off the bus and stay in Tashkurgan. I explained that I had had to get off *en route* because I was sick, feeling doubtful I would get much sympathy for having got off to look at the women's hats. To no avail. I was to get off the bus and stay in Tashkurgan. I produced what I thought was my trump card. My passport.

'Look,' I said. 'Date of birth 29.9.29. Today I'm sixty-five.

That's old. You can't abandon an old lady in Tashkurgan.'

It was clear from the officer's face that he could think of no better fate for troublesome old ladies.

'Many happy returns of the day anyway,' said the Pakistani fellow beside me.

Another then stood up and announced to the bus, 'Gentlemen. Today is this young lady's birthday. We will not leave without her.'

There was a general cheering and singing of 'Happy Birthday' and a show of such solidarity from those dear English-speaking Pakistanis that the bus driver and officer finally relented and the bus set off for the Pakistan border and Sust.

The sparse dry grass in the wide stony valley didn't seem adequate to support all the animals grazing there: camels, horses, cows, donkeys, sheep, goats.

'These animals', said one of the men, 'don't belong to the people. They belong to the Government. That's called communism.'

We climbed into the mountains and through snowfields dotted with *yurt* and yaks, past majestic lakes that held the sky and the peaks in their stillness, and then over the Khunjerab pass into Pakistan. As we continued through a tight gorge there was an ominous whistling. A tyre had burst. I got out and walked. It was two hours before the bus caught up with me and for those two hours I walked beside awesome rocks along a road that meandered above the river, trapped by shadow or blazing in open sun. The murmur of the water hardly disturbed the intensity of silence. It was the road towards Palas.

I journeyed then slowly down the KKH to Islamabad, by jeep and by bus, calling on the way at the Pattan Field Office. Herb had completed one suspension bridge but, in the first melting snows of spring, it had collapsed, pitching three cows into the raging torrent below. The contractor had cheated on the concrete.

Lawrence of Arabia

On my return home I dropped a friendly line to Alexandra, touching on the subject of my hundred dollars, but only in a most polite way, concentrating instead on enquiring after her health and the rest of her journey once we had parted. There was no reply.

The local library had the official biography of Lawrence on their shelves, a doorstop tome bound in the flock burgundy of many an Indian takeaway. I subtracted nine months' gestation from my own date of birth, then another three months just in case, and began reading at 26 September 1928. There was a report in the *London Evening News* that T. E. Lawrence was living in disguise in Punjab, posing as a saint warding off the evil eye and curing illness. In actual fact he was in Miranshah in Afghanistan translating the *Odyssey*. The author made no mention of Cairo, nor of any woman who might prove to be Alexandra's grandmother. The book was clearly most carefully researched and the facts irrefutable. I read on.

'On 12th January', the author stated, 'he returned to England on the SS *Rajputana*.' Could she have been on it? Might it have been a shipboard romance? 'Lawrence had a second-class cabin to himself, and rarely left it. He spent most of the voyage to England working on the *Odyssey*, and was able to translate three more Books.' Prospects for the return of my money were looking bleak. 'At Port Said there was a distraction.' But no, only that the police thought he was a dangerous spy and tried to arrest him.

When he reached England he had one month's leave in London, the book said. Did he meet her there? 'I am in London', Lawrence wrote, 'rather distractedly and jerkily, with one set of plain clothes, and two suits of uniform, and a motor-bike: I see hardly anyone, and don't know what to say to them, when I do see them.'

By this time I was in despair.

He stayed in Herbert Baker's flat in Barton Street. 'Your people have been very good', Lawrence wrote to him. 'Nobody has found me at Barton Street, despite efforts by callers and telephones.' He was then sent to the 'small and isolated' RAF seaplane station of Cattewater near Plymouth.

'Cattewater proves to be about 100 airmen, pressed tightly on a rock half-awash in the Sound; a peninsula really, like a fossil lizard swimming from Mount Batten golf-links across the harbour towards Plymouth town.' He had weekend leave from 1 p.m. on Saturday until midnight on Sunday, 'too little to get to London', he commented. The only woman he saw, it appeared, was Nancy Astor, Conservative MP for Plymouth: 'I like her: and admire her even more; but, for living beside, commend me to some vegetable.'

We had now reached September 1929 when, according to Alexandra, he became the proud father of a son. It seems he actually went to the Malvern Festival to see a performance of *The Apple Cart*, then spent a day with Augustus John and had his portrait painted. Then on to Calshot for the Schneider Trophy: 'The actual days and nights at Calshot were unmixed work. I hardly slept, and do not remember eating much.'

'In the end,' commented Charlotte Shaw, who mothered him, 'he was very dreadfully lonely.'

What's more the book made it clear that the manuscript of *The Seven Pillars of Wisdom*, lost on Reading station, was not a neat bundle abandoned on a GWR seat, but was inside an attaché case left behind in the station buffet. Had Alexandra fed me the story about the seat, or was that simply as I had visualized it?

I tried another letter to Alexandra, this time stressing somewhat more the little matter of the money, but not mentioning what I had since learned about Lawrence. This time there was a reply. It came from Essex.

Dear Sheila

    As usual on my travels I still have a shortage of money. Actually I wanted to give you the $100 but I

assume that has to wait till next week. And so I have a
reason to write you something about whatever. So take
care and till the next time.
       Yours,
          Alexandra

It arrived some weeks later, wrapped in tissue paper in a letter
from Germany. A bundle of dollars, adding up to one hundred.
'I send you small notes. This is good for travelling as you taught
me. You save my life.'
    In Samarkand Alexandra had gone down with dysentery, had
flown to Israel and, finding her man there did not share her
feelings on the planet in precisely the way she thought, had –
no doubt after releasing some venomous oaths – returned home.

RETURN TO THE LANDS OF THE GOLDEN HORDE:

RUSSIAN HEARTLAND

THE OKA

✠

Genghis Khan had styled himself 'ruler of all those who dwell in felt tents' and of 'all lands from the rising of the sun to its setting'. The share bequeathed to Batu and thus belonging to the Golden Horde stretched 'to the west as far as the hoof of a Mongol horse trodden'. In fact Mongol horses conquered as far west as Lviv in 1240 and then moved into Poland, Hungary and Austria. I set Lviv as my westernmost limit on Mongol soil and thought to begin my second journey by returning to their homeland around the Oka, the Volga and the Kama.

These rivers of central Russia are part of the system of waterways that formed the arteries between the Baltic and Byzantium and between the Caspian and the Orient. They also flow through much more of the territory of the Finno-Ugrics and the Chuvash and Tatars than I had seen so far. So Ivan's invitation to sail along them on another pilgrimage seemed fortuitous, but more churches? Should I really be looking at churches?

'The only future for Russia is Orthodoxy,' Ivan stressed. 'Not law, not democracy, but the Church.'

Amulets are the refuge of people who have little control over their lives, of people who inhabit a world they believe to be in the power of spirits, both good and evil. It seemed akin to the situation in the former Soviet Union today – a society in chaos, in the power of crime and chance, where the old and the vulnerable were taking refuge in the Church. Not in the triangle but in the Trinity, not in the fertility goddess but in Mary, not in horns but in haloes. By looking at churches, might I not also learn something of amulets? And in any case, it was a way of getting a visa back into Russia.

*

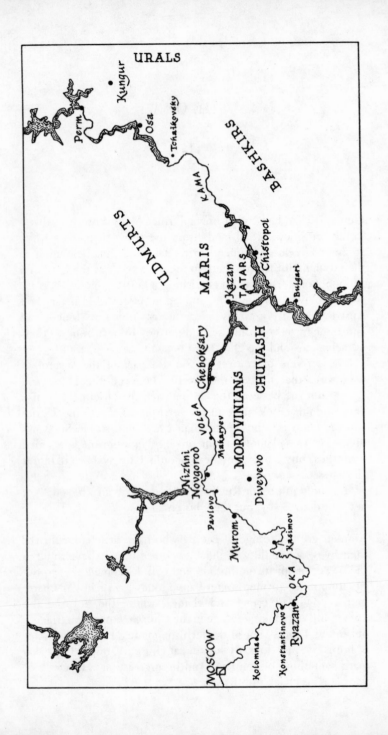

On the day of the Feast of the Pochaev Icon of the Mother of God the good ship *Gregori Perogov*, berthed at Moscow's South River station, was blessed by the five priests who were to accompany the pilgrims.

'At least Perogov was a singer, so an artist and not a bureaucrat,' said George.

The next day she set sail for the holy places of the rivers of Russia's heartland, Ivan shepherding his flock with the help of his sharply devout daughter, his plump motherly wife and an affable son who had come along for the ride.

George in the interim had taken two more of Ivan's river trips, one along the Dnieper ('Ruined. All hydroelectric falls'), the other down the lower Volga, which he could not even bear to mention. There was a Vladimir with us again, but not the same man. This one was a warm-hearted, slightly paunchy fellow who everywhere produced bags of lollipops for the local kids. 'The name's Vladimir,' he said, 'but call me Walt.'

I had been met at Moscow airport by a chubby young woman with smooth pale skin and hair and light eyes, who belonged to 'Our Church', as did the old Lada she drove. She crossed herself fervently before pulling out of the airport carpark and embracing the perils of the Friday evening traffic. She swerved to avoid a drunk fourteen-year-old. 'They kill our children with drugs, alcohol and sex.'

We were welcomed at the quayside by another pale young woman, with beatific moonlike face and soft voice. She was dressed in white and clasped her hands to her flat bosom, leaving her handbag unattended on a public bench. She hoped one day to be a *matushka*, a priest's wife.

It was soon evident that these river trips for pilgrims had slipped into fanaticism. The quota of resident priests had risen from two to five, with an assortment of *matushkas*, and every meal was a good hour late while the pilgrims prayed and chanted.

'I go to church once a week,' said Walt, 'but every day is too much. I feel like I got to heaven.'

The *Gregori Perogov* was an old-fashioned boat of cramped cabins with wooden doors, sash windows that didn't work, and outdated wall radios tuned to Moscow. Rumpled, threadbare carpeting of burgundy and yellow flowers lay rucked across the corridors, and smells of boiling fish permeated the atmosphere. Painted wooden benches lined the decks and the dining saloon was sited directly above the engines, so that conversation was drowned and grace was a triumphant bellow.

We sailed down a wide calm river, the Oka, at first overtaking slow tugs, then passing into a deserted landscape of low grass-grown wooded banks flattened under an immensity of sky, a sky of rain-washed translucency that seeped into the denser silken grey of the water, rippled by the boat's passage. Horizons were lost in blurred and distant tree-lines below a never-ending canopy of light. Here and there we passed the odd jetty and even a church – a stark cluster of verdigris domes rising above the trees – but we saw no villages. One or two fishermen disturbed the empty peace as they cast their lines and waved.

'It was all like this once,' said George. 'Why their brutal exercises, why the damages they did?' He stood staring, his jowls sunk into his neck, his black beret aslant, his jacket hem hoisted at the back by the stoop of his shoulders, his cotton bag of drawing equipment in his hand, ready for the first port of call and the first churches to sketch. As the boat pulled towards the old wooden landing-stage and its pale green and white ticket-office, he discussed the merits of Watteau's drawings and the paintings of the Mexican Diego Rivera, without ever mentioning his lady friend of the previous year.

Konstantinovo was our first port of call and the Captain's home. He had donned his gold-epauletted white uniform, which corseted him across the stomach, to meet his family waiting in the drizzle on the landing-stage. His granddaughter, a baby with a face like cottage cheese, swaddled in woolly garments though it was August, was one year old that day and was held aloft in greeting. Tow-haired men with ruddy cheeks and plump bottoms hauled the boat alongside and rigged up a makeshift gangplank. The land behind was hillocky. One or two cows grazed and a few boys skidded around on wooden bikes. The church and a row of little log houses lay at the top of the hillocks, above the river.

In one of them Yesenin, folk poet and icon of 'poor village boy made good', was born in 1895. The little birch house with fretted white windows was approached through rain-soaked high grasses and wild flowers – thistles and cornflowers – and patches of marsh. In the tiny rooms were a small bed covered by a patchwork quilt, Yesenin's bast shoes tucked underneath it, a cradle draped in a cloth embroidered with a horned goddess, and a stove hung with more embroideries. On the top of it, reached by a home-made wooden ladder, the old people had slept. The pilgrims remembered that from their own homes, they said.

Yesenin had been brought up by his grandfather and educated at the village elementary school. His poetry orbited him into political and public life, at first embraced by the Soviets, but then sidelined as his idealism proved to be at odds with theirs.

Dancing her way at the same time mellifluously around Europe, Isadora Duncan reached Moscow and there married Yesenin, seventeen years her junior. A photograph of him in the house showed him to be a good-looking young man, soft and blond and of rather playboy style. Isadora then took him along on her travels, but he became miserably homesick for Russia and for his small wooden house and its log cabin ('my green office') in the garden. He returned and three years later is said to have committed suicide.

'Murdered,' said George.

'Here,' said the Captain, 'is not only the home of Yesenin, but mine too. The heart of Russia. A land of great rivers. We call it the blue – even turquoise – heart of Russia,' he added, as we looked out on a scene of unmitigated grey as the rain pelted down. The sunset at least, when it came, was of molten fire, rolling to the horizon and scuffed by a few vagrant clouds.

Whereas the *Gregori Perogov* used to cruise the rivers with its full complement of about two hundred – and no room even for the captain's mother – now the pilgrims were the sole passengers, though they occupied only a quarter of the cabins. Many, but not all, were the same as the previous year, joined by a few of the other worshippers at Ivan's Moscow church, unfamiliar with Russia outside the capital. Mary and her friends had not returned, nor had the little old ladies from New Jersey, their savings exhausted on the trip north, their religious duties fulfilled.

Those who had come were almost all from the States and Canada ('I live in Toronto forty-one years') but could hardly be called American or Canadian. Their stories gradually emerged in response to curiosity about amputated fingers, about their unquestioning love of Canada, their tendency to fat – they fell upon every meal as if the years in North America had never existed – and their habit of always speaking Russian among themselves. 'We speak the Russian of Pushkin,' they said. 'Here it is polluted by the Soviets.' All had escaped from the Soviets. In freezing cold, on foot or by horse and carriage, by truck and wagon, but mostly on foot.

Sasha was the prettiest. A bosomy bouffant blonde wearing tracksuits of bright pink and black, and sparkling with real diamonds and gold, she was pursued by every man along the river. 'He invites me into the hay! A hotel I could understand, but the hay!' She had left a wealthy husband – 'We got a boat, then we had to get a bigger one, then another bigger one, always chasing something' – and now she spent her time at art classes, learning to paint roses: 'Real pretty, pink and with tears falling off the petals.' She was born in Astrakhan and had four brothers and a sister buried there. It was malnutrition – she was the only survivor – but then her mother was small and weak. Her father she never spoke of.

Irina's father was banished to Siberia, then arrested again and finally released, blinded and sick, without ever saying what they had done to make him so, before he committed suicide. Her young world of French governesses and piano and ballet lessons collapsed, to be changed for one of scavenging for frozen potatoes, branded the daughter of an Enemy of the People. It was while sheltering under a cart in temperatures of minus forty, escaping from the German/Soviet fighting near Rostov, that her fingers had been frostbitten. A Red Cross convoy happened to be passing through the next village as she reached it and an Austrian doctor had amputated her fingers on the kitchen table.

As for George, he had been brought up on his father's estate and gone first to Poland and then Germany, on foot through the snow. He said little about it but recounted with nervous laughter the memory of his nanny once getting him to school an hour too early, to find no one there. His laughter did little to disguise the childhood mortification never forgotten.

The *Gregori Perogov* sailed on, resounding with prayers and muffled by rain. Father Artemi treated the pilgrims to a two-hour dissertation on his visit to Taizé and the decadent West, while the cooks steamed the lunchtime fish over cauldrons to try to keep it warm.

Along the river banks the vast empty wasteland rolled on, its inhumanity extended in the mind's eye by the awareness of the immense marshy tracts of Siberia beyond and the memory of the unending forests to the north. Just occasionally the odd conical haystack, a few geese, a pig running along in the grass, a cow grazing and fishermen wading, indicated that there must be a few villages out of sight of the river. Otherwise we sailed through a crushing emptiness under the relentless orb of a sodden sky. Then a beautiful forest of birch and pine frilled the grassy bank, a few domes glistened beyond it and the boat drew alongside at the old wooden landing-stage of Kasimov.

Furs and fish, padlocks and nails had been traded along the Oka river, and the Tatar merchants of Kasimov had grown rich, building their solid houses – solid at least to the first floor where the stone ended and the wood began – along a rough road above the landing-stage. They had vied with each other for the pretentiousness of their Roman-style pedimented side porches, building them like fanciful theatrical wings on to the plain stage of their homes. They now stood tilted and chipped, their brickwork curtained with creeper.

The plight of Kasimov – and thus of rural Russia – was quickly apparent. Rampant nettles, thistles, foxglove and dropwort over cracked brick walls and in every unkempt space, locks hanging askew, rusting pipes, peeling plaster, broken windows – nearly one hundred years of utter neglect greeted our eyes as we climbed the potholed unmade road from the river up to the town, making our way past muddy rivulets, lumps of stone, stray cats and concrete drums to a street of crazily leaning wooden houses.

The pillared early nineteenth-century market hall close by must once have been splendid, a monument to civic pride. Now its dirty plaster columns were scabbed with exposed flaked pink bricks. The metal market stalls, rusted and twisted, stood forlornly behind it, like old garden chairs forgotten in the rain. One grandmother stood selling pears. Urchins played in the mud. Not like the kids of Konstantinovo in sweatshirts and trainers acquired from their proximity to Moscow and the shrine of Yesenin, but children with peaky faces and the old-fashioned woolly clothes of the forties. Men filled buckets from standpipes, an alcoholic staggered past. Lovely baroque buildings of pink and white and yellow and white, scaled and moulded with damp, housed the administrative organizations of the town.

'They were going to build a New World,' said George, 'but they couldn't even take care of the Old.'

But it was the churches we had come to see. One of our priests stood in the town square, one hand holding a bag of pears, the other outstretched to be kissed by the headscarfed women who came to him to be blessed. On this Feast of the Domition of Anne, Mother of Mary, the pilgrims and the Russians of 'Our Church' in Moscow – who had never been to these forgotten towns before – stood before the old church. It was now a sports centre: 'Not even a cross on top, only a lightning conductor.' One or two of them wept. Kasimov had been a prosperous town of many churches and mosques, where Russians and Tatars had lived peacefully together. Now four churches had been handed back to the Orthodox community.

'We need more. We must pray all the time,' they said.

And Saudi Arabia, Syria and Iran were all going to pay to renew the mosques. That they knew. They were proud that it was the Russians who had kept Orthodoxy alive through the four hundred years Greece was under Ottoman rule. They didn't want to lose out now.

It was in a former mosque that the museum of Kasimov was housed. There were Tartar embroideries – long net scarves tamboured in wool the girls would make ready for marriage, and *chapan* with *ikat* linings. And there were amulets, bronze ones of the eleventh century from the region round about and from the river. One was a goddess with a trapezoid skirt. I asked about triangles with pendants. Yes, they knew those. They came from the north.

I walked alone through the streets beyond the square and the church, past an old man, legs amputated, sitting beside his upturned hat, past another selling jars of sour cream. They led, those streets, into the old heart of the city, to the small wooden houses set in a neat grid of neglected concrete roads and grassy verges. Away from the pilgrims, in the space left silent, the new sound of distant church bells pealed and then died away, leaving only the soft footfall of passers-by, a child singing, the rustle of leaves and the smell of apples. The *Gregori Perogov* sailed away to sounds of music from a café and waves from young men fishing in the evening light. The rain had stopped.

The light, the translucency, the glistening and shading of sky and cloud became all-pervasive. There was nothing else. The washed shimmer of morning glazed like chintz the low sandy beaches and eroded sand cliffs that now formed the banks of the river, and sparkled for a few moments on the distant domes and gold crosses of Murom as we sailed by. A smoking chimney stack slurred across them.

'You see, always a factory right by a church. They did it on purpose,' said George.

There was a general movement as the old wooden landing-stage of Pavlovo came into view. Each stage along the river was slightly different but all were little plank buildings, floating on the water like so many Noah's arks, their edges rotting from the lap of water, the white paint of their windows, the red or green of their roofs pocked and untended. Behind them was always waste ground, sandy or grassy, always leading up to the small town or village they served. The pathway up from that of Pavlovo led straight to a stately brick house of curly nineteenth-century style, decorated with wrought iron, fancy turrets, fluted pillars and white urns. It was in immaculate condition.

New concepts of business patronage might have taken root in Moscow, but to be blown as far as this small place was surprising. Since 1992 the local bus factory had sponsored this merchant's house as a museum. They had thrown out the displays of Soviet achievements housed there and replaced them with local costumes, ironmongery, embroideries – all that related to Pavlovo itself. They had restored the beautiful ornate plaster ceilings, the carved wooden doors and their lion knockers, and had polished the parquet floors. The world of the nineteenth century that the museum portrayed was not only that of wealth and trade, of contact with the outside world – the dresses and *petit point* purses could have come from Victorian England – but also that of a deep-rooted peasant tradition. There were the shoes made of bast, of birch or linden, the breadboards carved with solar symbols, the handspun, handwoven linen towels embroidered with the old Russian legend of Sirine and Alconoste, bird sirens who charmed the saints in paradise with their singing.

Pavlovo otherwise was down-at-heel, only the church on the hill, pungent with the smell of rotting flowers, being restored. George watched the other pilgrims filming the iconostasis.

'They will never understand Art and Life, these family men with their camcorders and grandchildren,' he said.

There was by now a great deal of unrest among certain of the pilgrims: rumblings at the extent to which fanaticism had taken over. Sasha had just come for a nice boat trip, to sun herself on deck. The others had expected to visit churches and monasteries and see something of the great revival of Russian Orthodoxy, but for some of them it was getting too much. The informal 'happy hours' of a small faction of us, held outside our cabin windows, grew louder and jollier and longer and provoked the envy or scorn of the virtuous who passed by us on their evening promenades around the deck.

Through these roistering evenings – when we toasted the Serbs as Orthodox Christians while the rest of the world was condemning them for crimes against humanity – we observed subtle changes along the quiet river's edge, changes from flat grassy banks to eroded sandy ones, from bare slopes to wooded, and to lines of dead spruce along the shoreline and distant forest. The sunsets were a pale imprint of those in the north, their intensity bled out through cloud and high trees. We saw the odd heron, but otherwise rarely any sign of life.

The Oka had flowed into the Volga, and Sirine and Alconoste

– and the cover of Yesenin's cradle – had been the only glimpses of pagan mythology amid a surfeit of kissed icons and restored domes.

THE VOLGA

✠

The walls of the monastery of Makaryev, fortified against the Tatars, rose sheer and white from the Volga. Within them nuns in black robes and peaked black caps swept the paths, planted cabbages and carried around buckets of water. The artesian well in the grounds had become polluted with iron, so the nuns now boiled water from the Volga for their needs. In the glorious main church the icons were shiny new, collection boxes had been provided and tracts were offered for sale. Restoration of the walls was revealing old frescoes.

'It'll be attributed to some miracle,' said Irina.

Away to the side of the monastery lay the village of Makaryev, a scattering of wooden houses built here and there in the grass beside ponds and close to rough tracks. A few chickens pecked around, a woman carried baskets of washing on a yoke to rinse in a pool, others fetched water from the wells, a couple raked hay.

'We live how we can,' the woman said. How they always had, like all the village, from mushrooms, wood, chickens and goats. She knitted her own socks from unwound jumpers, she added, puzzled at my question, but knew nothing of embroidery or amulets.

The village had survived – the soil of the Volga banks here was sandy and unproductive – by making wooden chests that were sold at monastery fairs and later at Nizhni Novgorod. From six hundred houses before the Great Patriotic War it had dwindled to two hundred (exactly as at Konstantinovo – was it just a symbolic third?) and the forty-odd children in the one school were all likely to move away. The war memorial listed a hundred and fifty names, more than could be fitted on the panel, so that extra wings had been added, decorated by a hammer and sickle, a red star and lurid posters of gunfire. It stood on a small plot, surrounded by a metal fence, its gate tied with wire. An old couple sat outside it with a bucket of dank-smelling mushrooms that they had gathered from the woods four miles away, some butter-coloured, some spotted red and white. They sorted them into baskets to sell, while they ate their lunch of one tomato and a hunk of dry brown bread.

The small village church was locked and George rang the bell. A bent old woman in a headscarf – who else would it be? – slid the bolt and creaked the door open to reveal a dark interior shimmered with gold. She gave us each a *prosphora*, a tiny cottage loaf embossed with a cross and the monogram of Christ. We walked hushed over the stone floor towards hundreds of glowing icons, candlelight burnishing into pure gold the tawdry metal framing of thin saintly faces and aesthetic hands.

Three young priests in ponytails ministered to a crowd of old women whose names were undoubtedly the same as those on the war memorial. They knelt stiffly and tried, in praise of God, to touch the floor with their foreheads. They were like a puppet show in the centre of a stage, encircled by glimmering golden candlelight, brooding saints and mysterious hidden corners of dark.

We were about to sail on out of the golden light of Christ and Orthodoxy, I pondered, and into the dark corners of animal and human sacrifice and cannibalism. Into the territories of the once pagan Finno-Ugric subjects of the Golden Horde: the Maris, the Udmurts and the eastern Mordvinians.

The Maris were nomadic hunters living in the forests as isolated individuals, unfamiliar with the custom – among others – of washing themselves. They moved to the Volga region in about the tenth century – two bronze amulets of that period had been found in graves on the river bank. They were triangular, with pendants of chain – one with four, the other with eleven.

It was from their Turkic neighbours, the Tatars and Chuvash, that the Maris learned to abandon their hunting life for agriculture and cattle-raising. From the Chuvash they also copied an embroidery of exclusively geometric patterns and a costume of high horned headdresses and bibs of beads or coins. From their Muslim neighbours, the Bulgars, they learned about family life, but kept some revered customs of their own, such as fathers having conjugal rights over their daughters-in-law. From the Bulgars they also learned to put furniture in their homes and vegetable gardens around them, and to trade and wash. But the Maris remained pagan.

They worshipped the spirits of stones and plants, and divinities of the sky and of earth and abundance, and prayed to them to bestow on the faithful as much wheat as there is sand in the Volga. They protected their homes, not by amulets, but by hanging branches of white pine in a place of honour, and they chased out the evil spirits by hitting the house with sticks and stabbing knives into the floor.

A hundred years ago they still practised animal sacrifice in the forests around Makaryev, together with human sacrifice, as did the Udmurts further east along the Kama river where we were headed. But if the killing of animals to appease the gods seemed primeval, it had just happened in Pakistan, I reflected, to placate the god Mammon. When shares fell heftily on the Karachi Stock Exchange in March 1995 'panic-stricken investors offered a dozen goats' sacrifice to invoke God's mercy'.

From Makaryev to Kazan we sailed through Mari territory on the north bank of the Volga and Chuvash on the south. Kazan was Tatar country, though the Maris stayed around the shores of the Volga there when the Golden Horde lost Kazan in 1440 and their khanate became the property of the Tatars, shared with their neighbours the Bashkirs, the Chuvash and the Finno-Ugrics. And so it remained until 1552 when Ivan the Terrible floated numbered logs down the Volga from Moscow to construct the fortress of Sviashek on a hill strategically placed to attack Kazan, conquer the Tatars and claim this most northerly khanate of the Golden Horde for Russia.

Now the flooding of the Volga for hydro-electric power had turned the hill into an island, an island crowded with churches. Churches of plain wood, churches painted white, Byzantine churches of brick. Goats, cows, pigs, dogs, cats, chickens wandered freely around them and a woman sold bags of apples for twenty-five cents.

'Don't buy them,' said Irina. 'There's cholera here.'

Days passed – from the Feast of the Icon of the Smolensk Mother of God to the Feast of St Basil of Moscow (1557) – as the *Gregori Perogov* sailed north-east from the Volga into the Kama river towards the Urals.

In churches iconostases glowed with new gilding, some with their icons missing, stolen by the Soviets, others with theirs replaced by the old women who had hidden them away from harm during Soviet rule. Frescoes were retouched in bright colours or simply splashed with white paint as the walls above were decorated. There were summer churches, high, vaulted and cool, and winter ones nearby them, small and squat like the parish scout hut. We visited them all.

The pilgrims mouthed the liturgy with less and less enthusiasm. The priests resolved themselves into individuals: the white-whiskered Santa Claus, Father Roman from Boston; the rotund, hedonistic Alexander from Moscow; the sharp Tatar Alexander, who was mounting a political group against pornography and declining standards and who ignored his prissy wife and obnoxious, arrogant son; then stooped Sergei from Venezuela who, in contrast, solicitously cared for his equally bent wife; and the Russian intellectual, Artemi, who got off the boat at Pavlovo but whose wife stayed on.

It was she who seemed to be the head *matushka*. She had a devout pasty face devoid of make-up and wore sandals, long floppy skirts and various hand-crocheted tops in dull colours that she hoped would disguise her chubbiness. Her hair was always scraped back by kirby grips into a large scarf, usually white but occasionally changed for one of the batik-silk type popular in France, in Madonna blue, and certainly a gift from Taizé. When we stopped to dip into a holy pool, the pilgrims all put swimsuits on. But *matushka* dressed entirely in the purity of white, concealing herself in an enveloping scarf and demure long loose nightgown, which, as all could see when she emerged from the water, became completely transparent when wet and clung to her naked body underneath.

During the innumerable services in plain churches of wood, or in fancy ones decorated with gilded vines and pastel painted flowers, *matushka* stood primly by the iconostasis, hands folded, gaze reverent, only the red light of her tape-recorder disturbing the aura of righteousness.

As we walked round the small towns in their wake, our priests were stared at with some amusement, for we were now in Muslim Tataristan. The region had thrived on riverine trade – timber, grain and furs – and the merchants had endowed schools, hospitals, orphanages and, of course, churches. Now thistles and the tall tangled leaves and small pink flowers of tobacco plants were rampant and the merchants had been the first to be killed. They had been kept prisoner in the churches they had founded and taken to the cellars to be shot.

'You only need cellars to kill,' said George. 'You don't need anywhere special. That's where they killed the Tsars.'

Not all the churches had been used as prisons. One was a museum, its art gallery displaying paintings of nude women that Ivan and his solid wife could hardly bear to look at, so deeply shocked were they. But most had been floored over and converted into flats. People were often still living there, Ivan said, when the churches were handed back to the Believers. Cooking, drinking, their TVs blaring, while services were going on.

THE KAMA

✠

He was found exactly a hundred years ago lying in the road, beheaded, the cord of the copper cross on his chest cut in half: one of the three cases of human sacrifice with which the Udmurts were charged in that year of 1896. Witnesses had also seen families kneeling together in the forest praying to a goose and a duck and it was well known that ducks were sacrificed in holy forests. Sacrificed to Kiremet, the evil spirit, who was appeased in woods, near springs and at the bottom of ravines.

Greatest of the Udmurt gods was the god of the sky, but there were those of the forest, the house and water. The women's costume put them in touch with this spirit world. The deep red embroidery on the hems of their long skirts communed with the earth and the harvest, the belts round their waist protected them from the unknown and the inexplicable, and their high horned headdresses linked them to the air and the domain of the sky god.

Today it was in white cardigans and down-at-heel stilettos that the women of the local watch factory streamed out at sunset while the men, paid by barter, staggered out humping huge hessian bags of flour. This was Chistopol, where Pasternak once lived.

The town boasted the usual small museum exhibiting a stuffed hedgehog, a woodpecker, a couple of robins, a squirrel, a badger and a moose. Beyond this Natural History section were a few oddments of everyday life in the region: a pair of Tatar boots, appliquéd with leather flowers edged in couched thread, in the Pazyryk tradition; a Russian costume comprising bast shoes, linen pinafore embroidered with bright wool tamboured flowers and a pearl *kokoshnik*. And a few amulets. One was a carved-bone writing utensil like a small stick, others were crosses from the eleventh century and some small clay horses, dogs and goats. And a few metal horses pierced by holes, just like the gold ones dating from the fifth millennium BC unearthed in Varna on the Bulgarian coast. They came from Bulgari.

Bulgari? It was the capital of the Bulgars until 1236 when the Golden Horde conquered it and Batu made it his first stronghold before he established his court at Sarai. Then in 1536 Ivan the Terrible took it for Russia and it was now just a small village on our return itinerary.

Meanwhile the *Gregori Perogov* was heading along the Kama for Tchaikovsky's home. The banks changed from birch and pine woods to low hillocky grassland and distant forests, beyond which the evening sun sometimes caught the glint of pylons and the white clusters of Soviet blocks of flats, even their remoteness failing to disguise their mammoth size. A few working barges bustled past, there were still fishermen and haystacks and still the unremitting drizzle, until heavy black clouds rolled over the glowing horizon of sunset like a stretching cat, and it poured with rain.

At its confluence with the Vatkya the Kama was as wide as a lake, fondant pink and glacial blue in the light of dawn. Then, pinched again between dense forests of mast-high birch and pine shouldering each other for light, the river was released into an inland lake so that its course appeared on the map as a butcher's string of fat sausages. Pinched and released for the sake of hydroelectric power, though the electricity brought less income than the cut grass from the agricultural land had done before flooding.

'This was my home, this was where my family first came from,' said Irina. 'Now there is only water.'

The house where Tchaikovsky was born overlooked the river, a low pink house of plain colour-washed rooms, rather Scandinavian in style. In the room of his birth a mournfully tasteful arrangement of glass panels held his portrait above a gold vase of white flowers, and *Swan Lake* played softly. Proceeding eastward we had come West. The piano, the furniture, the embroideries – a beaded purse, a Berlin woolwork firescreen depicting the rural scene of a youth serenading a milkmaid – could have come from any nineteenth-century house in Europe.

It was only in the log house in the garden – the servants' quarters – which Tchaikovsky's father is said to have filled with 'typical' things from peasant homes of the day that we had not left the heart of Russia.

A cloth embroidered with solar symbols hung over the icon in the holy corner. A faceless doll lay on a pile of handspun, handwoven linen, faceless because once it has a face it becomes a person and so cannot be used as a toy. The wooden loom that stood in the room was carved with magic symbols and notches. These treasures belonged to people who confronted evil spirits with mystical decoration. But in the main house, as in any other nineteenth-century house of the Western world, the cradle was plain, the white baby clothes were trimmed only by a frou-frou of lace and flowers of pulled threadwork in which were invested no powers against malevolence. And the beaded bag was simply pretty to hold in gatherings around an evening's music on the piano, while the woolwork firescreen merely shielded pale white skin from the blotching of heat.

As the day of the Feast of St Herman of Solovetski (1484) drew to a close we sailed away past dark forests into a colourless void, until the next day, passing along the shoreline small towns of scattered bleak houses, gantries, abandoned cranes, rusting railway wagons and piles of thin logs tossed on the red earth like matchsticks, we docked at the town of Perm, a two-hour time zone east of Moscow. Facing us beyond the landing-stage was a small shop, its fascia of red plastic labelled in large blue lettering, SEX SHOP.

Ivan hustled us past it to the bus that was to take us to the foothills of the Urals, through an undulating land of grass and dense thickets of pine trees, dark as spinach sprinkled with soot, their branches deep to the ground, where a low frilly undergrowth was pierced by cow parsley and dogwort. Here and there were the beginnings of the marshy wastes of Siberia, betrayed by bulrushes. The old road that led there, the old road to Siberia, was just a mud track between trees. For one hundred and fifty years under the rule of the Tsars prisoners had had to walk the whole distance into exile and people would leave bread and milk on their windowsills in case they passed. This simple mud track was also the route to China along which the furs and minerals of the Urals were traded.

Beyond it the road to the Byelo Gorsky monastery was too muddy and too steep for our bus to negotiate and so Father Benjamin came down to greet us. He had been exiled here by the Soviets and had stayed on because of the old women. 'They shine,' he said. They had worked as horses during the Great Patriotic War, ploughing the fields while the men were away, and had buried the icons, prayed and kept the church alive through Communist rule. ('You see, it was the women and not the priests,' said George.) Now it was Father Benjamin who would look after the women. When he first arrived at the monastery he found that the abbot there had protested against Communism and so the Bolsheviks had come and cut off his arms and legs and thrown him in the river. Guided by the local people, Father Benjamin had discovered the bodies of the four hundred monks they had also murdered.

'I didn't know Russia outside Moscow,' said Ivan. 'It is lost.'

Father Benjamin was again waiting for us when we docked the next day at Osa, in black robes and gleaming cross, leaning on a huge sceptre. A woman held a large black umbrella over him, while he used his hands to bless us. A line of little old women in scarves – their cheeks fat and wrinkled, their eyesockets hollow – stood on the landing-stage throwing flowers and wheat at us. Behind them a circle of young girls dressed in tamboured pinafores and blouses, sheltering from the rain, held balanced on embroidered cloths large round loaves topped with salt, which they handed us in greeting.

Osa had been another small town of merchants trading timber and furs along the river, their wooden houses now neglected and shabby, planks hanging off, windows askew. It was founded in 1591 but an earlier, even 'prehistoric', wooden settlement had recently been unearthed in the centre of the town and then asphalted over to make the main square. From this bleak heart a grassy track led straight into woods of birch, fern and foxgloves, the pollen-dusted colouring of the trees a presage of the early advent of autumn.

There was no municipal electricity in Osa, as there was none in the much larger town of Perm, though temperatures here were normally minus 40° in the winter and could descend to 55° below. Nor was there any piped water.

Seven thousand men had left to fight in the Great Patriotic War and only two thousand had returned. The town still seemed bereft and in a general state of decay. The main shop remained as in Soviet times – a pigeon sat on one of its shelves between endless jars of pickled gherkins and tins of peas. Other shops were simply empty and there were none of the kiosks selling unaffordable Western goods.

But there were many churches. Some were still abandoned, trees growing out of their brickwork and windows boarded up; some were surrounded by shaky scaffolding, buckets and mops. One, its porch filled by two open coffins, the smooth bluish-grey faces of the dead men exposed for all to see, was taken over by our priests, dressed in red and gold, ornate jewelled crosses hanging over their stomachs.

They ministered to a full congregation. Short, stunted old women in flowered woolly headscarves, many tied the Muslim way, in cardigans stretched over ample bottoms, in thick stockings and boots, stood patiently for the three hours of the service. There were one or two men, a few young girls, but no boys at all, nor any men of working age. A ripple passed across the church as they bowed their heads and crossed themselves in unison. A few were given a spoonful of wine, but most drank blessed water poured from a kettle into small metal bowls. Hunks of dry bread were laid on a table and the little girls wolfed them down as if they were welcome food.

The Orthodox church takes its form from the Hebrew temple described in the Bible, Father Roman explained: the holy-of-holies, the temple and the court. The holy-of-holies for the Orthodox is the part behind the iconostasis, the sanctuary, accessible only to the priests and then only on certain days; the temple is the main body of the church and the courts are the four apses. The cupola symbolizes heaven and so is usually painted with a figure of Christ or with stars. As only one liturgy a day can be held at any one altar, the church of a big town will be designed with several altars. Here our priests had placed themselves in command of all of them.

Father Sergei took confession, and it was obvious now why his body was permanently bent forward from the hips, as he inclined to listen and covered each penitent's head with the deep gold cuff of his robe. Our priests spoke to the assembly in turn. Father Sergei broke down crying – Venezuela was so far away – Tatar Alexander mumbled pompously, Father Benjamin – a small, sandy-haired man – filled the church with power and distributed little wooden crosses from Jerusalem to the pilgrims. He stopped at me.

'Is she Christian?' he asked the others, before handing me one.

We had travelled to our most easterly point: Kungur in the Urals, a poor and desolate town built on a hill between two rivers, a place soul-destroying for the inhabitants, but once strategic. So I would find no more easterly amulets, bar those that came from the far north-east in Siberia. They were made of deer's antlers in the shape of a goddess, a fish, a penis and a bear. And in Osa, people had worn bronze ones depicting the earth goddess as part of the tree of life. But nowhere, absolutely nowhere, was there a triangle.

The *Gregori Perogov* was heading back westward in dreary weather, the pilgrims beginning a fast in preparation for the death of the Virgin Mary. But first we celebrated the birthday of one of them, drinking Russian champagne and singing mournful folk songs of love and Lake Baikal. Our next port of call was Bulgari. It was on no map, Ivan didn't believe it existed, the captain assured us it did. I hoped he was right.

BULGARI

✠

It seemed as if Bulgari could only be reached by river, though before the damming of the Volga it had been three miles distant. Now the small wooden landing-stage lay berthed alongside a line of low grassy hillocks where a few cows grazed. An extraordinary restaurant decorated like a circus tent stood empty directly behind it, and a flight of wooden steps led up to the village, as though visitors were expected. But there was no one there, though it was an archaeological site of some importance. In a fenced-off grassy area stood a small white Russian church and the few low stone buildings that were the only surviving monuments of the Golden Horde anywhere. But long before Batu's people the Bulgars had settled here.

The Bulgars were a Turkic race, one of the peoples pushed towards Europe by the Huns at the end of the fourth century, and were believed to have originated in the region of the Altai mountains, before being displaced. By AD 635 they had founded a kingdom near the sea of Azov. Pressured then by the Khazars, themselves a Turkic people, who from the seventh century dominated the lower Volga and the lands north and west of the Caspian, the Bulgars split into three hordes. One remained at Azov and was absorbed by the Khazars. The second moved to the lower Danube and, integrating more and more with the Slavs, formed the original people of present-day Bulgaria. The third followed the course of the Volga and by the end of the eighth century had founded a khanate with Bulgari as its capital.

The Russian director of the archaeological museum at Bulgari opened a cupboard drawer and tipped into it with a crash the previous day's findings of stones. He scowled at us. He spoke no English, while that of the woman assistant director was fluent.

Her Mongol features and gold teeth conspired to make me feel I was back in the right terrain. Indeed, she knew the amulet very well – the local Chuvash women wore them, three hung on their belt on each side of the buckle, each with three tassels. They were made of fabric and embroidered with geometric patterns or with dots representing animals' claws. Just as on the ancient pottery of the region. Such triangles worn on a magic belt, I told her, have been found on goddess statues of Ancient Babylon dating from around 4,000 BC.

'And in Bulgari women still wear them,' she said. 'But of course nowadays the women wear this traditional dress only for marriages or funerals. Or to visit a new mother, or to send their son away to the army and then to welcome him back.' Only last month they had had a wedding in the village and the women had worn their old dresses and amulets. The triangles protected them from evil spirits and from sickness.

The Chuvash were descendants of the Bulgars, with a bit of the local Finno-Ugric blood thrown in, and the triangle had had a deep significance for the Bulgars, she said, especially in the form of two triangles superimposed, the top one, strong at the base, representing power from heaven, the bottom one with a strong point, denoting the power of the earth. It was a cosmic symbol carved on many of their graves and stelae. Soldiers still wore such an amulet, made of wire, around their necks.

Then – as in so many places in the world – the triangle with pendants was a common jewellery design. They had in their museum, the assistant director said, a tenth-century mould belonging to the Bulgars, and Tatar jewels of silver triangles with three chain pendants that hung over a woman's temples. Both Tatars and Chuvash had become subjects of the Golden Horde and both claimed descent from the Bulgars, the Chuvash sharing many similarities of language, and the Tatars of myths, customs and traditions.

But some of the customs of the Chuvash too were perhaps taken from the Bulgars, or even the Mongols. They used a lot of blood in their rituals, smearing sheep's blood over everything, she said. And then fire. They jumped over fire at marriages, the men seven times, the women three.

'And have you come across a tradition like this anywhere

else?' she continued. 'People gather on the banks of the Volga and an old man takes two tree branches and plants them. On one he puts the skin of a sheep on which the feet, tail and head have been left – it's very skilled to do that – and on the other a white scarf with one tassel at each corner and one in the centre. He then takes this scarf and folds it, holding the five tassels and stroking them. Then he uses it to flick on each shoulder girls who want to get married that year, or very soon. All these things are still done.' No, there was no chance of witnessing such a ceremony, nor would it be possible to find an amulet in any of the houses.

The village lay a short distance from the archaeological site, but of course all the topography had changed. It was the only village left above water when the Volga was dammed in 1967, submerging all the others. Some had been very prosperous and the whole area was extremely important anyway because of its archaeological remains. 'Moscow' had sent a few students down to survey, they'd dug up this and that and taken everything away, using no system and leaving no records. From this 'Moscow' had decided the site was not worth keeping and could be flooded for cheap electricity. Now the people of Bulgari had lost all the fertile land as well as their history and the situation was very bad. They had no industry at all. They lived from the vegetables in their gardens and were starving. If Yeltsin didn't do something strong within five years, the assistant director said, Russia would be gone. 'I don't know who will take it, but it will be gone.'

Some excavation was in progress at Bulgari, undertaken by a man with a bicycle and a tin tray. The stone buildings that remained from the Golden Horde were fourteenth-century mausoleums, a fortress, and a Black Chamber that had once been a highly decorated prison. The small white Russian church had been built in the nineteenth century on the site of Batu's palace, so nothing of that was now accessible. In the mausoleums there were precious stelae with inscriptions in Bulgar and Tatar and stones covered in Runic script. It was only as I walked along the grassy track away from the site that I spotted it above the trees – a minaret. The Bulgars were Muslim, of course, I remembered. I was indeed in the right terrain.

*

From Bulgari we sailed westward back up the Volga to Cheboksary where, though prayers had been said, icons kissed and sins confessed – or Allah praised and vodka eschewed – no one could understand why the mushrooms that had always been gathered in the forests round about had suddenly become polluted and sixty people had been seriously ill and eight had died. The locals bringing their plastic buckets of boletus, horse-mushrooms and chanterelles off the ferry on to the landing-stage could not help but gather them still as they had always done. They touched the hem of Sergei's robe as he passed by.

Continuing on to Moscow the journey was a kaleidoscope – an ever-changing sequence of precisely the same elements of drab, hopeless small-town desolation, of golden iconostases and blue-starred domes with pigeon droppings on the earth floor below them, of grassy river banks, birch and pine, vaulted still by the vast canopy of the sky. The *Gregori Perogov* ran aground on a sandbank, and the pilgrims continued to fast.

The monastery of Diveyevo fed all those who came for the Transfiguration. Huge cauldrons of porridge, noodles and heavy beans eaten in silence. In honour of the Virgin there was no meat. And in honour of St Seraphim hundreds of pilgrims walked in a silent night procession around the periphery of the monastery grounds, through woods, past picket fences, skirting villages. Some touched and kissed the trees. They were pacing out in the dark of night, they explained, the domain of the Virgin Mary. Most interesting that they were touching and kissing the trees, I pointed out, considering the connection between trees and the mother goddess and how Christianity had taken over the goddess, together with the virgin birth, from primitive mythology and turned them into the Virgin Mary. No one listened.

The next morning I was somewhat ostracized and so I wandered round the village of Diveyevo. Its quiet car-less roads, flanked by grass verges and small wooden houses, were overshadowed by the brooding domes of the monastery. Chickens pecked around, a few cats and women sat in the sun – the roadside was still a homely place to rest. The old woman Feodorovna was good at embroidery, they said, but she'd just padlocked her door while she went to see to her cows.

It was a small plank house surrounded by an overgrown garden and a wooden fence. When she unlocked the door for me, we went into a dark log hallway up a short flight of steps made of whole tree trunks. The house lay to the side of the hallway and was a simple construction of plank walls, wood floors and plyboard ceilings. There was a bed in each of the three rooms, a plain table and kitchen chairs, one or two wooden cupboards, clocks on the walls and a holy corner of icons above the table. Onions and cucumbers dried on the windowsills. It was the first home I had been invited into.

Elizevietta Feodorovna was a small, thin woman a couple of years older than me. She had had a sad life, she said. Her husband had sworn at his brother, who had killed him instantly, leaving her with two boys aged nine and five. She'd done her best but now one was a drunkard and the other one she never saw, though they both still lived in Diveyevo. She shuffled to the bedroom cupboard where she kept her embroideries and fetched out first a long handspun, handwoven linen cloth which she had used to present bread and salt to wedding couples – as had been presented to us in Osa – or to hang round the icons, though when the Soviets had forbidden icons in the house she had hung it round the mirror instead.

Then she had the costume that belonged to her mother: a heavy hemp *sarafan* that she kept rolled and tied to conserve the pleating, a cotton blouse, an apron and a cap. All made by her mother who had had her own loom and grown her own hemp and flax. Elizevietta lent the costume around the village for marriages, at least she had until the fifties and had worn it herself twenty years ago at her nephew's wedding. Now she wasn't sure that the old ways would come back again. She looked at me quizzically and then thrust the apron into my hands. I thanked her and kissed her. She banged the cap down on top of the apron. It was a wonderful velvet *kokoshnik*, embroidered in the same style as the textiles of Pazyryk dating from about 400 BC, I explained. But she understood only my excitement. Though it was essential to insist I knew her offerings were gifts, I gave her money for grain for her chickens, food for the cows and flour to see her through the winter. I hoped her sons wouldn't call.

She didn't embroider any more, she said. She had bought up all the threads they had in the Univermart shop twenty-five years ago and hadn't been able to get any since. But she didn't think she could see well enough now anyway. And amulets? No, she used no amulets. 'The cross is our amulet,' she said.

Like a darning thread the *Gregori Perogov* called on its way back to Moscow at those towns it had skipped on the way out and left out those we had seen. The closer we got to Moscow, the more they buzzed. Bright flowers grew in gardens, park railings were being painted, nuns looked happy and about thirteen years old.

The box of farewell presents stood on the floor of the dining saloon. Ivan distributed them by saints' names until only one of the small earthenware pots wrapped in tissue remained at the bottom of the box. There was an embarrassed silence. 'You haven't got a saint's name,' explained Ivan.

'Sheila is Irish, a form of Cecilia, patron saint of music.'

There was a sigh of relief and the pot was handed to me. I thanked them, as the only non-Russian and non-Orthodox on board, for the warmth and friendship they had shown me – in truth they had mothered me like an orphaned kitten – and apologized for not speaking Russian.

Matushka sidled up to me and whispered in French, 'Embrace the Orthodox faith. Then you will speak Russian and understand the Russian soul.'

The pilgrims dispersed in Moscow, followed by trolleyloads of luggage and clutching plastic bags of the cartons of orange juice and tomato juice they had been given to drink on our excursions and had saved. I prepared to move on to Ukraine.

'It's much worse there than in Russia,' Ivan said. 'There's crime and cholera everywhere. And don't go near Crimea. They're fighting because the Tatars Stalin exiled to Central Asia are coming back and claiming their property. It's very dangerous.' He booked me a place on the overnight train to Kiev in a four-couchette compartment. 'That'll be safer than a double,' he said. 'You're sure to be robbed if you're alone with one person.'

I spent the last of my roubles on a bottle of vodka and two Mars bars, secreted my dollars around my underwear and mounted the train in some trepidation.

RETURN TO THE LANDS
OF THE GOLDEN HORDE:

UKRAINE

KIEV

✠

My travelling companions were two rather crumpled men sitting opposite and, by my side, a neat young lady with marcel-waved hair, wearing a white blouse and flowery skirt. As soon as the train pulled out she changed into a clean blouse, the briefest of pale blue satin shorts and a pearl necklace. The men, it transpired, were businessmen, though until very recently they had played in a dance band. They'd come non-stop from Finland, they said, where they'd been buying timber.

A woman came round to collect money for bedding and before I could sort out what she was asking for the men had paid for mine.

One of them, a big, strong, bearded fellow, introduced himself as Igor and then leaned across the table. 'You're lovely,' he said to me. My pleasure at this compliment was somewhat dampened by the realization that he was slightly drunk and thus probably not focusing too well. He gazed at me soulfully for some time. 'I love you,' he said and then added, 'You are like my mother.' He followed this by announcing that in the morning he would be forty. He looked rather misty-eyed as if he realized that this would finally mean dropping the apron strings. I handed round my vodka and pieces of Mars bar in celebration. Without even knowing that that was all I had, they brought out their bread and chicken and insisted on sharing it. The young lady declined, fetched out her own supper and, smoothing a small napkin over an expanse of bare thigh, munched her way through it.

The evening passed in a surreal conversation about the Beatles and the Queen and toasts drunk to George MaFarlane of Nazareth – at least that's what I thought they said – until Igor's vodka was finished.

'I love you,' he repeated with the last swig. They promised, he and Alexander, to look after me when we got to Kiev.

At the new border between Russia and Ukraine the train lurched to a stop and police and customs officers mounted it.

'This is fool! Fool!' shouted Igor. 'My mother Ukrainian, my father Russian. What am I? What am I?' he declaimed, pummelling the air, in the best tradition of ham Shakespearian actors.

The next morning he looked rather hangdog and held his glass out to me. 'Your vodka, please.'

I filled it for him and he downed it in one gulp.

'More please.'

I poured another glass. 'That's it,' I said, 'absolutely no more,' screwing the cap tightly back on. 'You're not having any more,' I added sharply, as his mother should have done years ago.

Kiev had once been two cities: the old town of wooden buildings of the 'commonplace' people, down near the Dnieper, and the fortified royal precinct on a hill above the river, enclosing churches and monasteries. Its crowning glory was the Cathedral of Saint Sophia, a cluster of green and gold domes gleaming above a white wall and a ruff of trees. Its approach was through a tall white-and-gold tiered entrance tower, itself capped by a golden dome. Founded in 1037 it was the major tourist site of Kiev. It was closed.

Outside it a small shrine had been erected on the pavement, flowers laid over it and candles lit. Hung along the white wall and the entrance gateway were hundreds of newspaper cuttings. People stood, in ones or twos, quiet and solemn, the stillness hardly broken as they shuffled along, reading intently. Some of the newspaper cuttings were about the good works and life of the Patriarch of Ukraine, who had just died. But the ones they were mesmerized by, as if they had never known the truth before, were contemporary reports of the Great Famine of 1932 and 1933.

Ukraine had already suffered the totalitarian terror inflicted by Stalin in the twenties – executions, purges, the exile of millions to the Siberian gulag labour camps. And in the thirties

he had intensified his policy of genocide in those years of
deliberate famine when the Soviets had exported Ukrainian
grain to America and the West, leaving almost ten million in
the wheatlands of central and eastern Ukraine to die of starvation.
And did the West not know? The front page of one American
newspaper of 1933 was covered with reports and photos of starving
peasants, stick-ribbed donkeys and dead horses yoked to carts.
I crept away.

Across a wide square and down a tree-shaded avenue lay the
church of Saint Andrew, a green and white baroque building
fluted with gold. Also closed. It stood at the top of a steep roughly
cobbled road with high stone kerbs that led down to the river
and looked as if it hadn't changed for hundreds of years. Lining
the street, on the pavements, against the walls of the old balconied
buildings, in the road, were hundreds of market stalls selling
paintings, hand-made souvenirs, woodcarvings – and old
embroidered dresses. These were long shifts and blouses of white
linen or harsh hemp, totally in the tradition of Eastern Europe
with their wide sleeves, gathered into shoulder and cuff, carrying
most of the embroidery. Roses, stars, lilies and strawberries in
red and black cross stitch, geometric motifs in pulled threadwork
and the distinct work of Bukovina in the west, shared with
Rumania: a heavy band of stitching on the shoulder and diagonal
lines of pattern below. The market was there every weekend I
was assured. I would buy on the way back home. In fact when
I returned it had vanished. That particular weekend had been
the celebration of independence and of Ukraine's traditional
crafts.

It was Alexander who came the next morning alone in his white
Lada to drive me around Kiev. His wife had a cough and had
gone to the doctor – 'She is tired of eating ice cream' – but had
given him precise instructions on what to do with me. He was
to take me on a brief tour of the city, then to the Pechersky
Lavra monastery and, most particularly, out to the folk museum
an hour or so south of Kiev, since it would be hard for me
to get there by public transport. As a new businessman he
undoubtedly had better things to do with his Sunday.

The entrance to the monastery was beneath the facade of

golden-haloed saints of the twelfth-century church of the Holy Trinity. Inside the monastery precinct were low white seventeenth- and eighteenth-century ecclesiastical buildings set around pathways, and in the centre a church bombed by the Nazis. Half still stood, the rest lay beside it in a rubble of stones and bricks and slices of buckled green roof. One or two monks walked around, bells pealed, the bell-tower clock chimed the quarter hours and people thronged into one of the churches to pray beside the pillars and walls of gold painted with saints. But Pechersky Lavra was in reality a collection of museums and not churches. Alexander had paid for us to go in, my ticket costing ten times his.

'How do they know I'm a foreigner? I'm not talking, I've got no camera or bag.'

'Foreigners have different faces from Russians,' he said.

The monastery of Pechersky Lavra was founded in 1051, when the Kievan-Rus princes had already established their city of Kiev, which was to become a great centre of civilization until Batu and the Golden Horde destroyed it in 1240. The monastery had been a leading centre of learning and guardian of the Orthodox faith. Now respectful little groups of tourists walked round the museums. We followed them. Books, the History of Printing, Folk Costume – 'All the decoration is amuletic, it keeps away evil spirits,' said the curator, 'but we wear no separate amulets' – and Scythian Gold, where jewellery for a woman's temples was a cascade of granulated triangles hung with three gold balls.

The golden domes of Pechersky Lavra are visible for miles around but from across the Dnieper they are dwarfed by an out-of-scale Soviet statue in aluminium of the Great Russian Mother with outstretched arms. 'They're going to get rid of her,' said Alexander. 'She'll be destroyed and a memorial to those who suffered from Chernobyl will go up in her place.'

Chernobyl was a suppurating wound. It had been the turning point in the downfall of Communism, he said. The realization that the Soviets didn't give a damn about the ordinary citizen, let alone the Ukrainians, the revelation of bureaucratic inept-itude and corruption, the negligence and cover-up, all that

twanged at the meek subordination that had lasted amazingly
for seventy-two years. After so many generations there was no
one alive now who remembered what life had been like before
the Communists. 'And we always thought it would go on like
that,' said Alexander. 'I have only one child, Igor has only one
child. Everyone the same. There was no future in the past and
there is no future now.'

And it was Chernobyl that had been the decisive factor in
Ukraine's bid for independence, he continued. The country was
in fact split down the middle, the industrial east and Crimea
considering themselves part of Russia, the west – subjected
to Polish and Lithuanian rule for a hundred years, from the
mid-sixteenth century until conquered by Russia – regarding
Russia still as an alien power. But Chernobyl had rallied the
people together as Ukrainians. 'We will never forgive the Russians for what they did there,' said Alexander.

The folk museum was one of those open-air collections of
peasant buildings, but lived in. Tethered horses cropped the
grass, women dug up silvery cabbages, old men stood chatting
in gardens of bright flowers surrounded by stake fences. The
small white houses, built of straw and clay bonded by horses'
urine, and thatched with straw, were totally unlike the wood
plank and log ones of Russia. We had left the forest and moved
to the plain – there were even old windmills – left the north
and moved to eastern Europe.

The houses were divided into two: a cold storeroom that went
straight up into the thatch, and a ceilinged living room heated
by a stove. Next to it would be the parents' bed, a rod fixed over
it where the family's clothes hung. Round two sides of the room
was a bench where the family sat and slept. In the corner an
icon hung on the wall with an embroidered cloth, the *rushnyk*,
draped around it. Otherwise the only furniture was a table. The
floor was earth, in the living room sometimes strewn with grass.
A few houses were laid out with souvenirs to sell, but there were
no visitors.

Embroidered clothes were everywhere, leather jackets with
metal studs and goddess figures appliquéd on, shifts of home-
grown, handspun, handwoven linen, decorated in natural linen

thread in simple pulled threadwork patterns, every seam finely stitched by hand. Some too were for sale and it was as if they had only just been discarded and the rural way of life preserved in the museum had ended only yesterday.

I spent days wandering alone round Kiev. It was a beautiful city of trees and gold and crackled plaster. Car tyres scrunched over old cobbles, muffled as over compacted snow. Puny chestnut trees, their leaves scorched brown and yellow as much by the fumes as by the approaching autumn, shaded every avenue. It was hot and sunny and the still, polluted air tickled my throat. I passed buildings of massive rough stone, carved with faces or with Bacchus and swathes of vines, and fronted by Egyptian-looking balustrades. Others were delicate baroque, painted white and turquoise or pink. Still others were brick, decorated by tiles embossed with rosettes, and topped by fancy turrets. And all around them, everywhere, were trees.

'It's hard to believe we're a capital,' said the man in the queue behind me at the opera house. 'We've always been a provincial town. We have to get used to everything being new. We have to find ourselves. We're moulded by the Orthodox Church, by Communism and the Russians. But we're not the same as the Russians. We're east Europeans.

'I think you should go for Khachaturian's *Spartacus*,' he added. Bookings would only begin after I had left Kiev and he offered to buy my ticket for me. I could call him to get it when I returned. I gave him the phone number of the flat where I would be staying, and the equivalent of fifteen dollars.

'No, no,' he said, 'it's only a tenth of that.'

When I returned to Kiev the ticket was waiting for me at the flat. So much, I thought, and not for the first time, for crime in Ukraine. But then many of my nights in hotels were disturbed by the sound of my phone eerily pipping morse signals.

My search in Kiev for the amulet – this was, after all, new territory and a different culture – was exhaustive. In the National Museum of Ukrainian History, I found metal ones from the period of Kievan-Rus that hung from the belt, as those in Bulgari had: a spoon for the well-being of the home, a duck and a horse – both solar symbols, the one believed to pull the sun

underground at night, the other through the sky in the day – a
moon for female fertility and a saw to guard the home. There
were jewellery pendants that tinkled and kept away evil spirits
and there were decorated circles that warded off the evil eye. A
trawl through all the Scythian displays revealed lots of stone
goddess and god idols and many fertility goddesses that were
pre-Scythian, but all massively curved of buttock and thigh. Of
the triangle with pendants there was no sign.

I called at the Bessarabian market, which was almost as grandiose as Harrods' food halls, and sniffed at the medicinal herbs,
the dried wild flowers, the rose-hips, poppy seeds, rosemary and
heathers, at the thistles, dried chopped mushrooms, and the
twigs and tangled roots. They were sold in twisted cones, in
crumpled brown bags or small cut pieces of paper folded into
rectangular packets and tied with bits of rag or old plastic tape.
Whether or not they were used for amulets I couldn't discover.

Out of curiosity I followed people into a large building labelled
the Ukrainian House. It had smart marble escalators and recessed
lighting, pot plants and comfortable plastic chairs. There was
nothing chipped or cracked or crumbling and the chairs had no
splits or holes stuffed with fag-ends. This was indeed Europe
and I had left Russia behind. As had Ukraine – the building used
to be the Lenin museum, but was now host to a music trade fair.
It was alive with hi-fi equipment, strobe lights, drum kits, blaring
pop, visiting Americans in rolled-up sleeves and Agassi bandanas,
and entranced local kids.

Two men from London in smart suits were selling oboes.
There was a very high standard of musicianship here on terrible
old instruments, they explained. They were mostly made in the
southern part of East Germany near the Czech border and the
best were sent to Moscow and only the second-best got to
Ukraine. Some were even exported to the West because they
were cheap. But now people could buy these good oboes from
London. More each year.

'There've been amazing changes in the few years we've been
coming here,' they said. 'Even since last year. They've now got
an airport that looks like an airport, you can get petrol and a
reasonably decent dinner if you're prepared to pay. You even
see Western cars, but most of them are probably stolen.

'At least that's true of Kiev. Kiev is good. But you shouldn't go to the north,' they added. 'There's still a risk of radiation there. And Crimea is dangerous. The Tatars are going back there from Central Asia, and Sebastopol has opted to belong to Russia after all, so the situation's explosive. Go west. The Carpathians are lovely and there's lots of folk art there.'

I booked a train ticket, with the usual hassle, to Simferopol in the Crimea.

CRIMEA

✠

Taking the usual precaution of choosing a four-berth compartment on the train, where a thief was less likely to operate, I found myself in the company of a kindly woman with a gaggle of children, who pressed on me huge hunks of fatty ham and slabs of stale bread. The journey was to take twenty-one hours.

The outskirts of Kiev seemed to consist of mile upon mile of rusty garages, so far away from any flats or houses as to effectively discourage car ownership. These gave way to an endless sunlit expanse of grass and corn, marred here and there by pylons, chimneys, huge lagged pipes, telegraph poles and silos, and softened by a few trees, cows and fields of marrows and then the occasional tin-roofed, brick house surrounded by sunflowers and geese. Such homely sights ended quite suddenly and there was nothing but black earth around us, the same steppeland I had journeyed through to the east and the same that extended west into Hungary.

The train jolted murderously along to the pungent odour of warm ham and queasy children. It crossed some causeways over water into the Crimea where the flat land was planted tidily with rows of trees and vines. At every station crowds of people pushed round with buckets of peppers, pears, aubergines, grapes, walnuts and melons, which the passengers from the north avidly bought, not by the kilo but by the bucketful.

Simferopol was a pleasant but boring town, on Moscow time but with Turks on the street selling doner kebabs. My hotel had no water, so no tea or coffee, and its restaurant had long since closed down. I pursued my usual priorities and began at the museum.

Here there was no sign of any archaeological remains from the original Scythian town of Neapolis or the subsequent Tatar one, only stuffed birds and an antelope or two. A different lady in slippers took me through each of the dimly lit rooms, each one her own fiefdom. I could see that after a lifetime of being harnessed into working boots, their feet had widened gratefully into these woolly slippers, and their hands, calloused and wrinkled, had slipped into a retirement of clanking keys. The last room had a chart of the Chernobyl fall-out, illustrated by a photo of a mutant cat. It had one duff leg.

My next thought was to look for churches, of which there were none. As for vodka, there was no Stolichnaya, though it is made in Ukraine, but only peach and melon vodka from Israel, kiwi vodka from Italy, and 'eagle' vodka from Germany. A man lay dead drunk on the pavement.

I caught a trolleybus to Alushta on the coast. The trolleybus line is the longest in the world and winds up and down through a landscape of hills and deciduous forest, even mountains. A tumble of cloud caught its hem on a sharp sunlit peak and I suddenly saw what had been missing in the vast open skies and wide horizons of Russia. It was that intimacy between earth and sky that tucks the land into valleys, enfolds villages in downland and nestles a cloudy sky around hillocks of grazing sheep. And that here in the Crimean mountains lit the steep and rocky forest floor with shafts of sunlight. Where the forest ended, the mountains spilled straight down to the coast in skirts of vineyards.

Alushta was a pleasant little town of whitewashed houses and a crowded pebbly beach. Impelled now by habit I looked for the church. A concrete shop had been built round it, enclosing it entirely. I walked past shelves of gherkins and shoes and found myself in a nave divided into floors of living and storage space that were slowly being dismantled. The icons were all framed prints.

The town museum displayed Ghanaian banknotes, newspaper articles about the mayor's visit to California in 1987, lead toys and some dust-encrusted minerals. Again no sign of any amulets or embroideries and I headed back for Bakhchisarai.

Crimea was a stronghold of the Golden Horde, who had conquered the local Turkic people – the Coumans or Kiptchaks – at the same time as they had ravaged Kiev, and it was at Bakhchisarai that Batu was reputed to have built his palace. The southern coast at that time was held by Genoese trading settlements, but the Greeks had been there long before then, at least by the fifth century BC when Herodotus writes of them and the Scythians. By 1419 the Horde had split into three khanates – those of Khazan, Astrakhan and Crimea – and it was the Tatars of Crimea who were the first to secede, in 1430. Together with the princes of Moscow, who refused to continue to pay the tribute that had helped to make them golden, the Tatars of Crimea were responsible eventually for destroying what was left of the Horde.

Crimea was now overwhelmingly Russian for on the night of 18 May 1944 Stalin deported the entire Tatar population to Uzbekistan as part of his policy of punishment for those non-Russians he deemed might have helped the invading Germans. This included the Germans of the Volga, the Chechen and other Caucasian people. In 1956, Khrushchev denounced the deportations and allowed the people to return, but nothing was heard of the Tatars and the Germans, some of whom must of course be the ones I had come across in Bishkek. While the Germans now hoped to go to Germany rather than the Volga, some Tatars were returning to Crimea, claiming land and stirring up trouble.

A couple of them were on the train to Bakhchisarai wearing the Uzbek cap typical of the Ferghana valley: four sections of green cloth, each machine-embroidered with a white squiggle that they told me represented the womb and hence the four wives allowed by Islam, though the usual, more pedestrian, interpretation is that it depicts a chilli.

We sat on wooden seats in a filthy tin train littered with cigarette ends, pumpkin seeds and chewed gum. People walked up and down selling papers and ice cream or simply begging. We passed through a rolling grassy landscape stabbed by dark cypress trees, almost like Italy except that the buildings were hideously functional, and industrial clutter disturbed the peace of sheep, cows and women carrying grain for their chickens. We had to drop down off the train and cross the dirt tracks to reach the town.

Bakhchisarai was a sleepy place, one of those towns where old crones swept the gutters with stiff broomsticks and goats could cross the main street unhurriedly. The palace of the khans had been built between the sixteenth and eighteenth centuries and was thus far too recent for Batu. But there were ruins in the tufa hills outside the town that could be the right date. I walked for miles and saw cave cities where people took refuge from invaders – including the Golden Horde – and monasteries where Orthodoxy was protected from Byzantine secular powers. But Batu needed no refuge and I returned to the palace of the khans. It was now a museum and was closed.

I returned to Simferopol to catch a bus the next day to the ancient Greek and Genoese settlement of Kaffa, now the seaside town of Feodosia.

The night was strangely restless and in the morning I threw away my bus ticket to Feodosia. I felt impelled to return to Bakhchisarai.

The embroideries in the palace museum were all entirely Turkish in style. Towels and sashes with floral motifs repeated three times, napkins embroidered with fruit and the knife to peel it, also repeated three times, all worked in pinks and greens and gold. They were not remotely like anything Ukrainian or Russian. They were of cotton not linen, they hung across the henna and marriage rooms and not around icons and windows, the dresses were goldworked velvet and not simple white linen shifts embroidered in red. But then Crimea had been under the protection of the Ottoman from 1475 until Catherine the Great seized it for Russia in 1783.

And then I saw it. It was lying in a display cabinet, a perfect example of the amulet. Just as it should be, a padded triangle with three tassels. It was made of dirty brown leather thonged together, embroidered in silver with the motif of a crescent moon and the solar symbol of an eight-pointed star, and had a loop to hang it by. The tassels were of twisted wool, the outer ones white, the central one red. An extract from the Koran was inside, said the museum director, a German-speaking lady in a pink nylon frock. It was for a man. To protect him from illness. Women's amulets, she pointed out, were always hung with gold coins that jingled and so kept the evil spirits away.

Perhaps the tinkling water in the Summer Room should have

alerted me, or the painted flowers of the Golden Study, or the cushioned divans around the rooms, without mentioning the fact that I should have noticed that the towers of the palace were minarets: my amulet lay firmly in the embrace of Islam. And they had displayed it upside down.

'Clear off! We're counting our money,' the receptionists finishing the day shift at the Feodosia hotel shrieked at me. This welcome was kindly translated for me by two Ukrainian women who had taken me there, as the only hotel in town that accepted foreigners. It was painful later to have to contribute to the takings of the night shift. The hotel served no breakfast, its restaurant closed from twelve to two and again at six and they allocated me the room directly over the town disco. I was woken in the night by terrible screams, assuming them first to come from that direction, but it turned out to be a woman being attacked in the corridor on her way to the loo.

Feodosia was, in fact, a sweet old-fashioned seaside town where people arrived on holiday by train and bus. Pleasures were innocent: little groups stood around licking ice cream and staring at a monkey on a chain, photographers snapped children on green blow-up crocodiles, and their parents sitting on white chairs by a small white table with a bowl of fruit and a palm tree, against the backdrop of the Black Sea. The entire setting made of plastic, bar the Black Sea. Between the seafront and the town promenade ran a railway track and shunting yard so that small queues formed of people carrying buckets and spades waiting to cross while lumbering trains belched to and fro.

Among the pretty little buildings fronting the promenade was the local museum, painted cinnamon with white trimmings. It was full of fragments of Greek vases, for Feodosia was a Greek city founded originally by the Milesians, at least as early as 570 BC, from which date an Athenian vase had been found. The museum also had dozens of amulets, of bronze, paste and clay, dating from the seventh century BC on. Wolves' teeth, supposed to protect against toothache, a host of fertility symbols – a penis and testicles, fish, three clay goddesses – bunches of grapes for fertility of the land, then a scarab from Egypt – symbol of the sun and of virility – and a cross. They seemed to cover every eventuality, but there was no triangle.

A bus ride to the far east of Crimea went again through black steppeland brushed by thin yellowing grass, limitless to the horizon and beyond to Asia. Pylons and telegraph poles were stuck in it like pins. It was here that the Scythians had erected some of the richest of their tombs, their burial goods including Greek jewellery and amulets. They were impossible to get to, those *kurgan*, I was told in Kerch. A young man grabbed my hand and led me into a lovely eighth-century Byzantine church, showing me how to cross myself correctly.

Back at Feodosia, a salty tang in my mouth as I swam, I watched an elegant cruise boat follow the shoreline out at sea announcing excursions over its loudspeaker. I could swear I heard the Russian word for embroidery, *vishivka*, and I most definitely heard 'museum', but then it cruised on and away out of my grasp like so much else. For I hadn't seen a single *kurgan*, nor a lonely stone goddess figure in the steppe. I had seen no embroidered towels hanging from birch trees in groves, either by moonlight or on St George's night, or forty days after whatever festival or birth or death was significant in the community. I was at least a generation too late.

In the days that followed, I scavenged through the museums and towns of southern Ukraine. I saw relics of Scythian settlement – torques, amulets of birds and eyes, plaques of animal art, gold gorgon faces, bulls' heads of clay. And of Greek – statuettes of Aphrodite and Pan, amulets of bulls, gold earrings of Eros – and gold embossed plaques to stitch on clothes that were both Scythian and Greek. But in all these searches I advanced not the width of a whisker in my search for the amulet.

In Odessa – a dignified city of flaking splendour, where a sharp wind of commerce and future prosperity blew round every corner – I looked for shipping routes to Turkey and on to the Greek Islands. There was just one company that had boats going from Odessa to Istanbul, but photos in their office window of passengers having a jolly time drinking cocktails on red plastic couches, or relaxing in the sauna in gold-trimmed bikinis, convinced me that the trail of my amulet, if not completely lost, was here smothered by modernity. What I needed was an ancient trader with lateen sail and an old salt for captain – his nose to the breeze and eyes to the stars – wearing on his hairy chest a triangular leather amulet, a tooth and a cowrie that would ensure fair winds and a clear berth from rock and reef.

Instead I caught a rumbling old tin train to the north-west confines of the territory of the Golden Horde, that region of the Carpathian foothills from where they rode pillaging into Krakow, shooting dead the town watchman, as he pealed his warning bell in the church tower, and terrorizing the populace before in the flick of a moment mysteriously vanishing to the oriental steppes from whence they came. I was thrown off the train, together with a young Syrian, as its route between two Ukrainian towns took us through Moldavia, where Ruritanian police officers demanded visas for their newly independent state.

THE CARPATHIANS

✠

'Deported' back to Odessa, there was no choice. After a three-hour struggle to buy a ticket, with just two people in the queue ahead of me, only a two-berth compartment was available on the night train by another route to the Carpathians. I would have to risk sharing with one man. He was a Dell computer salesman wearing dirty yellow flip-flops and carrying one of those huge striped plastic bags that spill their homely contents on every airport carousel east of Frankfurt.

'It's impossible to work as a salesman here. People can't imagine anything on their tables except a mug of water and a piece of bread. And as for a computer they can't understand what they would ever need one for. Even businesses are like that. So my job is hard. I've tried to leave, to settle in Israel. I've been there and seen what it's like. In that small country, mostly desert, they grow all kinds of things and have proper factories. Here we have these sad dirty useless factories and we grow only cucumbers.'

His colleague in Israel, he continued, his English lapsing under the emotion of recollecting his visit, 'does the same work, only his English is little and mine is greater, and he earns nearly a thousand dollars a month and has a flat, two cars and three children. Here the average wage is thirty dollars a month and old people get twelve. Most couples, like us, have only one child. There is no future for children.'

There was clearly no point in asking whether he had a car. And a flat? They lived with his mother-in-law.

'Then,' he continued, 'people don't invest here. If a foreigner puts, let's say' (he paused to think of a huge amount) 'ten thousand dollars into a business and he makes one thousand profit, he can't get it out. And he has forty-four papers to fill in, changing all the time. The government's corrupt and I can't see any future for Ukraine.'

I woke to a different landscape. Gone the hot sunshine, the arid, almost Mediterranean, feel of the Crimea. Here a watery morning sun silvered the heavy mist, the tufted grassland was sodden with overnight rain. Village houses nestled under trees instead of standing exposed to the open arc of the sky. Cows huddled in pastures, ducks splashed in their home ponds.

Lviv to the Ukrainians, Lvov to the Russians, Lwow to the Poles, Lemberg to the Germans, it was a busy town, a town of cobbled streets and tramlines, fountains of Adonis and Diana, heavy Gothic buildings, and worthy merchants' homes dating from the sixteenth century on, balconied and adorned with carved lions and balustrades. It carried the history of its various names in every stone and was wholly European. There was nothing, absolutely nothing of Asia. The Horde had pillaged, destroyed and left.

Though Orthodoxy lingered here, in churches of gold baroque with walls covered in mauve lino, like the Transfiguration in Lviv, this region was none the less the frontier with Catholicism. It wasn't evident. If there was a Catholic church in any town it would be almost hidden in some side street or small unfrequented square, otherwise all were Orthodox, and the single church of each village always so. Even when a new one was being built it was, without exception, Orthodox. Catholicism had retreated to Poland and the Vatican.

Lviv was a town whose solid grandeur I really only appreciated when I had left it behind. Its environs were again a nihilistic skyscape of half-finished brick blocks twenty storeys high, their roofs non-existent, their windows void. Glassless and frameless blanks in their façades. A massive hydro-electric scheme had petered out in a scruffy army of pylons paraded along the horizon and a deserted concrete-fenced enclosure of industrial waste: obsolete piping, motionless derricks, silent cranes, padlocked iron gates and an unearthly stillness through which only a hungry cat stalked. All one could possibly hope was that these heartless landscapes of blighted concrete, these abandoned factories, gas-ometers, silos, dumped like the toys of some giant who had never understood what they were for, would be dynamited into oblivion. As the Soviets had taken twenty blasts to destroy the church of the Assumption in Moscow, why not blast after blast until this travesty of a civilization and social system had been razed from these stepped and wooded lands and from the minds of men?

The rolling forested country south of Lviv was calming. Farming was in strips, couples were digging up potatoes, scything grass, cutting maize, men were ploughing with horses and wooden ploughs. Silvery cabbages and geese were like lace ruffs around the brick houses, whose ugly high-pitched roofs grabbed the space above them and spoke of winter snow. Old women passed, each leading one cow, men drove horses and carts, a pair of horses to every cartload of hay. Small white goats were frightened by the train and pulled on their tethers. As we approached Ivano-Frankovsk, the low evening sun gilded the tips of the cabbage leaves, glistened the backs of the sleeping geese and burnished the flanks of the horses pulling their loads into the villages before night.

Ivano-Frankovsk must once have been a peaceful little town of stone houses, their windows pedimented and pillared in white, their walls extended into white corbels, their balconies topped with stone lions, their heavy wooden doors ornately carved and hung with wrought-iron knockers. But it had been sliced through and brutal, megalomaniac Soviet buildings now crowded out the old streets.

I caught the bus on to the small town of Kolomiya, through more grassland and strip farming. The road climbed tortuously past them until – muted grey, fading in intensity as they increased in height – the distant Carpathians softened the horizon and we pulled into a poor, quiet town of cobbled streets and closed churches where people crossed themselves as they passed.

Roxanne was tall and fair, with intense blue eyes and a shirt to match. She was Ukrainian by birth, but her family had fled when she was a baby and she had lived in the States since she was seven. Now she was fifty-two, recently divorced, and had returned to her origins to help Ukraine get back on its feet. The Peace Corps had sent her to Kolomiya as a small-business adviser. She had wound up her own business in America, left her family the day after her son's wedding and said goodbye to her Argentinian tango partner, to spend two years in this godforsaken place. Home leave was actively discouraged as volunteers tended not to come back.

They had all been trained in Lutsk, some of them as TEFL English teachers, others as advisers, she explained. 'The younger ones, they usually find, don't do so well under stress. We all have to work terribly hard, particularly in business. They have no idea here what a "free market" is. They think it's nipping over the border into Hungary and buying mayonnaise and tomato ketchup and selling it here. They have no concept of unemployment either. The town council of Kolomiya is about the same number of people as run New York. Then the laws change all the time, so investors shy away. The government's really corrupt, people just lining their pockets.

'The future's bleak,' she added. 'Lots of people preferred Communism and, when you think, it came almost straight after serfdom, so there was hardly any period when they made decisions for themselves. Maybe it's the TEFL people who'll do more good in the end, by changing their attitudes.'

The one hotel in town was opposite the bus station and Roxanne's flat was nearby. I had been taken there after a tortuous and desperate search for someone who spoke English – or French or German or almost anything other than just Ukrainian. Even the director of the museum – a young man in a green lumberjack shirt, smelling heavily of tobacco – spoke nothing but Ukrainian. How could he do any research? I wondered. Was he just a Party man? Had nothing changed?

The weekend that I was taken to meet Roxanne was potato-picking weekend, she pointed out. Most people, even those living in flats in Kiev, have a strip of land in the country, otherwise they have no food. That's why when they find potatoes or onions, or anything, they buy them by the sack or bucketful and store or dry them. She was busy drying apples and plums in her cooker to help see her through the coming winter.

The hotel was terrible. Lunch and dinner every day was just thin cabbage soup, and inedible gristly fried pork with fatty potatoes which the cook ate herself each time I left them on the plate. Breakfast was non-existent, not even tea or coffee, and at the bus station there was only vodka. Roxanne rescued me and invited me to supper each evening that I was in Kolomiya, always managing to whip up something, though the shops had little more than yellowing cabbages, puny mud-caked carrots and endless rows of jars of gherkins. I contributed fearful wine and cognac.

My admiration for Roxanne was unbounded. Though it was a business as an interior decorator that she had given up to come to Kolomiya, she was as pleased as punch to have been able to buy some brown and orange winceyette printed with elephants to use as a bath towel, and a blue working overall for a dressing-gown. Boots for the winter were a problem. She'd have to walk a lot and women's ones here were made for soliciting. It would probably mean buying men's. If she could find them.

As we sat drinking cognac by the fading light, the strain on her face began to show and her hair looked greying, rather than fair. Her daughter and best friend had both been diagnosed as manic depressive, she said. When her two years here were up, she thought she might settle in Mexico.

Each night I went back to the hotel and again the phone always rang in the small hours. I left it to ring. But it was a knock on the door at the crack of dawn and the call 'Police' that did make me jump out of bed, barking my shin as I tried to get to the door through the small space. It was two policemen. I stood answering their questions with blood trickling down my leg.

Where had I come from? Where was I going? Why was I there? They commented that I had a stamp in my passport to say I'd been to Simferopol – what was I doing there? They searched through all my papers, apologized and left.

The rain never stopped and Kolomiya was miserable beyond belief. I walked round the overgrown cemetery where apples had been laid on the graves, and along the deserted streets. Where shops had nothing much to sell their windows were decorated with wedding photos, the brides always dressed in white nylon and carrying their bouquet, as in Uzbekistan, still wrapped in Cellophane. But many of the men wore embroidered shirts. They came, it seemed, from the villages high in the Carpathians.

In 1941 and 1942, the Soviets had swooped into these mountain villages and arrested people, deporting them and their families to Siberia and confiscating their lands and property. Even, the villagers said, their embroidered costumes. Still, they had managed to hide some and they carried on making new shifts and shirts which they wore at Christmas, Easter and the saints' days of St Peter and St John.

Then they all made *rushnyk*. They were tied on every cross, draped over every icon and picture, laid on every surface in the village churches. But among all the patterns – the village of Kosmach had fifty alone – there was no triangle. And the embroidery was in no way amuletic. That function was left to wild plants. These they dried and dyed and then held in bunches in the corner of the room, burning them slowly to stop children being afraid and to protect the household from devils and bad thoughts. And from bad people too, they added.

Then there was the festival of the River Jordan on the nineteenth of January, when the priest blessed the water in their wells and held a burning candle over their door frames, marking the wall with a black cross to protect the house. They used, on the same day, to tie bunches of the wild plants and wooden crosses on their gates, but now it was blue plastic flowers that they liked. They left them up all year. Then forty days after Easter it was a green holiday and they put bunches of leaves on every gate and window. And see what good luck such charms had brought them, they said. For this pretty region of mountain and forest was relatively wealthy. They made souvenirs that businessmen traded for them in Russia, Poland, everywhere in eastern Europe. Carved wooden boxes, spoons, that sort of thing. Look at the local doctor, they said. He sells souvenirs as well and he's building a new house with eighteen rooms just for himself and his wife and one child. Will he put blue plastic flowers on the gate and burn plants in the rooms? Yes, of course. And he'll have piped water.

Where villages were not inaccessible because of mud on the

road, I travelled around a nursery-rhyme land of small wooden houses painted blue and yellow and surrounded by apple trees, their little gardens fenced off from untended grassy slopes. Almost all had a well, a tethered cow and some geese, a small conical haystack and piles of drying onions to stock for the winter. And bunches of leaves round the white fretted windows, and blue plastic flowers and a wooden cross on the gate.

On my last return to Kolomiya the hotel was in darkness. The town's electricity had failed – the cook indicated the pots of tepid water and congealed grease on top of the cold stove, spread some of the grease on a hunk of dry bread and clapped her false teeth into it. I caught the evening bus back to Ivano-Frankovsk.

Taras had whiskers everywhere, long soft brown hair that fell in a fringe over his deep-set blue eyes and a curly beard that encompassed his gentle face. He was an ethnographer. His lower lip quivered whenever he was excited which, discussing the next morning at the museum the symbols he felt so passionately about, was very frequently. And as it quivered, so it shook with it a tangle of brown beard. His symbols were those on the pottery of the Tripilye culture of the region between southern Rumania and the Dnieper, dating from 4000 to 2500 BC and known as Tripolye in Russian and Cucuteni in Rumanian. He had filled one thick album after another with meticulous drawings of them, neatly categorized into those on the outer rim of vessels, those on the inner, on the body and the lid. They would never be published, these thousands of drawings. 'We have too many problems here,' he said.

The symbols were extraordinary, an infinite variety of curving lines within the circle of a pot, a display of amazing ingenuity and imagination in spirals, ellipses, wavy lines, whorls, loops, twists, mandalas, spinning swastikas and symbols of the moon, of snakes, rain and water. Within them, here and there, were small dogs, birds, slanting trees on hillocks, animals with horns like the moon and ladders to heaven.

'They put ladders on the graves at Kunya Urgench for the soul to climb to heaven,' I commented.

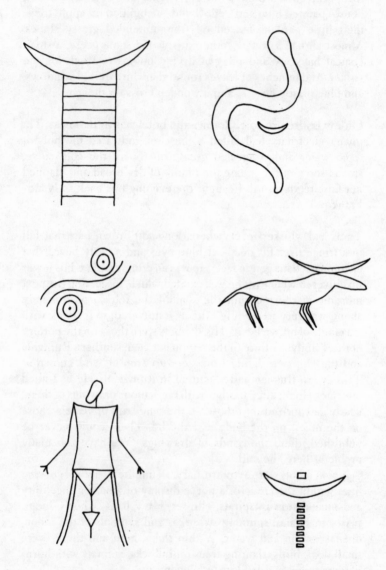

He nodded. That was not uncommon.

'And triangles with pendants?'

There were triangles only as the skirt of anthropomorphic figures – he wouldn't go so far as to say they were goddesses – but then not with pendants but with definite legs. But amulets they did have locally. Not as symbols or decoration but made of leather and metal in the form of belts, wristbands and headbands.

He returned to his drawings. Tadpoles, women's breasts. All were curved, only the occasional small details within the pattern lines were not, like the stylized dogs and 'goddesses' and the ladders. And the embroidery on the local shifts was quite different, he pointed out.

Naturally. Such magnificent twirls and whirls, incised with fervour into wet clay as if by some demented spirograph, or flicked gently in red ochre on the fired surface, and those goddesses giving birth, could never be subjugated to the discipline of linen, I suggested.

'Linen?' The beard shook. 'Linen?'

We were on a different wavelength. His thoughts were with the flowing ritual decorations of seven thousand years ago, mine with the relentless toing and froing of a weaving shuttle. We were both wrong. Mary had been to the Carpathians before me and if there was anyone in the world who could spot a goddess figure in an innocent sleeveband of cross stitch or a rough piece of leather sewn onto a sheepskin jacket, it was she. And goddess symbols were indeed on the village embroideries and folk art.

Firstly the birth and fertility symbol of a dotted quartered lozenge. That Taras was familiar with. It was a symbolic invocation to secure fertility. It was found in the Tripilye culture, in the upper Dniester valley, from the fifth millennium BC. But it was much older. They had found stamp seals and wall paintings from two thousand years earlier in Çatal Hüyük in Anatolia. And Mary had spotted it on *rushnyk* and painted Easter eggs, and 'on a rug stretched out under the apple trees in Yavoriv' she had seen 'a large fertile field full of seeds between the outstretched legs of the birth goddess'.

Then again the mother-and-daughter goddesses on the

Tripilye ceramics also featured on the wall paintings of Çatal Hüyük, and were appliquéd in leather, studded with metal and embroidered, on the sheepskin vests worn by both men and women of the Carpathian Hutsul people. But there were no triangles with pendants, and on the ceramics of Tripilye Taras had recorded only one, incomplete, with seven pendants, set between curving patterns with animals, waves, rain, ladders and trees.

We rushed out of the museum three hours after lunchtime and grabbed a small sweet coffee, and then returned to discuss the goddesses and gods of Old Europe – the neolithic society of pre-Indo-European culture that embraced geographically this region and the Greek islands.

'What about Carpathians and Karpathos?' I asked Taras. Was there any link in the names, linguistic or otherwise, or was it just chance?

Carpathians might mean trees, he said, or it might be the name of the people who used to live there. Now they were the Hutsul, Slavs from Slovakia, and the Boyko, who were a Celtic people. Of course, the Celts and the Greeks shared some of their mythology, the triple goddess, for example. A triangle could relate to that trinity? suggested Taras.

KARPATHOS

OLYMBOS

✠

The mythical imagery of Old Europe extended right through
to classical Greece, but Taras's trinity of goddesses and his
drawings were not the only link that could have drawn me from
the Ukraine to the Greek islands. Greek settlement of the
northern Black Sea coast was another obvious one. Others were
Sirine and Alconoste and the Greek mythological version of
siren and harpy; the women's linen shifts cut straight and
embroidered at cuff, hem and neck; the puzzling shared sounds
of the names Carpathians and Karpathos and of their string
music. And the most obvious one of all, the Orthodox Church.

Direct links to the more easterly parts of my journeys were
also there. Bearing in mind Alexander's campaign to the Indus,
there was the flouncy dress of Palas and the equally flouncy
foustanela of the Greek guards and nobility. And the horned
headdresses of the Hindu Kush that were also worn by women
in Russia and eastern Europe. Then the migration of Turkic
people from Central Asia to Turkey and their dissemination
throughout the Ottoman empire.

All these routes brought me to the banal one of a crowded
tourist flight, a wander through the golden cobbles and toppled
stone columns tumbled with yellow daisies and ginger cats of
Rhodes, a slow ferry to the cluster of tavernas hugging the shore
that was the port of Diafani on the island of Karpathos, and
finally a ride on the school bus up the mountain to Olymbos.

Olymbos is one of those thousands of villages of the Mediterranean and Aegean that cling to precipices beyond the clutch
of *condottieri* and pirates. Its main street is merely a narrow
cascade of whitewashed stone and step that here blazes in sunlight
a bent old woman in black, and there entombs in dark shadow
a laden donkey and a string of goats.

Olymbos is not only cut off from the sea, which churns
menacingly on the rocks thousands of feet below, but is also
hemmed around by mountains and just as isolated to landward.
Merely a spider's web of donkey trails and goat paths connects
it up to a narrow plateau where its fields lie, and down to the
small harbour of Diafani on the opposite side of the island. A
road – which is continually eroding at the edges, the missing
bits outlined with stones – was built between village and harbour
a few years ago, slightly more recently than the Karakoram
Highway, and in 1980 electricity was brought to the village so
that, while the women still bake their bread in wood-kindled
ovens, the men sit in the bars watching television.

The result of this isolation, together with a more recent strong
desire on the part of the villagers not to lose the dream and
memory of their home as they emigrated in droves to Baltimore,
has meant that Olymbos has kept its old traditions – even an
ancient form of the Greek language with many Doric elements
– to a quite extraordinary degree. And the women and children
still wear amulets.

Some of the links that had brought me there could be dispensed
with fairly quickly. The flouncy dress of Greece, the *foustanela*,
was not worn in Olymbos. Also its skirt was frilled by pleating
and not formed of hundreds of godets as that of Palas, and
in any case probably had nothing to do with Alexander and
Macedonia.

Then horns. Though it was pretty certain that 'pointed caps
must have been widely in fashion during the sixth and fifth
millennium BC throughout southeastern Europe', there was no
evidence of any horned headdresses or any patterns with horns
in Karpathos. I dumped that idea.

The Turkmenistan to Turkey route was pointed out to me
often as a possibility. But, though the Turkmen still wear the
triangular amulet and hang it over their thresholds, the Turks
do not. And, though the Ottoman occupation of the Greek
islands lasted almost four hundred years, it scarcely touched the
people of such a remote and unimportant village as Olymbos.
One link might be found in the way the women of Olymbos
edge their scarves with crochet and with small leaves and flowers
– though now of plastic and not needlework – a technique

known as *oya* in Turkey and *bibila* in Greece. It was hardly an earth-shattering association and I abandoned the Turkic connection.

Then the similarity of the shifts of Ukraine and Olymbos. Their embroidered edges at neck, cuff and hem derive from the common element of a decoration whose original purpose was to prevent evil spirits entering and attacking the body, a role now largely forgotten. Most of all there was the identical cut, dead straight with any insertions such as gussets adding up to a rectangle, but this comes simply from the fact that the strips of cotton or linen were woven painstakingly by hand – and in Ukraine were often of home-grown, handspun thread – so that not a scrap should be wasted and only the small curved piece cut out for the neck would have to be discarded. It would also have to be cut and could not be torn, so that in similar dresses in Rumania it was thrown into a river to magical incantations. And the rough weaving by hand left each thread visible and easily counted. And so delicate white pulled-work was a technique common to both, as was cross stitch, which would have been the basis of geometric patterns – goddesses with triangles as skirts, zig-zags, rhombs, stylized birds. The links lay in the logic of technique and not in history.

The women of Olymbos still wear these shifts but the geometric patterns have been replaced by flowers, particularly roses, ordered into the cross stitch discipline of the threads. I had been told that the women only put their costumes on when the daily tourist boat arrives in summer and then take them off again when the bus ferries the tourists back down to the boat at Diafani. But all the women wear their costume with such assurance and with such esoteric patching on shoulder and back where burdens of water and wood have rubbed the fabric away, that there is no possibility that this is a tourist enterprise. And even the women herding goats on distant hills, where no tourists venture, are always dressed in the same way. What they wear is a straight open coat of handwoven indigo or black cotton, held round the waist by a sash and a flowery apron, and machine embroidered around the edges with a small three-pointed motif like a chicken's foot, which they said symbolized a flower. Underneath they wear the white linen or cotton shift that is so like that of Ukraine – which should be two fingers longer than the coat, they said – and white pants gathered into a band at the knee. They twist a black scarf bordered with painted flowers around their head and wear boots of soft beige goat's leather with a red or brown shoe base.

When Dawkins visited Olymbos in 1903 he recorded exactly the same costume, but with the pants tied at the ankle and worn with bare feet or simple rough shoes. He mentioned no embroidery, but then men seldom do. He commented even then that: 'Here alone have the women preserved their peculiar dress, for it hardly survives at Mesochória, and elsewhere, I think, not at all.' He then added that Olymbos was 'another world. It is the most primitive village in Karpathos, and many things survive there which have disappeared from more accessible places.' They still do.

As for the link of Sirine and Alconoste, the half-woman, half-bird sirens of Russian pagan mythology that decorated the towels of Pavlovo, there are almost identical figures on the embroideries of the island of Skyros in the Northern Sporades, which represent the sirens and harpies of Greek mythology. Such human-headed birds and animals appear in the arts of Ancient Egypt, and Persia of the Achaemenid period. They also decorated Turkish pottery made in Asia Minor and exported to Greek islands in the sixteenth and seventeenth centuries and could have come from that source. But as embroidery they seem to be peculiar to Skyros and are not found on the islands, of which Karpathos is one, that were the Southern Sporades until political expediency renamed them the Dodecanese.

What are found there, particularly on Rhodes, are small stone figures, half-woman, half-bird, from the period of the late eighth and seventh centuries BC, when the East Greeks had close contacts with the Orient. Earlier still the Minoans and Mycen-eans carved similar figures in stone, and both these peoples had settled on Karpathos. The Minoans first migrated there around 1600 BC, the Myceneans around 1350 BC and by 500 BC at least four thriving settlements were established on Karpathos, of which Vurgúnda was one. It lay on the seashore, a three-hour hike away from Olymbos over rough terrain, beyond the plateau

of tiny terraced fields belonging to the village that they called Avlóna.

Anna was a stocky woman of about my age, though she insisted I guess it. She had a tanned face with a broad flat nose and pale eyes, one of which was slower to open than the other. She dressed in shrieking purple and turquoise anorak and trousers, with a matching purple sweatband holding back her short tufted dark hair. Her hiking boots she had bought in the sales and had only now realized that one was stitched in red and the other in brown. She was travelling alone without wishing to be alone, and, speaking only German, was having problems.

'You're by yourself, too?' she asked. One eye glinted when she perceived a useful interpreter. 'Where shall we have dinner tonight?'

I recoiled but her pursuit was relentless. She had spent eight months the previous year hiking around Greek islands and was doing the same now for six. Yet she expected everything to be on time and was perpetually exasperated by the Greeks.

'Will you tell them this, will you ask them that,' she commanded me. Then she snapped incessantly at me: 'You walk too fast. You should eat at seven, not later. You shouldn't bother with lipstick. You should give me your bath plug, I wash more than you do.' She was divorced and her son was gay, she confided in me. No, it hadn't been a worry or a problem at all. He had his own life to live and that was it.

She pursued me with a thousand and one suggested improvements to my behaviour until I was obliged in the end to point out diplomatically that she was the Gestapo personified and I'd had enough. After that, we achieved a *modus vivendi* for two days during which I ate where and when I wanted, put on lipstick, refused to part with my plug and walked at my own pace. It didn't last.

'You don't walk, you run like a deer. What point is there in that? How can you see the red dots?'

The truth was that Anna had come for the hiking, and in that stony and empty countryside it was safer not to walk alone on the more isolated and distant paths. Not that there was the slightest danger from any people one might chance to come across – the odd goatherd dressed in her traditional costume, or a man tending his olive trees – it was just that the going could be rough and a fall or twisted ankle could mean being left to lie on the ground for a considerable time before being found.

Anna had her German hiking guide with her and refused to go anywhere that wasn't fully described in it. 'The path goes up over the rocks to the left,' it said. There was no path there, but there were signs of one to the right. She wouldn't try it. Then the Swiss Hiking Association had marked one or two noteworthy walks with red dots on stones. She wouldn't budge an inch until she could see the red dot and only when I was disappearing out of sight would she risk following, calling after me triumphantly every few minutes, '*Rote Punkt!*' Otherwise her conversation was a litany of problems and indecisions and it was an unfortunate twist of fate that I needed her to be able to get to Vurgúnda.

The donkey path that led there began as a steep descent between the old stone windmills to the windward side of Olymbos. The village straggled up both sides of a long ridge on which a line of these windmills squatted like pigeons on a municipal roof. I had taken a room in a house on the leeward side looking down over the cleft that separated Olymbos from the mountains between it and Diafani. Anna had chosen a small hotel on the windward side and complained perpetually of the cold and damp, but, paying a visit to me with the thought of changing, fortunately found the accommodation at my place too 'primitive'. Our walk to Vurgúnda thus logically began with my calling for her at her hotel. At nine, we arranged.

As I walked up the quiet morning alleyway towards the ridge, a familiar figure of garish hue came striding towards me.

'Why didn't you come earlier? Last time the weather was fine you came early. I've been ready since half past eight,' she bawled down the street.

'Good morning,' I said, wondering whether Vurgúnda was going to be worth it.

We climbed to the ridge. The windmills were of stone, horse-shoe-shaped, and faced out to sea in a clustered line that almost formed a battlement. Only a few had their wooden sail mechanisms intact – one even with sails – the rest were left merely with the wooden shaft sticking out like a gun from a tank. We walked past them, turned to the lee and then for an hour or so scrambled along a rough track – which was here neatly laid with steps of boulders and there disappeared into a maelstrom of wild flowers – up to the summit of a hill and the small white chapel of Agios Constantinos.

Its blue door stood ajar. Inside was a simple faded iconostasis, draped in frilly curtains held back by a circle of pleated brocade and hung with bright wool fringed cloths printed with huge roses, just like Russian headscarves. Bronze lanterns, candles and matches lay around. Such small chapels were scattered everywhere around the mountains and the villages and from the smell of candlewax seemed to be in regular use.

From the chapel the path widened into the sandy track that led to the cultivated plateau of Avlóna, the stones along its sides cracked where wild yellow orchids grew, a view over the plateau opening up as the path turned a bend. This small stretch of flat land between mountains was zigzagged by low stone walls and chequered with small stone huts, half house, half animal-stall. Until recently, except when the villagers of Olymbos moved in for the harvest, the only people living there were a couple of young girls left in charge of the animals. Now one or two families had settled there but still it had the eerie feel of an abandoned and empty place. With its circular threshing floors, tiny fields of corn and grass, and fruit and vegetable gardens, Avlóna was the only agricultural land available to the people of Olymbos, apart from one or two small terraces and vineyards in the cleft deep below their village.

There was a wire fence around the settlement and, at the entrance through which the sandy track passed, rags were hung on it. Rags from clothing, but also a cut plastic oil container and a twisted bright yellow fishing net. I had seen such things at the entrance to villages in northern Thailand. They were to protect the people, should they fall sick, and to pray for good harvests.

'Wonderful,' I said. 'They're for the wandering spirits.'

'It's a scarecrow,' said Anna. 'For the birds.'

We walked through the deathly stillness of Avlóna on to a narrow path of loose pebbles between stone walls. A donkey, hung with pompoms round his neck, stared at us. Then for about two hours a precipitous track of boulders and rocks led down to the coast through a wild barren landscape where only the bells of goats disturbed the silence. Ahead lay a curved bay – which must have provided a small harbour – and a narrow peninsula thrashed by high seas, on which the town of Vurgúnda had been built, most likely by the Myceneans but certainly occupied by the Dorians. Another tiny white chapel, that of Agia Marina, stood beneath the rockface, this time its door hook so rusted that we had to bang it open with a stone. The woolly rose-patterned shawls over the iconostasis were chewed to pieces where they had been left folded and never touched.

I don't know what I had expected to find in Vurgúnda – evidence of half-woman, half-bird sirens? Triangles? Minoan flat-headed goddess figures with raised arms? Two-tailed mermaids as on the embroidered skirts of Crete? What had been found there were a stone broken in two, bearing a Dorian tribute of the third century BC to a local doctor and now in the British Museum, some scraps of city wall and votive tablets to the goddess Athene and to the Roman emperor Domitian who 'passed the greatest part of the day in catching flies and killing them with a bodkin'. But what we saw were only early Byzantine rock graves, a massive stone rolled across their entrance, just as across the tomb of Christ.

The following weekend was Easter. And there was still the link of the Orthodox Church.

EASTER

✠

And that of Taras's drawings. The Tripilye culture of the Dnieper valley was the northernmost extent of the civilization of Old Europe, and Rhodes and Karpathos were its southernmost. The people of neolithic Old Europe were settled farmers, peaceful and, above all, a matriarchal society, whereas the Indo-Europeans, who conquered them, were nomadic hunters, belligerent, patriarchal.

While the patterns Taras so meticulously drew of his beloved Tripilye culture would be sought in vain in the stitching and woodwork of Olymbos, the structure of its society had here survived. It was matriarchal, matrifocal, matrilinear.

The inheritance laws of Olymbos decreed that the eldest daughter, who was always given her maternal grandmother's name, would receive as her dowry all the houses, fields, furniture, jewellery and household goods brought by her mother to the marriage, while the eldest son inherited the father's share. However, the system ensured that, once the father's wealth had passed to a daughter for lack of a son, it never reverted to the male line. In this way, over generations, the wealth of the village had devolved almost entirely into female hands. The men were thus mostly obliged to emigrate to find work in America, Germany, Belgium, wherever.

'They have only their trousers,' said the priest.

It was at Easter that the matriarchal aspect of Olymbos society shone openly in the guise of hundreds of candlelit gold coins, for it was particularly on Easter Sunday, and at the celebration of the Resurrection on the following Tuesday, that the eldest daughters appeared in church with their wealth hanging round their necks. As much as forty thousand dollars' worth of gold, in coins bought from the bank in Rhodes: English sovereigns, Dutch guilders. These eldest daughters also used to receive from their mothers, as part of their dowry, a paving stone in the women's antechamber of Olymbos church on which to stand through the Sunday service. If they didn't have this patch of their own they had to worship elsewhere. But now things were softening a bit. Younger daughters were beginning to inherit something, too, a minimum was left for the parents to live on and the paved floor of the antechamber had been plastered over. But still the young men had to move to Baltimore.

Celebration of Easter began with Palm Sunday. As I had been told that one of the contents of the triangular amulet was the candle grease from that service, I was there. In fact, remembering the pilgrims and their devotion, I was already at the Saturday Vigil of Palm Sunday. There was no one else, only the priest and his assistant, a fat, rather stooped, man who seconds before had been slumped over a half-empty bottle of retsina in the bar.

The candles were non-drip, stuck in sand. I stood for the statutory three hours of the service and watched them sputter, greaseless, to neat, trim stumps. As the priest walked in and out of the iconostasis doors, like a little figure on a Swiss town clock, he carried aloft icons and holy books and incense swingers, muttering over each, and then a basket filled with basil and olive branches, over which lay a huge round loaf. This he blessed. The bread was then normally cut up to share among the congregation but, as there were only two of us, the regular attendant, bent in anticipation, quite rightly got a large hunk and I a small piece. As I took it away I noticed it had triangles incised in it. Triangles in bread instead of crosses on hot buns. I was much too thrilled to eat it.

On Palm Sunday itself the church was half full, the women in a more fanciful version of their everyday costume, extra roses embroidered everywhere, their gold coins round their necks, flowered scarves trimmed with sequins over their heads. They stood motionless in the antechamber, a candlelit blaze of colour and golden sheen. The ritual was the same as at the Vigil, but this time the priest put a candelabra of five candles on the basket of leaves and bread, perambulated round the church with it and then laid it on a table before the iconostasis. He blessed it, swung incense over it, and then carried the candelabra round the church, replaced it and blessed the leaves and the bread again. At the end of the service the fat man from the bar cut the bread into chunks and handed it around the congregation. As the people filed out they each took some basil and olive from the basket: could it be these and not candle grease that they stitched inside their amulets?

Outside the church, the granddaughters of an old man who had been buried a few days before gave everyone chocolate and a bag containing ground wheat, sugar and silver dragées. And with them a small loaf. To each person as they walked down the steps away from the church, even running after me as I passed them by. It was the bread that was important, they said, not whether I was a tourist or a villager.

The bread of Olymbos is still baked in the old stone ovens, twenty or so, scattered around the village. The women light them with dried olive branches and then start baking as the flames subside into ashes, each woman having her own recipe, and using the ancient tools that have never changed. Some women make dry bagels, baked slowly all night with the metal door of the oven propped to with their old wooden shovels. Some loaves are glazed and covered with sesame seeds, some are matt and heavy, others taste of a spice like the smell of incense, others can be identified as tasting of caraway. The huge loaves of holy bread, two foot in diameter, baked for the church at Easter are the work of several women together, while the bread for the Resurrection each woman makes for the dead of her own family. All is shared among passers-by. The gift of bread is for the redemption of the souls of the dead, to atone for their sins in life, the women explained. And as the bread passes into the living, so too do the dead.

The funeral of the old man whose granddaughters now distributed bread outside the church had taken place the day I arrived in Olymbos. The small white funeral chapel and its cemetery stood on a spur down in the cleft below the village. Its bell pealed twice, answered by a double peal from the village church of Mary the Mother of God on the top of the hill. The responses, the bell of the living chiming twice for each double toll of that of the dead, continued while the funeral procession led by three priests wound its way up the steep path from the chapel to the church. All the people of the village attended, the men in their working garb, the women in their traditional costume. Some were wailing, some crying.

Then came an old woman with her hair uncovered. Whereas the others had all plaited their hair and hidden it under their black scarves so that maybe only the tips of the plaits could be seen, as they always wore it, this woman had wild grey hair cascading down her back for all to see. It was the tangled hair of the otherworld, the world outside the picket fence, and shocking in its disorder. She wailed like a demon possessed. She wailed with the power of chaos beyond the labyrinth.

By the time Good Friday came and the people's wailing was for Christ and not for a beloved old man of the village, Olymbos was full of photographers and tourists. The narrow main street, its whitewashed walls previously slashed like Elizabethan sleeves only by shuttered windows and doors, was now festooned with table cloths from Taiwan, furry slippers from Athens, silly hats from Rhodes and a plethora of tourist knick-knackery laid outside the small shops that before had been invisible.

Only the workshop of the old shoemaker remained the same. He was still at his last at seven each morning, a tall thin man with weatherbeaten face, whose own shoes squeaked as he walked up to the bar at mid-morning to take a break. The boots he made weren't authentic, the villagers said. The decorative strip of leather across the top wasn't traditional, it was for tourists. But then he had always been a farmer until he decided to become a cobbler. In all his years in the mountains, he told me, he had never come across any evil spirits, not even at night. But the goatherd women always wore amulets.

They had come gradually, the tourists and photographers, by taxi from the relatively new airport in the south of the island, each day one or two more. I had attended every church service during the week and their presence and lenses had become day by day ever more intrusive. I had escaped by walking into the mountains, along paths that disappeared into scurries of slate or ended at sharp drops by waterfalls. Everywhere there were lovely lacy wild flowers of the kind that thrive in dust and stone – small white, mauve and yellow-petalled fragile blooms – and low-lying meshed plants whose thorns always seemed to be under my hand when I stumbled. In pine woods there were bee orchids and tiny daisies. I walked alone as such hikes were not in Anna's guide.

When I wasn't away walking, I was invited into people's homes. They were beautiful – a simple room at one end of which, opposite the entrance, was a raised wooden platform with storage space underneath for clay jars of wine and oil. Here the family slept. It was approached by a couple of steps through a wooden arch and enclosed by a carved balustrade. Covering every inch of space on the platform and the walls around were cushions, weavings, decorated plates, family photographs, plastic dolls.

Just to one side of the entrance arch stood one strong post that carried the weight of the roof beams. This symbolized the man of the house and was covered with richly embroidered and finely crocheted cloths and was sometimes topped with his photo. The old cloths were of pulled threadwork in geometric patterns which included the goddess with a triangular skirt, but the new ones were of nothing but roses. Spectacular as this post was, it seemed a poor substitute for a plethora of gold coins.

In the evenings I wandered down to the cemetery and its red-roofed white chapel. As darkness fell, old women would come and light candles – glasses of water topped by olive oil and a wick – on each family grave. From down in the cleft, the candles flickered through the night, seeming to communicate with the lights of the village above, as if the dead were still among the living, the one welcoming the other.

The living grew ever more raucous as the disinherited men, and the children sent away to school in Rhodes, returned for the holidays. The bars were thronged, the church packed, fire-crackers and cap guns exploded everywhere. The services prolif-erated and were lit by photographers' flashbulbs. On Good Friday, the women arrived holding baskets filled with small posies of flowers in memory of their dead, which they placed on the church steps. The photographers rushed up, unconcerned by the women's tears. Outside the church it was the recently bereaved women who had the privilege of covering the *epitaphios*, the wooden cradle-like coffin and cross of Christ, with these posies. Photographers climbed the bell-tower above them, stood on the walls, ran up and down the steps.

At the last event, the festival of the Resurrection, the women, dressed at their most magnificent, again carried baskets, this time filled with bread, coloured eggs, coconut cakes, chocolate bars and home-made cheese, down the pathway to the cemetery. Photographers accosted them at every turn. The women laid their offerings on the graves as a prayer for rain, a good harvest and prosperity. The priest walked slowly round the cemetery, slipping into his pocket the wad of money each family gave him, and blessed each grave in turn. As he passed on, the women took up their gifts again and distributed them among the crowds, among villagers, tourists and photographers alike.

Later, on that day of Resurrection, a table was set at the top of the steps outside the church door, laden with sticky doughnuts, bowls of syrup and bottles of ouzo and Cutty Sark. Round it sat a couple of musicians, the priest and some men of the village, drinking and eating. One musician blew into a goatskin, the other drew a bell-hung rod across a three-stringed fiddle, the *lyra*, that emitted a pained screeching. Around them a circle of men, and a couple of girls, arms linked, began to dance. They simply swayed from foot to foot moving almost imperceptibly anti-clockwise. The music had no beginning and no end. The dance had no beginning and no end. Its purpose was to achieve a trance, the *glenda*, a trance intensified by the glasses of whisky and ouzo drunk by the musicians and handed to the dancers as they passed.

'I've seen the same dancing, this same total concentration, in the Balkans, the music played on a one-stringed fiddle called a *gusle*. It's Slavonic,' said one of the German tourists.

He was a man called Walter, always dressed in a hat inscribed 'Lumberman' and a woolly scarf for his bronchial affliction. He had spent three years as a prisoner-of-war in England and had returned continually ever since. It had left him with a longing

for the place, he said. He loved every stone of every cathedral:
Wells, Lincoln, Exeter. His conversation was as interesting as
Anna's was tedious and, whenever I could escape from her, I
spent my evenings with him. He was someone whose knowledge
I could trust and I asked him hopefully whether this music and
dancing would be found as far north as the Carpathians, seeing
it was Slavonic. He didn't know.

I asked him too if he knew the origin of the name Karpathos,
as I had already asked the men from Baltimore. No one was at
all sure, they had said, but as a people they believed they might
have come from the Carpathians – they mentioned the name
spontaneously. The Greeks were known to have come from the
north and east and perhaps there had been a direct settlement
on the island of Karpathos. I tried hard to remember Hutsul
faces – were they like Greek ones? Did people have curly black
hair? But then it could have been the other way round, that it
was the people of Karpathos who had settled in the Carpathians,
the men from Baltimore added, destroying their argument. The
gazeteer of geographical names merely listed Carpathians
(ancient Carpates), followed by Carpathian Ruthenia, Carpatho-
Ukraine, then Carpathos Greece (see Karpathos, Italian: Scar-
panto), giving no derivations. I wrote the whole idea off to
coincidence.

The music shrilled on. More girls joined the circle, laden with
gold coins, the young ones wearing pleated dresses of shiny
polyester that came from America or Athens, in acid yellow,
puce and sharp green, with bright fluorescent tights and clogs
and aprons of glittering brocade. Their headscarves of roses and
sequins ended in a cascade of gold beads and ribbons.

The Orthodox Church all this might also be, but I thought
of grey Russian skies, of the peace of weathered brick softened
by rain and neglect, of aspen domes in northern summer light,
of the flow of the river mirroring grassy banks and crumbling
stone. Then of a rediscovered faith that might save the beauty
of structure and ritual, just as surely as gawping tourists and
insensitive photographers might destroy it here.

THE AMULET

✠

Conquering Turks, seafaring Greeks, neolithic Europe, alliterative names – all these may have drawn me to Karpathos, but the real reason I had come was for the triangular amulets of Olymbos. The one I had received in the post and that had first drawn me here turned out to be merely a souvenir, of the kind that had failed to protect me in Uzbekistan. The women while away their winter hours making them for sale to the tourists who came on the daily boat in summer to spend a few hours in the village.

But I knew that real ones were made and worn by the women, and had heard they contained not only candle grease from Palm Sunday church but also dried flowers from Good Friday. Within a day or so of arriving in Olymbos I had learnt that they were called *philaktari*, a name that made their prophylactic role eminently clear. I had also become known as the '*philaktari* lady' and I had gathered a list of what went inside the amulets.

Essential were the dried olive and basil leaves from Palm Sunday and bits of dried flowers from the *epitaphios* of Good Friday. Then the recipe was unique to each woman, as her bread was. It could include a selection of ingredients, which were a hotchpotch of religious paraphernalia, strong smells and sharp objects that evil spirits don't like, bits of specific belongings of the enemy casting the evil eye, confusing threads in which spirits can entangle themselves, and objects with innate magical power.

The selection was made from the following: three grains of wheat, three or seven black sesame seeds, candlewax brought back by pilgrims from the Holy Sepulchre in Jerusalem, any other holy relics, three pieces of broken needle, garlic, some fishing net, a branch of black thyme, a fragment of white cloth (preferably from the gown the bishop wears to consecrate the church, but anyway some white cloth to represent Christ's shroud), a snippet of fabric from the enemy's clothing, holy wool from a lamb, a cord knotted twelve times for each apostle (which must be made by a woman who has stood through the entire Easter service), a short length of umbilical cord (this was then taken out and shown to the child when he started school as it was known to promote learning), salt, a sliver of wood from the threshold of the church or from the house of the enemy, snakeskin, cloves, red thread, three cuttings of palm used for the feast of Lazarus, a lump of stone struck by lightning. This last they found in the mountains after a storm. '*Astropaleke,*' they said, but couldn't explain what it was geologically, just that it was earth that had fused.

The recipe continued: smoke the ingredients with incense, sew them inside a triangle, hang along the bottom three blue beads or gold discs stamped with the saints Constantinos and Eleni. Pin inside a woman's coat over her breast, or on the back of a baby's left shoulder.

I set out to have one made.

Rigo led me down steep whitewashed steps, past an old woman holding two donkeys by tasselled cords, to her workshop. It was just as an untidied garden shed used by a witch casting spells might be expected to be. Dusty unidentifiable bottles were lined up on shelves, along with packs of 1930s embroidery threads, opaque plastic bags of dried herbs, esoteric heaps of rubbish. She plonked herself down on a chair, smoothed her apron over the fat stomach that had so recently miscarried and delved into a large plastic laundry basket. Unerringly she picked out a reel of red acrylic thread and a bag of remnants of hideous shimmering brocades. Turning suddenly to take a better look at me, she put these back again and picked up instead a piece of bright pink polyester. 'You like?'

I nodded wanly.

'Big you want?'

I nodded again.

She settled into her lap a blue plastic bowl that contained everything one could wish for to make amulets: dried flowers from last Easter's church, blighted sequins in star and circle shapes, strands of gold beads. All that was lacking was everything I wanted to see: candle grease, umbilical cord, fishing net and trophies from my enemy. She got me to hold the pink fabric while she snipped off a square. This she folded into a triangle, stitched down one side and then turned inside out, stuffing it with the dried Easter flowers wrapped in cotton wool.

'Why a triangle?' I asked.

'Tradition,' she snapped, stitching down the other side and then breaking the thread off between her teeth. She then threaded up some burgundy acrylic and deftly scooped out of the blue plastic bowl the necessary beads and sequins. I noted that those stitched on the outside in the centre of the amulet were merely a subterfuge for carrying the thread through to the top where it could form the loop. But she didn't make a loop, needed logically for the safety pin to hang the amulet by, instead she worked a kind of ridiculous cockatoo flourish.

It was the most miserable, meaningless amulet I had ever come across. Even one gold bead on one of the three pendants was missing, which, in another time and place, might have signified 'only Allah is perfect' but here set one corner pendant at right angles so that it simply seemed to be cocking a leg at the whole endeavour. It was nothing but a commercial sham. But then the priest had said scathingly, 'She's only a merchant.'

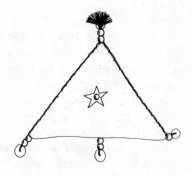

Rather than using amulets, the church did have its own
ceremony to deal with evil spirits, the priest explained. If he
were called he knew exactly what to do. It was usually a matter
of the evil eye. A woman would complain that when she milked
her goats the milk turned out to be no good for butter or cheese.
The evil eye was upon it. The priest would intone incantations
over the milk and all would be well. Then there was the evil
eye cast on babies. The priest was not expected to help there,
only the woman 'who knew'. Not so long ago there was an old
man in the village noted for his evil eye. He only had to look
at a baby and say 'good boy' or 'what a poppet' or any such
admiring remark and the child would instantly fall sick. The
woman 'who knew' would be called in immediately. She would
pour water on three plates and cast some sort of spell over them,
muttering words no one could hear. She then dripped oil into
each plate of water. If it spread over the water the baby was sick
with the evil eye and, because of her spell, would soon be better.
If the oil remained in a separate blob, the case was even more
serious and more spells would be needed.

Most of the villagers believed in the evil eye, even Nicos,
who had lived in Baltimore, then worked as a taxi driver in New
York and returned to his home in Olymbos to marry the girl his
mother had chosen for him. He ran the bar by the church that
belonged to his mother-in-law and remembered well that a
blue-eyed Danish tourist had come in and admired his video,
so that it immediately went wrong, though it had been working
perfectly well before. Then he had done the same with the
shutter of his camera.

Pinned up in Nicos's bar was a large triangular amulet, hung
with three tassels. The real thing. It was made of green fabric,
bordered with dull sequins and decorated with a ring of pleated
brocade, just like the ones that held back the curtains over
the iconostases of remote chapels. Its tassels were red. His
grandmother had made it, but he had no idea what was inside
it. It just always hung over the coffee machine, in case any more
Danes came in.

Though most of the women made amulets there seemed to
be one or two who were considered especially gifted. One,
Vastarkoula Vasilaraki, had died fifteen years previously but was

still remembered. Another, Irini Dariragi, had been gone only two years and some of her amulets were still treasured. One was given to me – a sparkly affair of shiny red fabric with jelly-baby beads dangling all round. Of the present-day makers two were particularly prized and were slightly different from the run-of-the-mill women of the village.

One had been abandoned by her husband and had made good by going to Baltimore and doing piece-work in a factory until she had earned enough to set up her own little shop in Olymbos. The husband had 'buggered off with a blonde tourist', she said, and, now that the German woman in turn had left him, he could be found wandering aimlessly around Rhodes, unable to return to his home village and his wife and family.

The other was Nicos's grandmother, who, now that she was really old and found the steps of Olymbos difficult to cope with, lived in Diafani. She was said to be completely mad. I set off to walk across the island to Diafani.

The old path ran straight, the massive stones that men had carried thousands of years ago and laid where the ground was friable now shattered where the new road zigzagged across its track. A kestrel hovered above. Where the path followed the river valley it was more difficult to find as floods in 1994 had ripped through, depositing mud and shale and tearing up stones. At the approach to Diafini it passed a Venetian watermill and wooden olive press that Dawkins had drawn and that was still there. By it was a small grove of ancient olive trees that belonged to the church. A rag was tied on one. There had always been an ancient belief that trees, most especially fig trees, were haunted by fairies and dragons and the spirits of the dead, but olive trees were considered holy and their power could be captured by cloth.

The closer the river valley drew to the harbour and the sea, the more desolate it became, littered with rubbish that the flood waters had uprooted and dumped. Then in the village itself, among whitewashed walls and crumbling steps, I was greeted by mangled tabby cats, the smell of orange blossom and the drone of bees.

The church was relatively new, rebuilt after an earthquake and spared by the flood. Its priest, Papa Minas, was a lively

intelligent man with white whiskers and twinkly eyes, who spoke
fluent English, German and Italian. Whereas most of the men
of Diafani were fishermen, or tinkered around in boats – on
which they painted eyes, as Japanese fishermen did, to ward off
the evil spirits of storm and wave – Papa Minas had been a
shepherd and disliked the sea. He knew many of the ancient
lost goat trails and walked them frequently, contemplating the
changes in society and the role of the church. His teenage sons
zoomed up and down the thirty yards of the seashore on noisy
motorbikes.

Nicos's grandmother lived close to the harbour and Papa
Minas confirmed that she was considered mad. She waited for
the daily excursion boat from Pigádia to land and then threw
stones at the tourists. Of course, this might be considered eminently sane. It was a matter of opinion. But certainly it was no use
talking to her about amulets. He himself might be able to help.

I asked him first about the possibility of prayers being placed
inside amulets. After all, those of the Islamic world always
contained excerpts from the Koran or prayers written by the
mullah. I mentioned that I had met a man in Olymbos, Michael,
who had returned to his home village from America for the
Easter holidays, and I had talked to him about amulets. He had
told me that he remembered the dried flowers in the ones his
mother made. He also remembered that, because he had been
to school, he used to have to write something for her, then she
would fold it and put it inside the amulet. He couldn't say
exactly what it was as it was in ancient Greek, but he knew the
gist of it.

He recounted: Christ was walking along one day when he
met a man and asked him where he was going. This man was
really an evil spirit in disguise and he told Jesus he was going
to do bad things to someone. Find a couple he could drive to
divorce or someone he could make suffer. 'Go home, Buster,'
said Jesus. That was about it.

Papa Minas nodded sagely and then went into the sanctuary
behind the iconostasis and fetched out some books. 'We have
prayers for amulets,' he said. 'Anybody can write them – like
this Michael – but it's usually the priest who does because we
have the books.' He opened the first one at page 493. 'I can't

actually read it,' he said 'because it's in ancient Greek. These prayers were written by the Holy Fathers of the Orthodox Church before the schism with Catholicism. This one is against devils, then there are others to St Basil and St John Chrysostom, Patriarch of Constantinople. There are special ones against the evil eye, then ones for every illness, or to bless fruits, wine, wheat, cows, sheep, cheese, eggs.'

'And the amulets themselves? Why are they a triangle?'

'That of course represents the Holy Trinity, as do the three pendants. But an amulet with pendants is special. It's called a *khaivali* and not a *philaktari*. It's especially potent against the devil. Of course the Church believes in the devil. We protect people from him.'

He had a couple of amulets beneath the altar at that very moment, he said. They had been there for three or four years. Not triangles, but powerful none the less. Cases of people being pursued by the devil in the form of their neighbour or an unknown enemy, and asking for the protection of the church. He fetched them out.

The first had been placed in his care by a woman who had fallen ill with a strange sickness. Medical care was always haphazard. Nowadays it was a bit better as all doctors training in Athens had to spend a year in a village somewhere, so that if the people of Olymbos and Diafani were lucky they had a doctor for a year – at the moment a young woman – but they then always moved on. The sick woman had had no medical care and her mysterious illness had persisted. She had placed a few charms under her mattress to no avail and then had found in the courtyard of her house, hanging hidden in a pergola, a bundle tied in a flowery handkerchief. She had taken it immediately to Papa Minas to place under the altar so that the power of the church could overwhelm that of the evil spirit – or neighbour – causing the sickness.

Papa Minas unwrapped the bundle to show me. Inside was a shrivelled lemon with a needle stuck in it, and a small handwoven white cotton bag made from someone's death shroud, tied with green wool. It was like the calico bags hung to catch the bounties of wandering spirits that O'Donovan had spoken of at Merv and had claimed were Scythian in origin.

The bag contained earth from the grave, lots of bits of fabric, presumably from the clothing of potential or past or immediate victims of the evil spirit, or of the neighbour or the devil, Papa Minas explained. Also some long hair, fine, so clearly from a woman's grave. That was it. As it had been there for so long and he had heard nothing further, Papa Minas could only assume that the woman had recovered.

There was a second, that had been lying below the altar almost as long. Papa Minas picked up a pink plastic bag. 'Devilish in itself, don't you think?' he said, holding it at arm's length. He untied it and brought out a tangle of cord. Four strands, about six foot long, had been knotted sixteen times. Not twelve for the apostles.

'Why sixteen?' I asked.

'I have no idea,' said Papa Minas. The woman who brought it had got up one morning and found it hanging from a lemon tree in her garden. She had taken it straight away to the church for the evil to be undone. 'Obviously, when one family or person wants to harm another they do it by magical means, and only the power of the Church can prevail against magic,' said Papa Minas, with a twinkle in his eye. 'So it is for several years that these magical devices lie below my altar.'

The days rolled on to the climax of Easter Sunday. Goats and sheep were herded down from the hills for the slaughter. Penned, and then – lambs too small, rams too important and unwanted riff-raff separated off – they were surveyed by prospective buyers, selected, removed from the pen squeaking and bleating, their legs tied together, and then hauled a few yards down the road to have their heads chopped off and be skinned, struggling to the end. Nevertheless, I shared a family Easter dinner – as an honoured guest – of a whole roast goat stuffed with spicy rice and served with fresh goat's cheese the grandmother had made that morning. For they milked the female goats before slaughtering them. The special Easter soup, *magiritsa*, made of goats' intestines with bits floating in it I couldn't face, though Anna, who had read about it in her guide and had made a point of eating it at one of the village bars, assured me it was delicious, if a little too salty.

*

Easter Sunday dawned cold, dry and windy. There was now an accumulation of about fifty tourists, photographers and a television crew from Athens. The priest of Olymbos, Papa Yannis, who seemed to be responsible for the entire running of the church, was sweeping it out and scraping up candle grease from the stone floor. He was dressed in a paint-splattered T-shirt and a silly 'Rhodes' tourist hat. I had spoken to him before, but his English was rudimentary and we had not got very far. Now there was a holidaying emigrant to interpret.

Amulets? Yes, he knew I had been in the village a long time and had seen me at every single service, often the only worshipper, 'but I hadn't known you were looking for amulets. I have one here, on the altar. A woman whose husband left her for a German tourist ('I know her, I know her,' I almost shouted) has become a master at making amulets. She says this must stay in the church for forty days and forty nights. On the altar. Come and see.'

I was astounded. Step behind the iconostasis? I remembered Father Roman's words. And now I was being invited to enter the holy-of-holies. Diffidently I drew over my head the scarf I always wore just in case – feeling I was back in Muslim territory – and followed Papa Yannis.

The amulet – large, stuffed no doubt with a worthwhile collection of the items I was by now aware should be found in the best amulets – sat regally on the high altar. A triangle, as yet without its pendants though they would come. Gold and green sparkling brocade, luminescent below the altar cross, tucked quietly in among olive leaves, basil, flowers and more crosses.

When are the forty days and nights over? I ventured to ask.

Next week. After that the woman would open it and make smaller amulets from it to protect her entire family.

I would have left on the weekly ferry.

The Easter Sunday service began at three in the afternoon. Women and girls at their most resplendent were pestered by photographers. One, a Frenchman, even came into the women's antechamber and set up his tripod there. I had an unpleasant altercation with him – it's my job, he said, and anyway the Bible doesn't say men and women should be separated – but he left to join the fracas of his colleagues in the main body of the church. Papa Minas might have agreed with him. In his church, he had told me, he let men and women stand together, except at weddings when the men were usually drunk and couldn't be trusted among the women. He had also said that when he has such photographers in his church, he stops the service and goes home. Papa Yannis let them be.

'So where is the beauty and peace in such a service?' said Papa Minas when I told him.

I positioned myself where I could see through one of the doors of the iconostasis to the main altar, in the manner of a medieval squint. The amulet was there. An ungodly, cheap, if not to say kitsch, bit of shiny fabric, bright green and gold, a pagan device sheltered under the shield and aura of the cross. It was ridiculous, but the little display on the altar was the calm order, the small cosmos, of the labyrinth against the chaos outside. For chaos there was.

The boys and youths, mostly those on holiday from Baltimore, though it mattered not, had declared war on the tourist photographers. As they set up their tripods, the kids exploded Chinese firecrackers in their faces and, as they peered through their telephoto lens, they fired cap guns into their nostrils. As the photographers rushed from one side of the church to the other to capture some fleeting image of a tradition that, thanks to them, was doomed, the kids hurled the firecrackers onto the floor of the church at their feet. Papa Yannis had totally lost control. It was mayhem.

I stood through it all, my eyes steadfastly fixed on this triangular amulet that had absorbed so much of my life and my thoughts over so many years. The last place I had ever expected to see it was set on an altar amid holy crosses. And if I had ever thought my search might lead me to some geographical source, this intruder beside Christ's cross set its origin in history and not geography, I decided. Whereas Islam might have appropriated the amulet rather successfully, the Orthodox church had left its pagan origins undigested, broken needles and stones struck by lightning held in the calm of the holiest spot in the church.

Around it explosions, reports like gunshot, sparks, fizzing splatting fireworks sullied the church.

When everyone had left and the altar remained like a still small voice of calm, I looked at the debris on the church floor. Cartridges from the firecrackers stated in Italian that they should only be used in the open air and away from people, though they had been hurled into a crowded church and their black smoke had over the years – this was clearly not the first time such bedlam had occurred – destroyed the ceiling frescoes with their blackening fumes. So that now, when everyone including Papa Yannis had left and I strolled around the church, the green and gold amulet lay inviolate on the high altar and a scattering of rubbish lay on the church floor. I tidied up spent boxes of matches depicting Diogenes – a Cynic of course. And a multitude of firecracker cartridges. Some were yellow and labelled 'Ground Mouse. With Two Reports. Whistling. Zig-Zag. Bang-Bang.' But most of the cartridges were red and labelled simply 'Mephis- topheles'.

Postscript

The fractured journeys, the seasons illogically melded, the stops and starts described in *The Golden Horde*, seem now like the demented trajectory of a zapped bluebottle. Travel books should be clear, a neat trek from here to there and maybe back again. That *The Golden Horde* was not.

I described my journeys as a drycleaner's coat hanger, one of those thin devices that always snap in the middle if you try to bend them. And it was in Russia that the itinerary snapped and there that it had to be picked up again. Whether I have been back or stayed away has also snapped the recollections of those journeys into pieces. I have since returned often to Central Asia but very little to Russia and not at all to those lost small towns along the Oka and the Volga rivers. Nor indeed to Karpathos, though I imagine that picturesque village has changed little, buttressed as it was into the pinnacle of its tourist potential.

Nothing destroys like the smothering march of tourism. Where it follows the Silk Road, Bukhara and Samarkand have metamorphosed into theme parks. Where it stays away – as in deep Russia – I imagine it has left a survival of cabbage soup, of meticulous stitchery on dowry aprons, of faceless amuletic dolls, of the village goose girl. The collapse of the seeming featherbed of communism changed nothing overnight but did so invidiously, through poverty, insecurity, and escalating rents and electricity bills, where all had been supposedly free. The old couple in Makaryev must still be wandering in the forests, collecting mushrooms to survive. The sufferers, profoundly, must be the peasants of that forgotten Russia through which I travelled.

Not, of course, the oligarchs or the cities. Moscow's streets of frozen scruff, ice and slush on cobbles, that I first saw before the journeys of *The Golden Horde*, and then again during them, are now a razzmatazz of rebuilding: underground shopping malls in Red Square, where Lenin once lay pallid, are now watched over by armed guards, while McDonald's, chain stores, the flotsam and jetsam of the West, crush the austerity of GUM. Bare midriffs and punky metal low-slung belts have ousted the tow-haired girl's sober shift and apron. Beggars, propelled by a new comparative poverty, hassle those who once were simply stared at as though they were visitors from Mars.

When I returned to Cheboksary, the bananas and German apple juice sat on shelves in supermarkets, instead of being sold one by one in small kiosks, and the town boasted a couture salon. The town's new fashion designer, dressed in flowing white robes, his hands heavy with silver rings, watched his pale Russian models parade his latest designs in front of the velvet drapes of his peach and white, chandeliered and mirrored salon. The clothes were so theatrical they could only be worn in Las Vegas or Monaco and, as his customers would be unlikely to come to him, making the river journey down the Volga and then up into the town from the old wooden landing stage, he takes the clothes to them.

How could I have imagined such opulence among the factories and power stations, where 'monumental and monumental-decorative art, in particular, has been greatly developing'? How can we ever know when we are there what will change in the future? What disappear, as those Soviet shops stocked with only fifty tins of gherkins and a lost pigeon: what blossom into celebration, as the new turquoise bathroom tiles of Samarkand, the kitsch gold statues of our dear ruler in Ashkabad; and what remain the same, untouched by every century alike, as the blood feuds of the high valleys of the Himalaya? But do those also change?

'To begin again where our travels began, I can only surmise that the annual cycle of maize and pre-puberty brides, the men 'in fort' and the scratching of the few semi-fertile, precariously cliff-hanging terraces of the Palas valley, continues as it always has. Nothing apocalyptic appears to have happened to have changed this. The western tragopan, I imagine, is still endangered', I had thought. How wrong I was. Within a week of writing this, the most devastating earthquake ever recorded in Pakistan's history struck that fragile region where the Karakoram highway clings precipitously to slithering scree. At least seventy thousand people were known to have been killed, though the precise number will never be known. As first reports spoke of Kashmir, it was a while before I learned that the Palas valley had also suffered: 'this remote Himalayan forest region best known for its unique population of the regionally endemic Western Tragopan Pheasant' said the World Wide Fund for Nature, who were unable to get help through as the highway lay blocked or crumbled. And life in Palas had seemed unchanging.

As the latest gold image of Turkmenistan's ruler revolves with the sun, bestowing his blessing on the Disneyland he has made of Ashkabad, it seems unbelievable it was not that long ago 'one of those towns that seem to drain from the memory like sand in an hour glass'. Now the emptiness and deprivation is swept into quarters of the city where houses have been razed and water cut off, to create promenades of guzzling grass and fountains along Niyazov's route back home from his turquoise and gold palace in town to another, more coolly placed in the Kopet Dag mountains.

But no one's heart could be in Ashkabad – in Samarkand maybe. But there the locked and abandoned rooms of the Ulug Beg *madrasa*, deep in dust, are now like a US shopping precinct. Its 'reconstruction' goes three storeys high in ever more blatant turquoise. But is there any point in such a comparison with what was and is now, in trying to archive years like a lepidoterist's pinned butterflies? Does the value of travel lie in what it was like then compared with now, or in the eternal why we move and what we see reflecting ourselves? And what we remember and what sinks into the subconscious.

We remember when we fall in love with a place. And for me that was with Bukhara. The tranquil heart of Central Asia that was the pool of Lyab-i-Khauz, where the storks had long gone, but the old men still sat, grizzled under their embroidered caps, playing chess around the old tables. Tables like king-size beds, space to rest forever. The rickety wooden *chai-khana* at the edge of the pool, where they relit the fire to cook some food for me, any food as long as I didn't go hungry, has been pulled down to make way for red Coca-Cola umbrellas sheltering rows of garden centre white plastic chairs, while iron pipes and sprinklers circle the pool, jetting fountains for the indifferent amusement of tourists. And the old men are banished to the back of town, to teahouses once of low repute. Why does tourism always kill what it comes to see?

Then there's Mubinjon, with his notice 'Welcome to House Museum. Come and take green tea' long gone under the onslaught of official harassment. His wife has left him; he seems lost, unshaven and slightly boozy. Though he has modernized his house, pulled down the carved wooden balustrade, killed off the tree and lost his dog, the odd backpacker does still call. Even so, though he was the first to see the potential of Bukhara, the tourist boom has passed him by completely.

As for Kurban, he set up a little stall, a piece of cardboard on the ground in front of the Kalyan minaret, where he laid out a few miserable trinkets. Many of them I bought to keep him going, but as his 'shop' failed to attract the attention of the new tour groups in town, he gave up in despair and emigrated to Korea, holding back the tears as he told me he was going. The horror of his attempted assimilation there, without his wife and sons, and speaking only Uzbek, drove him to Dubai. Here he earns enough to send money transfers to his wife to replace his lovemaking and his fatherly disciplining of his sons.

And what of Stoddart and Connelly? Though the guide books still recount their story, the stuffed cloth models have gone – along with the old coupon money thrown down to offer sympathy – as have the more vicious instruments of torture. Less offensive to tourists, the chained effigies of local common criminals still sit in the Zindan, waiting with their begging bowls to be let out on Fridays.

And what of Nukus, that hellhole of salt, disease and despair? Médecins Sans Frontières now battles there against TB, drug-resistant and rampant among the salt-sickened populace and mothers still sew triangular amulets filled with salt to hang round the necks of their children, salt against salt like the blue eye bead against the evil eye.

There were wonders on my journeys that I did not miss, but whose significance I did not appreciate. Before seeing them, I knew nothing about them, because nobody else did. They were the mummies in Urumchi and the Savitsky collection in Nukus.

The true significance of the Savitsky collection was easy to miss. In the town museum I had stepped around the tin buckets that caught only some of the relentless rain pouring through the mouldering fungus of the ceiling, deeply reverent before forgotten treasures of 1930s Russian art. But what treasures they were I had not entirely appreciated. They had reminded me at the time of the annual display in the village hall of some local painting group, lacking a selection committee. Everything hung cheek by jowl, hundreds and hundreds of paintings jostling for attention, the strident obliterating the gentle, the heavily allegorical, the simple. Before them I was rudderless. My experience of museum collections and exhibitions of art was that, whether I liked the paintings or not, they were considered of merit and therefore should be appreciated. Here I was on my own. Some were unforgettable and haunt me still. Why were they there, in that remote godforsaken place?

Ivor Savitsky was a painter and in 1950 he joined an archeological and ethnographic expedition to Karakalpakstan. He collected folk art and sent it to Moscow and to what was then Leningrad, but felt uneasy about its fate there. He settled in Nukus and set about collecting all the Karakalpak art and craft that was disappearing, establishing the museum with himself as director. He gave up painting but gathered thousands of works by other artists, forgotten or denounced and persecuted by the Soviets and brought them back by the trainload to Nukus. He went to Moscow and Leningrad visiting artists' widows and heirs, finding paintings piled in attics and basements or used to fill gaps in ceilings and windows. He had no money of his own but managed to get some funding from the Uzbek government, which had no idea what he was doing with it. He signed IOUs, and lived in penury, squirreling works of art into this small remote museum, far from the eyes of Moscow.

Each time I returned more rooms were closed because of leaking ceilings. The director, Marinika Babanazarova, who had known Savitsky as a child, guarded the museum like a lioness her cubs and the staff worked for no wages. Perhaps the defiance of the place, and the knowledge that many of the artists died in gulags or disappeared without trace added a frisson to the paintings. Elena Korovaï's Jewish dyers of Bukhara up to their elbows in blue dye; Viktor Oufimtsev's woman by a railway track selling milk to the passengers; Mikhail Ivanovitch Kourzine's old man in a white cap and black robe squatting on the ground cutting carrots with a pitcher of water and a bird in a cage beside him – none of these paintings seemed in any way subversive. Yet Kourzine spend ten years in a Siberian gulag and on his release went to live in Bukhara. Then one day he travelled to Tashkent without permission, was arrested and imprisoned again for eight years.

Now the government has built a new museum, a sanitized marble construction teetering already on future decay caused by the salt incrustations from the nearby Aral Sea. An imposing hallway and grand staircase lead to individual groupings of each artist's work, so that the paintings no longer fight with each other, a café serves Coca-Cola and there is a trickle of visitors. An exhibition of some of the paintings in Normandy, 'Survivors of the Red Sands', has alerted the outside world to the collection's existence. The locals cannot afford the entrance charge.

Further along my journeys the importance of the mummies of Urumchi, like the Savitsky collection, also escaped me when I saw them. My memory of the mummies is still vivid, a man, woman and a baby, though there may have been more. Perhaps not so vivid after all then, though I can still see them lying in dusty glass cases in a dark room of the Museum of National Minorities and History in Urumchi. Since there was no one else around and no information, I seemed to be meeting them as owners of the place. They looked like a family of wandering Swedes, dressed in their best for market day. They were not really mummies at all, but were desiccated by the desert climate and salty air of Central Asia, so that their features were fixed as in life. They were clad in homespun woollen clothing of tartan patterns, white leather boots and felt hats. The man's legs were wrapped in brightly coloured felted wool bindings of the same kind that Romanian peasants still wear today. The baby's eyes were replaced with blue stones, perhaps to denote their original colour. Hairy people – blond or red, the woman with plaits, the man with a beard – big noses, round eye sockets, they were also very tall, and clearly European. They were almost four thousand years old.

It was so extraordinary to find them here in remote western China that I felt sure the world must know about them. Just I had not heard about them. But no, they were in fact unearthed in the late 1970s and, though experts were told of them in 1988, they were not publicized until 1994, long after my visit. The reasons were mainly political. China's hold on this Uyghur region was still disputed and these clearly European inhabitants from so long ago weakened considerably China's claim that the territory had always belonged to them.

Later writings disclosed that other mummies had been found in the Tarim basin, in the desert south of Urumchi, and that the people were Tokharians, a group of Indo-Europeans. Sir Aurel Stein had come across some of these bodies in their desert graves in the early twentieth century and had commented on their clothing and on the fact that their heads were of the *homo alpinus* type, found in the West and in the Hindu Kush. I had noted that their felt caps with horns resembled those of the women of Eastern Europe and the high valleys of the Hindu Kush, though this was far from being the most important thing about them. Stein, unaware of their great age determined later by radiocarbon dating, had also thought them of no great significance because it was not unusual for Western travellers to venture into China.

Venturing east into China to seek the source of the amulet was a route I could have chosen but, since I had already travelled through the northern and southern regions of Central Asia, I attempted to close the circle to the west. These journeys, described in *The Linen Goddess*, took me from the Red Sea through East and North Africa to the Balkans and Albania. By this time it was clear that the triangle was far from the only amulet, or even the most important. Alchemy and magic, religion and superstition, the exotic and the misshapen, sex and fertility, all are harnessed against disease and danger, sometimes as stones or cowrie shells, blue beads or red pompoms, surahs from the Koran, even garlic and salt.

In time, the source of the amulet is impossible to pinpoint, but goes back to the prehistoric. In place, its source remained equally elusive, a kind of Shangri-La situated neither in the Hindu Kush, where I began my travels, nor in Prizren where I ended them, but in human frailties and fear of the inexplicable.

GLOSSARY

alimgash: black/white edging of Turkmen coats
Aurignacian: period of prehistory, *circa* 30,000 BC
Bactrian camel: two-humped camel
bast: inner tree bark, especially of linden
chai-khana: tea house
chapan: quilted straight-cut coat with no fastenings
charpoy: simple wood-framed bed strung with rope
cheongsam: tight-fitting, high-necked Chinese dress with side slits
chowkidar: caretaker
condottieri: mercenaries of the Italian city states
foustanela: official Greek court costume
ghee: clarified buffalo butter
godet: triangular gusset of fabric
Great Patriotic War: Soviet name for the Second World War
hujra: communal guest house for men
iconostasis: a screen bearing icons and separating the sanctuary from
   the nave
ikat: weaving technique where the design is dyed into the threads
   before weaving begins, giving a blurred effect
iwan: high vaulted hallway
jehek: Turkmen braiding technique
karavod: large square wooden bench
karez: underground water channel
kesdi: lacing embroidery stitch of the Turkmen
khan: a prince, or local chief
khanate: area ruled over by one particular khan
kokoshnik: Russian woman's headdress
kurgan: Scythian burial chamber
laghman: traditional noodle-based dish of Uzbekistan
langur: entellus monkey
lateen: triangular sail common in the Mediterranean
madrasa: Islamic seminary
malek: a local chief
manti: envelopes of boiled dough, usually containing meat
markhor: mountain goat

matushka: wife of a Russian Orthodox priest

mihrab: niche in mosque showing direction of Mecca

morel: mushroom of the genus *Morchella*

mullah: Muslim teacher

naan: flat, slightly leavened bread

plov: common rice-based dish

prosphora: bread of the Orthodox Church

remont: closed for repair, usually long-term

rushnyk: Ukrainian ritual towel

sarafan: pinafore dress of Russian costume

schist: crystalline foliated metamorphic rock

shabrack: saddlecloth

shalwar kameez: loose trouser and long tunic outfit worn by both men and women in Pakistan

Shin: inhabitants of Indus Kohistan who probably originally came from the lower Indus Valley, also their language

suzani: Uzbek embroidered cloth

tamboured: type of embroidery worked with a hook instead of a needle

tarbaza: hostel

TEFL: Teaching English as a Foreign Language

tomar: amulet

yurt: round felt tent of nomads

BIBLIOGRAPHY

Max Allen, *The Birth Symbol in Traditional Women's Art*, Birth 19, Toronto 1992

Baron Joseph de Baye, *Notes sur les Votiaks Païens des Gouvernements de Kazan et de Viatka*, Paris 1898

John Boardman, *The Greeks Overseas*, London 1988

Klaus von Bolzano, *Karpathos*, Salzburg 1986

William Craft Brumfield, *Lost Russia*, Durham 1995

Mary Burkett, *The Art of the Felt Maker*, Kendal 1979

Joseph Campbell, *The Masks of God: Primitive Mythology*, New York 1959, 1991

Johannes de Plano Carpini, *Voyage into the North East Part of the World, in the Year of Our Lord 1246*, London 1900

Georges Charrière, *L'Art Barbare Scythe*, Paris 1971

R. M. Dawkins, 'Notes from Karpathos', The Annual of the British School at Athens, 1903

Dawn Newspaper, Financial News, Karachi, March 1995

Adele Getty, *Goddess: Mother of Living Nature*, London 1990

O. Grabowitz and L. Wolynetz, *Rushnyky Ukrainian Ritual Cloths*, New York, n.d.

Marija Gimbutas, *The Goddesses and Gods of Old Europe: Myths and Cult Images*, London 1982

W. L. Hildeburgh, *Japanese Popular Magic Connected with Agriculture and Trade*, Transactions of Japan Society of London, vol. XII, 1913

W. L. Hildeburgh, *Some Japanese Minor Magical or Religious Practices Connected with Travelling*, Transactions of Japan Society of London, vol. XIV, 1916

Peter Hopkirk, *The Great Game*, London 1990

Schuyler Jones, *In Search of the Horned Headdress*, Ethnologie und Geschichte, Karl Jettmar, Wiesbaden 1983

Tatiana Kara-Vasuleva, *Ukrainian Embroidery*, Kiev 1993

Mary B. Kelly, *Goddess Embroideries of Eastern Europe*, New York 1989

Mary B. Kelly, *The Changeless Carpathians*, The Ukrainian Museum, New York 1995

Sheila Kitzinger, *A Celebration of Birth*, Washington 1986

Gyula László, *L'Art des Nomades*, Paris 1972

Oleg Lysenko and Svetlana Komarova, *Fabric, Ritual, Man*, St Petersburg 1992

Sir Fitzroy Maclean, *To the Back of Beyond*, London 1974

Robert Marshall, *Storm from the East*, London 1993

David Morgan, *The Mongols*, London 1986

M. G. Morozova, *Traditzionii Kostum Narodov Prikamya*, Moscow 1990

D. L. Mukhametshin and F. C. Khakimzyanov, *Epigraficheski Pamyatniki Goroda Bulgara*, Kazan 1987

Mixala M. Noyapoy, *Laographica Symmeikta Karpatios*, Athens 1965

Edmond O'Donovan, *The Merv Oasis*, London 1882

Sheila Paine, *Embroidered Textiles: Traditional Patterns from Five Continents*, London 1995

Sheila Paine, *The Afghan Amulet: Travels from the Hindu Kush to Razgrad*, London 1995

Dimitris Philippides, trans. Philip Ramp, *Greek Traditional Architecture: Karpathos*, Athens 1992

Jill Purce, *The Mystic Spiral: Journey of the Soul*, London 1994

The Mission of Friar William of Rubruck, trans. Peter Jackson, *His Journey to the Court of the Great Khan Mongke 1253–1255*, London 1990

Jessica Rawson, *Chinese Ornament: The Lotus and the Dragon*, London 1984

Sergei Rudenko, trans. Dr M. W. Thompson, *Frozen Tombs of Siberia: The Pazyryk Burials of Iron-Age Horsemen*, London 1970

Véronique Schiltz, *Histoires de Kourganes: La redécouverte de l'or des Scythes*, Paris 1991.

Jean Sellier and André Sellier, *Atlas des Peuples d'Orient*, Paris 1993

Leon E. Seltzer, ed., *Columbia Lippincott Gazeteer of the World*, Columbia, New York 1962

John Sharkey, *Celtic Mysteries*, London 1975

Jean N. Smirnov, trans. Paul Boyer, *Les Populations Finnoises des Bassins de la Volga et de la Kama*, Paris 1898

Yuri Tkach, *History of Ukrainian Costume*, Melbourne 1986

M. Tkachuk, M. Kishchuk and A. Nicholaichuk, *Pyanska: Icon of the Universe*, Saskatoon 1977

A. A. Trofimov, *Chuvash Folk Art*, Cheboksary 1981

C. E. Vasileva, *Chuvashski Narodni Iskustvo*, Cheboksary 1991

Gertrud Weinhold, *Zeit und Raum zur Ehre Gottes*, Berlin 1984

Giles Whitwell, *Central Asia*, Cadogan Guides, 1993

Jeremy Wilson, *Lawrence of Arabia: The Authorised Biography of T. E. Lawrence*, London 1989

Viktor Witkowitsch, *Eine Reise durch Sowjet-Usbekistan*, Moscow 1954

F. A. Wright, *Lemprière's Classical Dictionary of 1788*, London 1949

L. Yefimova and R. Belogorskaya, *Russian Embroidery and Lace*, New York 1987

INDEX